Handbook for the Financial Analysis of Real Estate Investments

Other Books by William T. Tappan, Jr.:

Real Estate Exchange and Acquisition Techniques (Prentice-Hall)

The Real Estate Acquisition Handbook (Prentice-Hall)

Handbook for the Financial Analysis of Real Estate Investments

William T. Tappan, Jr.

McGraw-Hill, Inc.
New York St. Louis San Francisco Auckland Bogotá
Caracas Lisbon London Madrid Mexico Milan
Montreal New Delhi Paris San Juan São Paulo
Singapore Sydney Tokyo Toronto

Library of Congress Cataloging-in-Publication Data

Tappan, William T., Jr. date.
　　Handbook for the financial analysis of real estate investments /
William T. Tappan, Jr.
　　　　p.　cm.
　　Includes index.
　　ISBN 0-07-062891-2
　　1.　Real estate investment—Evaluation.　2.　Investment analysis.
I.　Title.
HD1382.5.T36　1992
332.63′24—dc20
92-20939
CIP

1 2 3 4 5 6 7 8 9 0　DOH/DOH　9 8 7 6 5 4 3 2

ISBN 07-062891-2

The sponsoring editor for this book was Theodore C. Nardin, the editing
supervisor was Fred Dahl, and the production supervisor was Donald F.
Schmidt. It was set in Baskerville by Carol Woolverton, Lexington, Mass.

Printed and bound by R. R. Donnelley & Sons Company.

Contents

Foreword

Until about one or two hundred years ago, the real estate investment business consisted mostly of investments in farmland. In fact, the largest investor in U.S. real estate today, The Prudential, made its mark in the 1930s as an important lender on agricultural property.

Over the next 50 years, technological advances made most of these investments obsolete. Developments in mechanical irrigation and chemical pesticides made U.S. farmland so efficient (in yields per acre) that they effectively wiped out much of the demand for agricultural property.

Fortunately, over this same 50-year period, investors in real estate shifted from farmland to much more productive investment property—office buildings, apartments, houses, shopping centers, development land, and industrial property.

During the past five years, the field of real estate investments has experienced cataclysmic changes that can only be compared to what the original agricultural investors experienced over the past 50 years. And many sophisticated analysts of the real estate industry feel that the events of the past five years may only be the beginning.

In shopping centers, for example, we have seen certain types of retail tenants increase their sales per square foot almost 300 percent, at the expense of other types of retailers whose sales seem headed for extinction. In office buildings we are experiencing a massive increase in the demand for ex-urban office campuses at the expense of traditional downtown and suburban office towers. And in speculative land (i.e., land held for development), we have seen the virtual demise of a marketplace even with declining prices approaching one-tenth of values achieved during the previous decade.

Underlying these cataclysmic events is the phenomenon that, throughout our society, changes that used to take place over 50 or 100 years now take place in only five or ten years.

It took the United States 50 years to go from needing 30 million farmers to feed 100 million people in 1930, to needing less than 3 million farmers to feed 300 million people in 1980. But it took only five years, from 1980 to 1985, to go from needing 300,000 people to make and repair automobile carburetors to needing less than 30,000 as electronic fuel injectors replaced them; or only five years, from 1985 to 1990, to go from needing 100,000 people manufacturing vinyl records to needing virtually none as vinyl records were displaced by digital CDs.

And when it comes to the changes that our economy will experience in the future, about the only thing that the "experts" can agree on is that the speed with which the changes occur will continue to accelerate.

In the field of real estate investments, changes such as these create great havoc and great opportunity. Great havoc is created because rapid changes in our underlying economic structure threaten the viability of much of our existing commercial real estate. However, great opportunity is created since the same rapid changes are creating even greater requirements for new types of real estate.

Moreover, this increasing speed of economic change has dramatically accelerated the need for more frequent financial analysis of real estate investments. Where traditionally such quantitative and qualitative analysis has only been made at the beginning and end of the investment cycle, today it is imperative that such in-depth analysis be accomplished at least annually for each investment in order to stay ahead of a rapidly changing market.

Until now, one of the problems with the financial analysis of real estate has been the lack of a comprehensive handbook encompassing all areas of real property investment analysis. This is not to say that the many excellent books existing today did not fulfill their mission when they were published. They did. However, our knowledge base has grown so much during the past few years that a critical need has been created for a comprehensive up-to-date handbook for real estate financial analysis.

This need has been filled by the *Handbook for the Financial Analysis of Real Estate Investments* by William T. Tappan.

Most commercial real estate professionals are already familiar with Mr. Tappan's work. At some time or another, almost every sophisticated practitioner has needed knowledge on how to perform a tax-free exchange and turned to his modern-day classic, *Real Estate Exchange & Acquisition Techniques* (Prentice-Hall, 1989). Now, in the *Handbook for the Financial Analysis of Real Estate Investments,* he may have created a second classic for real estate professionals.

The initial value in the *Handbook for the Financial Analysis of Real Estate Investments* is in its comprehensive approach. In taking us on a long and thorough journey through the many nuances of real estate investment analysis, the book serves as a checklist of both pitfalls to avoid and opportunities to find in structuring almost any real property investment.

But the real value of the *Handbook for the Financial Analysis of Real Estate Investments* is in the author's open-book approach to reaching his conclusions. Despite how far we have come in quantitative and qualitative analysis of real property investments, successful real estate investing still remains more of an art than a science. Yet today's "artist" in a highly technological environment must have similarly technologically advanced tools. This book, thanks to the way in which the author openly explains the rationale behind each of his conclusions, is such an advanced tool—even for a reader who may disagree with some of the author's conclusions.

There is so much to like in the *Handbook for the Financial Analysis of Real Estate Investments* that it is difficult to tell the reader where to start. As a book for the practicing commercial real estate professional, most readers will turn to specific sections as they need them. But the book is so good in putting all the pieces into perspective, that great opportunities await the lucky student or professional who has good fortune to be able to read it from cover to cover.

Perhaps best of all, Mr. Tappan's new work brings to real estate investment analysis a fundamental approach—a return to traditional values—that many areas of the real estate industry have critically lacked. He recognizes that the true value of real estate lies in its productive value in a much larger economic model highly dependent on underlying changes in credit, employment, and population. And, in creating what is sure to become his second classic, he has provided a comprehensive framework for fundamental analysis that, in the author's own words, "is intended to encourage independent thought and decision making."

PAUL ZANE PILZER

Paul Zane Pilzer has been the principal in over 70 real estate transactions exceeding $1 billion. He is a Contributing Editor of *Real Estate Review* and an Adjunct Professor of Finance at New York University. He is also the author of two best-selling books, *Other People's Money* (Simon & Schuster, 1989) and *Unlimited Wealth* (Crown Publishers, 1991).

Introduction

This book is designed to help you measure the financial performance of real estate, simply and accurately. Cash flow received from all sources during the entire holding period is the measure of financial performance that objectively determines the worth of an investment. Although the financial performance of real estate is influenced by numerous market factors, each one of them can be simplified and expressed as cash flow invested or received at specific times.

The normal cycles of the real estate market produce exciting visions of wealth as well as fears of financial insecurity. Both extremes are reflected in cash flows. If you only see part of the picture you are vulnerable to unexpected price drops and lost opportunity. But if you recognize the patterns behind public expectations you can time your decisions to take advantage of the trends inherent in the real estate market, rather than being swept along passively. No self-promoting individual, no savings and loan institution, and no insurance company is immune from the consequences of ignoring the trends of the real estate market. The market is bigger than all and treats all equally, without privilege.

The principles that you will find in this book apply to the financial performance of the smallest residential rental in middle America as well as the largest office building in New York City. As you will see, the concepts here can be applied to the financial performance of all types of real estate in all locations regardless of size or the apparent financial strength of the building owner. When you learn to think in terms of market trends and realistic measures of cash flow, size is no longer a measure of success or superior market wisdom. In the world of financial analysis, size means nothing other than more zeros.

This book is intended to encourage independent thought and decision making. For example, there are times when it is to your advantage to go with the crowd and realize the price appreciation that may have taken years to develop. But there are also times in the real estate cycle when it is to your advantage to go against the crowd and sell when everybody else seems to want to buy; or, to buy when everyone else seems to expect real estate to remain in the graveyard of financial markets forever. This contrary approach is not always an easy strategy to implement, but there are specific guidelines that you can apply to buy and sell real estate without exposing yourself to the dangers of unrealistic market expectations typical of public participation.

It is said that generals tend to fight the last war. In other words, they expect the next war to be the same as the last, and they prepare for that one at the expense of flexibility and effectiveness under new circumstances. It is also too easy to expect market conditions influencing real estate during the recent past to continue forever. Thinking independently with a long-term perspective can help generate a different expectation for the real estate market. What may now seem random to you has more than likely occurred in past real estate markets repeatedly from cycle to cycle with predictable effects on financial performance. As you will see, the impact of these cycles can be used to your advantage.

Real estate is a relatively illiquid market. It is not always easy to sell real estate for cash when you want. As a result, price changes often take years to be realized as cash flows. Although real estate liquidity is essentially a function of price, in certain regions of the country at certain points in the cycle, there simply may be no buyers (or rental tenants) at any price.

Furthermore, real estate is a credit-dependent industry, and that has a very significant effect on the ability of the market to meet demand. At certain points in the cycle the availability of credit for commercial real estate ventures tends to stimulate new building, bringing additional supply on the market when demand is perceived to be strongest and is expected to continue, but is actually about to weaken. At other times you simply can't get credit for real estate, even though it may be the best time to buy or build in anticipation of the next positive move in the cycle.

Expectations that the future will be the same as the present are based on lack of appreciation of change that is fundamental to our market economy. In fact, the real danger is in basing investment decisions on the expectation that the present market conditions will never change.

For example, public popularity leads the crowd to buy at the top of the real estate cycle when they should be selling and to give up all hope at the bottom when they should be buying because in both cases they expect no change in trend. We all are subject to this tendency, whether an analyst for an insurance company or a small individual investor. But there are sound fundamental factors within the real estate market that you can use to evaluate the balance of supply and demand that is so crucial to financial performance. These fundamental elements can be factored into the financial analysis of any real estate venture and used to avoid the trap of popular expectations.

One of the most important forces influencing the real estate market is regional population growth, which in turn depends on employment growth. People follow jobs. Employment growth is the single most reliable source of population growth and, therefore, the single best support of real estate demand. The size of the population and the wage scale of the workers have a ripple effect on the demand for real estate and the stability of financial performance.

Eventually, as the cycles unfold, demand for real estate tends to absorb existing supply and in turn stimulates new building. It is this interaction between demand and the response of the market place in an attempt to profit from demand that is expressed in rental rates and price appreciation. This is also the same process that serves as a check on demand as prices rise higher than rational people are willing to pay.

The cyclical interaction of supply and demand, in part, determines financial performance. This market process is as much a function of solid fundamentals, such as employment growth, as it is public expectation that real estate is the place to make a speculative killing regardless of the time in the cycle. The key is to recognize change as the true opportunity that it is. The difficult part is recognizing the actual change as it is happening. There are a few guidelines that can help. Look at the pattern of public expectations. Look at the regional real estate cycle. Look at the employment base and the prospects for expansion or recovery. These are the factors that influence financial performance. Understanding how these factors are affecting real estate performance in your market region can help provide a perspective for financial decisions that goes beyond the current crisis or public euphoria.

Public expectations for change in economic conditions; the business cycle; the housing cycle; and, the supply-demand balance for real estate all interact and influence financial performance. Although these market forces as well as others cannot be controlled by any investor, they are direct influences on financial performance that are dangerous to ignore, but advantageous when understood and made part of the decision-making process. They can be and should be factored into your real estate decisions.

Ultimately though, all market forces must be viewed within the limited context of the financial performance of a specific property. Fortunately, each property has its own characteristics, which can serve to offset some of the influences that are beyond individual control. There are characteristics unique to individual properties that can help ensure financial success even under difficult economic conditions, as well as characteristics that sometimes prevent profitable performance even when economic conditions are stable. Both can be isolated when analyzing a specific property and translated into cash flows that can be measured financially.

The financial analysis of real estate is a process of translating (1) market conditions and (2) specific property characteristics into (3) cash flow received over time. Cash flow can come from several sources. The lump sum you receive when you sell is a cash flow just as much as the monthly proceeds of rental income. They differ only in amount and time of receipt. The amount and time that you receive cash flow are the primary components of the financial value of real estate. The challenge is to determine what the cash flows were in the past, what they are in the present, and what they are likely to be in the future. The timing of cash flows can be as significant as the amount.

Translating market conditions and property characteristics into cash flows is not difficult. The mathematics are clearcut. The difficulty is in accurately assessing the risk factors and allowing for them in your calculations. Diversification can go a long way toward compensating for risk. It is possible to build a balanced portfolio in real estate that accounts for investment risk and protects you during normal as well as severe economic cycles. You can also diversify geographically, taking advantage of regional differences in employment cycles.

Furthermore, you can diversify into different types of properties that have different risks at various times in the economic cycle. You can also manage risk by limiting the leverage you use to acquire real estate to an amount appropriate for the economic cycle. Reducing the debt on investments you want to hold during economic downturns may be the single best way to ensure long-term financial security. All of these risk strategies can be expressed in terms of cash flow, and their financial value can be measured.

Ultimately, the financial performance of your real estate investments must be tailored as nearly as possible to meet your personal or corporate goals. The *Handbook for the Financial Analysis of Real Estate* is intended to help you measure how well you are actually accomplishing that task.

Chapter 1 covers the influence of cycles on the real estate market. There is a long history of capital investment cycles in the economy, and the role of real estate is central to them.

Chapter 2 covers the fundamental factors contributing to real estate cycles and how they can be applied to investment strategy. Cycles have causes, which are in many cases more important than knowing the exact timing of peaks and troughs.

Chapter 3 covers the process of specifying real estate cash flows. Cash flows from a number of sources contribute to real estate performance, but they must be specified before they can be measured.

Chapter 4 covers the standard methods used to analyze real estate. Many are ingrained in daily use and applied almost automatically.

Chapter 5 covers discounted cash flow analysis and the crucial role of time value in measuring financial performance. The internal rate of return and net present value are both time-tested real estate analysis tools.

Chapter 6 brings together the essential elements of analysis into a model, which includes cycles, cash flows, and discounted cash flow analysis.

Chapter 7 presents techniques for applying net present value to various real estate situations.

Chapters 8 through 13 cover the specifics of financial analysis as applied to different types of property, including land, office buildings, rental houses, apartments, retail centers, and leases.

The appendix contains the formulas and discount rate factors for future reference.

There are many people who have contributed to this book in one way or another through the years. Although I cannot begin to mention them all I would like to especially thank Bill Turner, Ed Henry, Ben Butler, Mike Elliston, Steve Erickson, Laura Heflin, Bill Cornelius, Vic Bruno, Carol Rickert, Ken Kamerman, Jack Campbell, and Paul Zane Pilzer.

WILLIAM T. TAPPAN, JR.
Corrales, New Mexico

Handbook for the Financial Analysis of Real Estate Investments

1

The Crucial Role
of Cycles in Real Estate

Change in the real estate market is the basis of opportunity. Cycles are crucial to financial analysis because they reveal the time and sequence of recurring events and their effect on the real estate market. Consequently, cycles provide a structure for timing real estate investment decisions in preparation for competition, price risk, fluctuations in supply and demand, inflation trends, and economic change, all of which have an impact on financial performance.

The Purpose of the Real Estate Investment

The purpose of investing in real estate is to transfer purchasing power through time while increasing real wealth (adjusted for inflation). An increase in the general price level of goods and services is a natural part of U.S. economic history since World War II. In fact, prior to the current economic adjustment, the only extended periods of falling prices during the past 120 years occurred from 1870 to 1898 and from 1920 to 1933 [1, p.7]. These two periods marked the troughs of long wave economic cycles and had a direct impact on real estate investment activity.

The investment objective of transferring purchasing power through time while increasing wealth is a natural function of the free market system. It arises from an understandable desire to maintain the present value of funds by protecting them from in-

1

flation, taxes, and deflation while receiving a reasonable increase in real wealth. An increase in real wealth is essential to maintain our capital base so that new investment can be made to bring new technology and, therefore, new jobs and prosperity, to the economy [2, p.127].

To accomplish this, the net amount of money received during the holding period and at liquidation of the investment must purchase at least the same in goods and services as the total amount of money invested, while also increasing in an amount sufficient to allow new investment necessary for maintaining economic growth. Anything less is a loss in purchasing power and a missed opportunity for profit and, therefore, unsatisfactory financial performance.

Example

An 8 percent annual return during a period of 4.5 percent inflation must be virtually management- and risk-free to offset the effects of inflation and income taxes.

Tax Effect:
Investment	$100,000
Yield	8%
Income	$ 8,000
Tax rate	33%
Tax due	$ 2,640

Inflationary Effect:
Investment	$100,000
Inflation rate	4.5%
Inflationary loss	$ 4,500

Investment Effect:
Investment value	$108,000
Less tax paid	(2,640)
Less inflation	(4,500)
Purchasing power of funds	$100,860

The net after-tax, inflation-adjusted return is $860 on a $100,000 investment nominally yielding 8 percent. This represents a return of less than 1 percent (0.86 percent) net to the investor. Careful examination of real financial performance raises questions about traditional interest-bearing investment instruments and explains the motivation behind speculation in price-sensitive assets. Price appreciation and the speculative nature of real estate investment is central to the goal of increasing real wealth.

Financial performance is measured by the cash flows an investment produces. The financial worth of an investment is the net present value of the total of all the cash flows it generates during the entire ownership period, whether from monthly rent or at the end of ownership from sale proceeds. This simple principle has stood the test of time as the one reliable way to compare different types of investments on an equal time value basis.

Financial analysis is relatively easy when the cash flows are fixed and known, as in the case of a lease or the terms of a note and mortgage. The challenge arises when the cash flows are not known. Typically this occurs in a real estate purchase when future cash flows can only be estimated from income and expense data likely to be incomplete and of questionable accuracy. Nevertheless, the analysis process must be completed in order to measure past cash flows and establish the assumptions necessary to project future cash flows. This is where cycles can help. They provide a perspective of market forces that goes beyond the present moment to the history of repetitive economic patterns that are often difficult to see from within the daily real estate battleground. Cycles provide a structure for understanding how market forces contributed to past financial performance and for estimating their impact on future performance.

There is nothing mysterious or new about cycles. They are natural fluctuations in market activity, alternating between expansion and contraction. There are several cycles of differing lengths which are now working through our national economy. Also, many industries, including real estate investment and construction, have identifiable cycles. In fact, investing in real estate may involve years of exposure to several stages of market activity, involving different, but overlapping cycles. This consequence of the long-term nature of real estate makes it all the more important to understand how cycles influence the financial performance of real estate.

Four Cycles that Influence the Real Estate Market

There are four cycles of importance to the financial performance of real estate and the transfer of purchasing power through time. Two are general economic cycles, and two are real estate cycles.

Economic Cycles

   The long wave cycle (about 54 years)

   The business cycle (about 56 months)

Real Estate Cycles

   The real estate investment cycle (about 18 years)

   The housing cycle (about 7 years)

Each of these cycles has its own time period that is generally regular from trough to trough and peak to peak. The tendency of market activity to peak and bottom within approximately regular time periods allows anticipation and preparation for the events that characterize the different phases of each cycle.

Fortunately, cycles do not have to recur in precise time periods to be useful. It is normal for them to vary in length from trough to trough and peak to peak. Nevertheless, they do tend to stay within average time bands over the long term. It is this average that defines the length of the cycle. The average time periods associated with cycles have developed through observation of several time series. However, the timing of the expansion wave and the contraction gap is only part of the picture—it is what happens to real estate during each phase that is important.

Practical use of cycles comes from understanding the effect on real estate and the adjustment implied for investment strategy. Adaptation to the change in market activity during different phases of a cycle is of greater financial benefit than trying to predict timing exactly. Timing tends to vary, but the patterns of market activity in real estate have characteristics that tend to repeat with a high degree of consistency.

For example, knowing that the economy is approaching the time frame for a long wave peak would be ample reason to question the purchase of an office building that depends on high debt that can only be serviced if office rental rates continue to increase. Conversely, knowing that the regional economy is coming out of a recession as part of the normal business cycle is essential if you are weighing whether to commit funds in that region. Furthermore, knowledge of an approaching peak in the housing cycle would give pause to any builder who is considering acquisition of additional lot inventory.

Slight strategic adjustments based on the level of market activity anticipated during an approaching cycle phase can help make real estate a less risky venture. But a real estate investment program that does not consider the crucial role of cycles is a seriously incomplete view of the market that ignores the practical lessons of history.

The long wave and shorter term business cycles are primary economic fluctuations. The long wave is a period of major capital investment during which technical innovation is produced and distributed throughout the economy. The shorter term business cycle is also a period of capital investment and an attempt to bring innovation to the market but on a smaller scale, possibly involving different innovations [4, p.172].

The expansion phase of these economic cycles of varying length is followed by a period of contracting economic activity and debt liquidation in preparation for the next wave of innovation. The business cycle with its periodic recessions results more directly from the manipulation of credit and interest rates by the Federal Reserve Board in the attempt to control inflation or stimulate the economy. But during the contraction phase of the long wave cycle, interest rate manipulation has little effect on the stimulation of economic activity.

Real estate activity (buying, selling, and leasing) is directly affected by the expansion and contraction of these two economic cycles. In addition, the real estate market is affected by its own cycles. The 18-year real estate investment cycle tracks commercial-investment market activity. The 7-year housing cycle reflects new residential construction and existing home sales. Both real estate cycles are part of, and are directly influenced by, the broader economic cycles.

Fundamental and Governmental Factors Affecting Cycles

The forces of innovation that underlie economic and real estate cycles are influenced by identifiable elements within the market. There are three fundamental and three governmental factors that influence market activity at different stages of all four cycles.

Although we tend to think of cycles as changes in prices within the broad trends of inflation and deflation, there are internal factors acting on the economy and the real estate market that are at the core of cycles. These factors are primary influences on the cycles of real estate market activity.

Fundamental Factors

1. Capital availability—both equity and debt
2. Supply-demand—absorption/employment-income
3. Expectations—optimistic and pessimistic

Governmental Factors

1. Changes in tax laws (incentive-disincentive)
2. Changes in regulations
3. Changes in monetary policy (inflation)

Together these factors comprise the primary cyclical influences on real estate market activity. They are significant determinants of the cash flows produced by a property that appear as rent and sales price. Consequently, capital availability, the supply-demand relationship, and investor expectations have a direct effect on financial performance. Certainly anyone involved in real estate during the 1980s knows the see-saw effect of changing the tax laws as well as the consequences of deregulating the savings and loan (S&L) industry.

It is understandable that popular real estate investment attention focuses on inflation, price change, and deflation. But there is much more to the cycles in real estate activity than popular investment wisdom or the current political crisis. Understanding the fundamental and governmental factors that contribute to price change is a good first step beyond the limits of the obvious. It is also a move toward market-based financial analysis.

For example, tight credit is the primary cause of the business cycle phase we see as a recession. This regular reduction in available capital, usually caused by raising the price of money (interest rates), has a direct impact on the financial performance of real estate. These periods of recession are closely tied to the housing cycle.

Furthermore, a reduction in the availability of capital plays a role in the long wave cycle. But during long wave contractions it seems as though capital is restricted out of fear, or by regulatory accident. And in this case the efforts of the Federal Reserve Board to control market activity through lower interest rates has less effect. Here the market needs time to allow cash flows to catch up with debt service payments. Consequently, the process of debt liquidation overpowers the influence of lower interest rates.

Therefore, making a long-term financial projection that anticipates uninterrupted appreciation and rent increases is as historically unrealistic as a forecast that anticipates continued decreases in rents and values. A meaningful investment strategy should anticipate change and fluctuation in market activity and possibly in rents and sales prices. Awareness of the fundamental factors that contribute to cycles is one way to anticipate change in market activity and the impact on the financial performance of real estate investments. As we will see, the supply-demand relationship and the interplay of investor expectations work with equal influence at different stages of these cycles.

Characteristics of the Long Wave Cycle

The long wave cycle is characterized by major capital investment followed by debt liquidation. During the expansion phase, capital investment is driven by the entrepreneurial urge to bring technical innovation to the market. This process creates new jobs and increases the prosperity of the country. New plants are built to manufacture new product innovations. People have money to spend for homes, furnishings, clothes, and cars. More plants are built to supply the demand for consumer goods. More jobs are created to meet the new level of demand. New housing is built with each model growing in size with the expanding prosperity. Shopping centers increase in size to distribute the growing list of consumer goods. Office buildings spring up to service the growing prosperity with accounting, legal, and financial services. Finally, the prosperity flows to financial speculation in stocks, real estate, art, and diamonds. Debt expansion accelerates. Interest rates increase. Inflation gets out of control. Fortunes in the favored speculative medium are made virtually overnight. Expectations of a new era abound.

During the contraction phase of the long wave, cash flows become inadequate to cover the extreme debt accumulated during the final excesses of the expansion. Getting out of debt becomes a personal and corporate priority. The process of debt liquidation takes years to complete. Corporations restructure by permanently eliminating jobs by the tens of thousands. Confidence in the future drops, and people stop spending. Office buildings already in oversupply from the previous expansion remain vacant as law firms and financial services cut back. Shopping centers are no longer meeting percentage rent targets as retailers struggle to avoid bankruptcy. New homes shrink in size to meet the lower income levels of new buyers. International competition becomes vicious and politicians call for protection, blaming unfair foreign trade practices for domestic unemployment. Bankruptcies mount. Banks fail. Confidence drops. Government leaders try once again to figure out what went wrong, having never understood what went right in the first place.

The long wave economic cycle is the major economic cycle of the free market system and typically results in major changes in the banking regulations of the country. Popularly referred to as the *Kondratieff Cycle* (named for the Russian economist who discovered it), this long-term expansion-contraction process consists of about 30 years of expansion and 10 years of transition and confusion followed by about 10 years of severe contraction [3, p.2].

The expansion phase is characterized by massive capital investment in the national economy. The infusion of capital creates jobs and demand for goods and services accompanied by general economic prosperity as the expansion phase of the cycle produces and distributes technical innovations throughout the country.

Long wave expansions peak with high inflation and public speculation in a favorite investment, such as the stock market or real estate. Easy credit and readily available capital attracts abuse and white collar crime, which also appear during the topping process of the long wave cycle.

As the expansion phase of the long wave matures, personal, corporate, and government debt accumulates beyond manageable limits. Competition increases among businesses and between countries. With competition comes decreasing cash flows and difficulty in servicing debt. Eventually, debt service outweighs cash flows, and the restructuring and debt liquidation period begins. Unemployment increases, and the level of income drops nominally and in terms of purchasing power. The debt that financed the long wave expansion remains to be paid after many of the jobs created during the expansion phase have been eliminated.

Attempts to stimulate the economy with lower interest rates seem to have no effect. Each region has its own problems related to the condition of its dominant industry. Large corporate layoffs begin as the restructuring process gets underway in preparation for the new long wave expansion and eventual production and distribution of a new emerging technology.

The contraction phase ends with price deflation in the favored investment and public disdain of speculation—especially in the most popular investment asset of the previous expansion.

The Central Role of Real Estate in Long Wave Cycles

There are two theories that explain the long wave cycle. Historically, it appeared that the expansion and contraction was actually caused by technical innovations that worked through the economy. More recently, a new theory has been discovered through computer modeling. This econometric model demonstrates that the cause of the long wave is overbuilding of the capital plant of the country. The subsequent contraction, or gap between long wave expansions, occurs as the necessary process of financially and physically clearing the accounts of the old capital plant so a new wave of rebuilding can begin [3, p.6]. Buildings are depreciated and wear out physically. Only then can new construction begin and with it new long wave expansion.

Consequently, long wave expansions are directly linked to new capital investment in real estate and capital equipment necessary to bring new technical discoveries to the market. This indicates that the construction industry is more important to employment and economic prosperity than is commonly recognized. It also implies that overbuilding beyond the level justified by the ability to produce a return on investment is more dangerous than commonly recognized.

The role of real estate in the long wave is illustrated by the extreme overbuilding between 1981 and 1986. This obvious creation of oversupply was triggered, in part, by the capital investment encouraged by the investment incentives of the 1981 Tax Reform Act and formed a well-defined top to this fourth long wave cycle in our economic history. The bottom line that must be acknowledged is that the long wave is essentially a real estate investment cycle characterized by rebuilding of the structures that support the production and distribution system we call the national economy. Long wave economic contractions have occurred during the 1830s, 1890s, and 1930s [3, p.2]. It appears now that the 1990s must be added to the list.

Evidence is strong that we are in the contraction phase of the fourth long wave or Kondratieff Cycle. There have been three other long wave cycles in our economic history. They are of importance because they define the very long-term time periods of capital investment in real estate. They are also important today because of the timing implications for future real estate investment. After the current contraction ends, we will enter the fifth long wave expansion. Clearly, the opportunity for long-term investment in real estate ties directly to the timing of long wave contractions that result from overbuilding in the economy.

Long Wave Cycles	
The First Long Wave	1787–1842
The Second Long Wave	1843–1897
The Third Long Wave	1898–1933
The Fourth Long Wave	1934–199?

For the history of economic cycles prior to the Great Depression see Schumpeter [4].

Each long wave cycle had its period of real estate investment which was a prerequisite to the production and distribution of the technical innovations of the time. For example, the new inventions and revolution in manufacturing of the late 1700s and early 1800s characterized the first long wave. The growth of the railroads and westward expansion after the mid-1800s characterized the second long wave. The development of the automobile and related industry during the first part of the 1900s characterized the third long wave. The capital expansion after World War II into air travel, computers, and an improved quality of life through consumer goods and services and housing reflects the technological basis for the most recent long wave expansion.

Contractions are time periods needed to absorb oversupply and overcapacity, to physically wear out buildings, and to liquidate related debt. These gaps between long wave expansions appear unavoidable because the debt that financed the overcapacity cannot be supported by the cash flow produced by the investment. Thus, a primary purpose of a long wave contraction is to liquidate the debt that financed the prior capital expansion and to restructure the corporate base for more effective business competition during the new expansion; and most importantly, to prepare for the next wave of building.

Effects of the Current Long Wave Cycle on Real Estate

Long wave contractions represent a once-in-a-generation opportunity to acquire real estate. There is typically a 10-year period of debt liquidation during which bankruptcies and foreclosures drive prices down. In fact, one of the telling signs of a long wave contraction is the significant number of real estate sales as a result of bankruptcy and foreclosure.

Acquisition during a trough and sale during the topping process of the long wave cycle illustrates the ideal application of the investment principle of transferring purchasing power through time and increasing wealth for future generations.

For example, in 1936 a rancher acquired approximately 50,000 acres at the price of $3 per acre. His grandchildren's corporation carved 5,000 acres out of the property and sold it in 1986 for $500 per acre.

This transaction represents a compounded return of almost 11 percent in land value before taxes, expenses, and inflation. In effect, an investment of $3 that is held for 50 years which generates a one-time cash flow of $500 is comparable to a savings account that compounds at a 10.77 percent annual rate without payment of income tax until the funds are withdrawn. Certainly, at the time this land was purchased, an 11 percent rate of return was not part of the expectations of the rancher. But it was within the expectations of the market when the land was sold.

Although this rate of return may seem high (or low to you now) the fact is that about 5 years prior to this sale, interest rates had peaked at over 20 percent, and at the time of the transaction long treasury bonds were yielding 11 percent. Such high interest rates are another indication of a long wave peak. This land sale is an example of buying low and selling high over a 50-year period. Both the acquisition and the sale were once-in-a-generation opportunities.

Furthermore, a few years variation in timing of the sale would not have met with the same success. Five years earlier the economy was entering the double-dip recession of the early 1980s, and five years later the economy was trying to absorb the real estate holdings of the failed S&L industry. In addition, selling large parcels of land for actual development whenever you choose is not consistent with the illiquid nature of real estate.

Timing transactions in accordance with the long wave cycle is simple recognition of the nature of real estate and the obviously rare opportunity available for the transfer of purchasing power and building real wealth.

This transaction, of course, appears to have exceeded the minimum objective of transferring purchasing power through time. Keep in mind that this is a before-tax return, and there were holding costs associated with the property. Taxes are paid on the portion of gain attributable to inflation as well as the real profit after inflation. These expenses reduce the funds received and consequently must be charged against their purchasing power.

Therefore, we can reduce the gain in wealth by income taxes, expenses, and the loss in purchasing power to inflation.

Sale price	$500/acre	
Less expenses	(50)	
Less basis	(3)	
Realized gain	447	
Times tax rate	35%	
Equals tax due	$156	
Gross sale proceeds ($500 less $50)		$450
Less tax paid		(156)
Net sale proceeds		294
Less inflation of 85% over 50 years		(250)
Real gain		$ 44/acre
Real rate of return	5.52%	

This is not as high a margin as you might expect given the close timing and the relatively small window available to sell at top dollar (much less sell at all). Fortunately, good timing is not the only contributing factor to maximum financial performance. Regional employment growth, income level, location, and the physical characteristics of the property can all enhance or detract from the financial performance.

Nevertheless, timing is of major importance in the cyclical real estate business. The 50- to 60-year time frame for the long wave contraction puts the 1990s in the target zone. The topping process probably started in about 1980 with the peak in interest rates and commodity prices. This compares with similar peaks of interest rates and commodities in 1920. Farm and ranch land prices topped out about 1982, and the overbuilding of offices and commercial real estate probably peaked with the disincentives of the Tax Reform Act of 1986.

Furthermore, with the 20-20 vision of hindsight, the surge in real estate speculation during the 1980s is likely to be viewed as a market top extended by favorable depreciation for real estate enacted in 1981 and the liquidity provided by the looting of the S&L industry. Unfavorable depreciation was enacted in 1986, and the failure of the S&Ls was acknowledged a couple of years later. These two events are examples of governmental factors that can trigger turns in a market cycle toward confusion and then contraction. The Tax Reform Act of 1986 tore the real estate industry of this country into shreds and exacerbated the mounting real estate related problems of our lending institutions.

The failure of the S&Ls and the resulting attempt by the government to avoid a national panic by forming the Resolution Trust Corporation (RTC) are indications of the seriousness of the trend during the contraction phase of the long wave that is unfolding during the 1990s. The RTC was formed specifically to hold and sell real estate acquired by loan default. Much of the property in the RTC inventory was mortgaged far in excess of the real world value. As the speculation with S&L funds ended, it became clear that the likely sales value based on natural supply-demand relationship was much less than the property debt.

If there is a long wave parallel between the 1920s and the 1980s it can probably be found by comparing the leverage applied to stocks (10 percent margin—90 percent loan to value ratio) with the leveraged acquisition provided real estate through the S&Ls at 90 percent or more of value. These appraisals were based on peak market values that ignored the cycle turn. In the 1930s as well as the 1980s and 1990s, the end result was continuing bank failures.

The main contrast between the two contractions is that the federal government did not guarantee loans for stocks in the 1920s as it has for real estate. In effect, the deregulation of S&Ls combined with federal insurance of deposits to serve as government guaranteed loans for real estate speculation. This inadvertent underwriting provided the one thing real estate has typically lacked—liquidity. Debt-based liquidity facilitated the boom and virtually assured that the resulting collapse would be of equal magnitude and far reaching in cost and consequence.

It is hoped that this long wave cycle correction will not warrant use of the word *depression* on a national level. In fact, depending on the region of the country under examination, the worst may be past. The rolling recessions of the 1980s when viewed in sum appear to be a national depression occurring on a region-by-region basis. Here we can make a distinction between recession and depression by recognizing that a recession is caused by tight money policy and ends when the Fed (Federal Reserve Board) eases. In contrast, a depression is a slowing of economic activity caused by lack of cash flow to service debt, followed by debt liquidation, and corporate restructuring (laying off workers), which continues for an extended time despite the Fed easing interest rates.

Because of the regional nature of our economy, the full impact of the long wave contraction can only be appreciated by looking at specific regions of the country. This new phenomenon of a rolling recession (or depression if you lived there) started after the 1980 peak in commodity prices and interest rates. It hit the farm belt/rust belt of the Midwest, then it rolled into the Southwest as the price of oil dropped, hitting the mineral extraction industries of the West. Following the 1987 stock market panic, the recession rolled into New England, carving up the financial industry and placing the banking industry at risk. Unlike the early stages of the 1930s depression, the federal government has provided timely support to offset the effects. Unfortunately, government support comes in the form of more borrowing and yet again a new bureaucracy—the RTC.

Long wave corrections are natural economic adjustments to the excesses of financial speculation and overbuilding, flowing out of the prosperity of the previous expansion. Although painful, the minidepressions of a rolling national contraction do liquidate debt one way or the other. In doing so, the region is being prepared for the next expansion, unencumbered by the need to service debt on projects that have long ago stopped providing benefit. Just as the infusion of capital and rebuilding is the major characteristic of the expansion phase, the liquidation of debt and depreciation of buildings is the major characteristic of the contraction phase.

The one remaining question is when the rolling recession will finally hit the federal government. The federal government may be the lender of last resort, and consequently, the last to be hit with forced debt liquidation. This potential for further economic contraction has a direct tie to real estate. As underwriter of the S&L and banking industries, the government is also the ultimate owner of the properties that were once security for the loans that in part put the S&Ls out of business. The unavoidable fact is that the government is supporting the real estate market by holding foreclosed properties off the market. Doing so costs money. The initial estimates for the bailout were in the $20 billion range. The current cost is now moving steadily toward $200 billion and is likely to go higher.

There are two strategic points in the long wave cycle related to the investment purpose of transferring purchasing power through time. The first is an opportunity to sell during the acceleration of the inflation at the end of the expansion phase. The other is an opportunity to buy during the years of debt liquidation while the cycle is forming a base for the next expansion, which is likely to end in an acceleration of deflationary forces.

The long wave peak is a once-in-a-generation opportunity to sell with its characteristic inflationary excesses, high liquidity, and, therefore, active market. The contraction phase is an opportunity to buy as the basing process is complete with its characteristic deflationary excesses and lack of activity and the widespread need for cash.

The entire process of long wave expansion feeds on itself, producing optimism beyond reasonable expectations. Conversely, the contraction phase feeds on itself, producing pessimism that is far from justified.

During the expansion phase, technical innovation produces jobs, which provides money for consumer goods and housing, which creates more jobs in the less capital-intensive sectors of the economy until the capital structure for technical innovation is complete and overbuilt. Excess capacity and overbuilding are primary indicators of the end of a long wave expansion. Working out the overbuilding is one reason long wave contractions last as long as they do.

During the contraction phase, construction drops off, and construction-related jobs come to an end. Because of the overbuilding, rents are competitive, vacancies are high, and real estate debt is difficult to service. Foreclosures increase as the contraction gains momentum.

Indications of extremes in the long wave can be found in the perceptions and expectations of the public. Usually the optimism-pessimism measure is focused on one investment that tends to stay in the forefront of public attention. Best-selling books and get-rich seminars appear on the subject. It is the subject of social conversation. Everybody is in the market. At the peak, all are optimistic to the point of self-righteous indignation that anyone would question their investment belief system. After all, it is the road to financial security. But, it is also security for the debt used to speculate. In the 1920s it was the stock market; in the 1980s it was the real estate market.

The Effect of the Business Cycle on Real Estate

The United States has a history of business cycles reaching back over 130 years. Eight cycles have worked through the economy over the last 45 years, averaging 56 months in length. The expansions have averaged 45 months, and the contractions have averaged 11 months. The longest expansion was 106 months and the shortest 12 months. The contractions range from 6 to over 17 months, which is the current as yet unended and longest recession since the 1930s [7, p.2].

There is a sequence to the business cycle as it works through the economy. Generally, the financial markets react initially to lower interest rates. Then as housing construction and sales pick up, durable goods follow, such as appliances and cars, machinery and capital equipment.

Leading indicators of the business cycle are changes in interest rates, money supply, stock and bond prices, and housing starts, which tend to respond to the cycle 9 to 12 months before the rest of the economy. Changes in interest rates control the normal business cycle. Because of the sensitivity of housing and cars to interest rates, activity slows as the cycle matures and interest rates increase. As a contraction unfolds and interest rates drop, housing construction eventually starts again, leading the economy out of the recession with increased employment in construction and related industries [For more on the business cycle in action see "The Early Warning Forecast Method"(7)].

The business cycle is contained within the long wave cycle and is officially measured by two successive quarters of negative Gross

National Product (GNP). Measuring a recession on a national basis by consensus among economists has meaning in the practical world of regional real estate investment only to the extent that the recession has hit your investment region. And then a recession is significant only to the extent that it reduces local employment and income levels. Certainly, our recent industry- and regional-specific contractions have emphasized the primary importance of local market activity and the questionable use of questionable government statistics.

Employment and the availability of credit connect the business cycle to real estate. Local real estate markets are directly dependent on local employment and the availability of affordable credit. Real estate development simply doesn't happen unless the job base of the region is expanding, providing the requisite demand, while lenders provide funds for new construction. With the exception of retirement communities, demand for real estate follows jobs that provide a living wage. For that reason the normal business cycle has a direct influence on real estate financial performance.

The business cycle also has an influence on investor confidence. For example, a city with a history of net job gains over job losses will have a higher likelihood of loan availability for real estate development during a recession than a city with a history of not snapping back from the loss of major employer.

Lenders look at net job gains as an indication of economic health. Developments in cities with net job losses are not prime candidates for real estate financing because they do not recover quickly from recessions. However, financing is more readily available in cities that gain new jobs even while they are losing existing jobs in different industries during a normal business cycle. Net employment growth protects an area during the ups and downs of the business cycle. It is a prerequisite for the confidence of lenders and for real estate financing.

Activity in real estate consists of buying and selling, building and leasing. Real estate activity depends on the availability of credit. During the expansion phase of the normal business cycle, credit tends to be readily available for new construction and investment, as new jobs create new demand. Rates of return are high, and demand for rental space is strong. Investors and lenders expect the existing market activity to continue, based on current perceptions of its strength.

The normal business cycle is a short-term balancing of supply and demand and inflationary pressures and interest rates. New jobs during the expansion phase create new demand for more commercial and residential real estate. During the contraction phase, demand drops relative to supply.

As the long wave cycle progresses toward a peak, the business cycle swings to greater extremes with increased volatility in interest rates. Speculation increases as money moves toward assets that provide inflationary protection. The Fed steps in to increase interest rates trying to control inflation, thus edging the economy into recession.

Risk and uncertainty increase. Gradually, as interest rates rise, price appreciation as protection against inflation becomes a less important factor in real estate investment. And as expectations of inflation subside, cash flow and the ability to service debt replace inflation as the primary concern during the trough of the new recession.

Timing the Housing Cycle

Real estate market activity cannot be separated from the long wave and business cycles. Both have a great influence on the two major prerequisites for real estate market expansion—employment growth and the availability of credit. The long wave and business cycles are economic phenomena, both of which are more closely tied to real estate activity than generally acknowledged. The real estate investment and housing cycles are market cycles driven by supply and demand for real estate. Nevertheless, they are interrelated. For example, the housing cycle is typically expected to lead the economy out of recession. As interest rates drop, more people buy homes, increasing construction employment and stimulating related demand for furnishings and appliances. As the cycle matures, interest rates curtail housing sales and construction leading the economy into recession. The housing cycle is a residential cycle and therefore has a direct effect on demand for land needed for single-family subdivisions and apartment construction.

Housing cycle peaks occurred in 1972, in 1979, and in 1986—at 7-year intervals. Is the next peak due in 1993?

The indicator used for the housing cycle here is the volume of new home sales. Housing starts tend to peak slightly before home sales. Sales of existing homes when compared to new home sales tend to be less pronounced in cyclical amplitude and less related to the business cycle.

The 18-Year Real Estate Investment Cycle

The 18-year cycle in real estate activity is closely tied to the cycle of interest rates. Ideally there are three 18-year waves of real estate activity within the 54-year interest rate cycle [8, p.150]. This relationship fits well with the interaction of real estate, inflation, and the long wave. This cycle may be one of the more important time series in the real estate market. It is also one of the more difficult to track because of the monetary elements involved and the individual nature of the industry segments within real estate.

During the first half of the 1970s, the real estate investment cycle was beginning to rise out of a multiyear base culminating in a major top in the 1980s. This blow-off phase of real estate activity in the first half of the 1980s followed a top in gold and interest rates. Public infatuation with real estate as an inflation hedge continued well into the 1980s until the Tax Reform Act of 1986 ended many of the benefits. This extension of real estate construction and investment activity long after the primary indicators of inflation had signaled a change in trend illustrates the power of expectations to overcome market reality and produce excess supply.

When the peak or trough of any two cycles occurs during the same time period it tends to increase the intensity of that cycle phase. This is illustrated by the extreme unemployment of the 1930s depression during the bottom of a 54-year long wave that accompanied the bottoming action of the 18-year real estate investment cycle. More recently, the concurrent peaks in the real estate cycle and the long wave cycle in the 1980s illustrate the important influence of inflationary expectations in producing an oversupply of real estate. It also illustrates the influence of capital availability and investor expectations in overcoming the supply-demand reality of real estate.

Current projections for the ideal 18-year cycle indicate a potential bottom forming in 1996 [8, p.153].

Cycles are useful to the extent they help us understand the past, learn from it, and plan for the future. Clearly, there are events currently under way that point to a coincidence of the 18-year real estate cycle and the long wave 54-year cycle. There was a peak in the 18-year real estate cycle in 1925 followed by the foreclosures during the trough of 1933 [8, p.150]. Compare that with the speculative extremes of the early 1980s, the foreclosures of the late 1980s and 1990s, and the failure of the S&L system. The timing between peaks and troughs that defines a cycle is not the only way to use it in a real estate strategy. In fact, cycle timing may not be as important as knowing and adapting to the characteristics of cycle phases.

Peaks and troughs in the real estate cycle are not precise points in time when prices start rising or falling. Peaks can vary by a couple of years either side of the ideal timing. The real estate investment cycle is a process that can take years to complete and varies in time and intensity from region to region of the country.

Furthermore, cycle timing can be lengthened or shortened by outside events. The 1980 real estate cycle top appears to have occurred over several years (1981 to 1986) due in part to the favorable depreciation treatment of the 1981 Tax Reform Act and the liquidity pirated from the S&L system. In retrospect it is clear that the removal of the favorable treatment of real estate by the Tax Reform Act of 1986 increased the damage.

Guidelines for the Use of Cycles in Real Estate

All cycles can be divided into manageable units regardless of their length or the nature of their impact on real estate. The trend of a cycle is its phase—expansion or contraction of activity. There are two phases to a cycle. For example, the long wave, business, real estate, and housing cycles go through the expansion phase as the direction of each turns upward as the cycle's respective market activity increases.

The direction toward expansion is most apparent in the effect on five fundamental factors:

1. Prices increase as demand picks up.
2. Investor optimism dominates the market.
3. Interest rates trend upward; credit is available.

4. Inflation becomes a topic of concern.
5. Real estate market activity increases.

Both the long wave and business cycles progress through time and reflect change in these five fundamental factors. During the expansion phase of a cycle, the trend is up until a trigger event occurs to change the trend. It is the scope of investment activity that differs in each. For example, long-term capital investment necessary to bring technical innovation to the market characterizes the long wave. Shorter term consumer and durable goods demand and interest rate manipulation characterize the business cycle. And real estate construction and market activity for commercial, industrial, and housing characterize the real estate cycles.

Consequently, the nature of the change during the expansion phase varies from cycle to cycle. And the degree of impact on the financial performance of real estate also varies. The important thing is to know how cycles affect real estate financial performance. Then appropriate action can be taken to adapt to the change by gauging the degree of effect.

During the contraction phase the trend reverses.

1. Prices stabilize or drop as demand slows.
2. Investor pessimism dominates the market.
3. Interest rates trend downward; credit is restricted.
4. Deflation becomes a topic of concern.
5. Real estate market activity slows.

Government action is a triggering factor in the transition between cycle phases. Usually, some action is undertaken to control prices or influence interest rates or the money supply, or to raise revenue by changing the tax law, or instituting some change in banking regulations. There is always a reason such as the control of inflation or to stimulate the economy, but occasionally the reasoning is overshadowed by one or more unexpected or even accidental outcomes. The accidents often mark major trend changes, in public confidence, and the investment funds flowing into and out of real estate. For example, the deregulation of the S&Ls while providing deposit insurance must have been an accident. The real estate boom triggered by the 1981 Tax Reform Act and the real estate bust after the restrictions of the 1986 Tax Reform Act must have been accidents. Government by accident requires anticipation of the impact on the real estate market if the objective of transferring purchasing power through time is to be accomplished.

Using Cycle Characteristics for Investment Timing

Characteristics of the real estate market during expansion and contraction of various cycles can be tracked through the events typical of different stages of market activity. Phases of the real estate investment cycle occur in sequence. Although the business cycle and the real estate cycle may vary in time and even in location within the country, the sequence of events tends to remain constant.

Furthermore, turning points in the cycle are often triggered by a specific policy change or legislative incentive. During the final stages of the expansion phase, government action focuses on controlling inflation; during the final stages of contraction, it focuses on stimulating growth. The constant worry is that market forces will become so strong that even government action will not be able to influence them, and inflation or deflation will become uncontrollable.

Practical application of real estate cycles can be made with approximate investment timing, given a knowledge of the specific characteristics and sequence of the phases of the real estate investment cycle. Simply recognizing that there is a real estate investment cycle with a timing band that runs about 18 years from peak to peak and a housing cycle of about 7 years can be a helpful step in investment strategy. But knowing the specific characteristics of each cycle phase is even more useful.

Perception of the real estate market as strong and growing results in the expectation that demand will continue, at least long enough to absorb the new supply of rental space that secures the loan of the lender in question. But a perception of the real estate market that doesn't expect a change in the cycle is dangerous. It is a prescription for bad loans and foreclosure. Expectations that the present will continue without change, whether expanding or contracting, indicates a lack of awareness of financial history and an unnecessary exposure to risk.

It is difficult to see changes in the market as they occur because of the long-term nature of real estate investment. Construction of office space is characterized by the tendency to overshoot demand. Public speculation is characterized by the tendency to buy at the top, following the advice of get-rich-quick gurus who write popular books without mention of the down side of the real estate cycle. In this case the public includes the investment divisions of many large insurance companies and pension funds.

Special note should be made of the relationship between inflation and the objective of obtaining a real rate of return on invested funds. Prolonged periods of negative real interest rates tend to precede investment interest in real estate. Negative real rates dominated the market from late 1970 to the first half of 1978 [1, p.165]. During this period, inflationary expectations became entrenched and in part contributed to the boom in gold and real estate that followed, peaking in the 1980s as inflation slowed in response to high interest rates.

The real estate cycle is a dynamic process that unfolds through time with the lack of precision and error that is natural to investment life. Cycles may not always be precise examples of scientific reality. But they are very much examples of market reality. They can be understood, anticipated, and used to increase financial performance while avoiding costly mistakes.

Using Real Interest Rates as a Cycle Indicator

Real estate investment is ultimately a business that requires close management and an ongoing series of decisions. Pricing of rents, negotiation with tenants, meeting market competition, managing expenses, meeting debt service, and the impact of economic change are as much a part of the real estate investment business as any other business. And with real estate, as with any business, cash generated must sustain the purchasing power of the invested funds and generate a profit, or eventually the business will fail.

Maintaining purchasing power and earning a profit requires that an investment generate more money after taxes and expenses than is lost to inflation. This requirement is often expressed as a percentage rate of return or interest rate that is higher than the rate of inflation. Therefore, achieving an annual rate of return higher than the annual rate of inflation is one way to determine if an investment is protecting purchasing power.

This investment objective is accomplished by obtaining a positive rate of return or interest rate. Positive interest rates exist when they are higher than the inflation rate. Negative interest rates are lower than the inflation rate. Extreme fluctuations of rates between a positive and negative relationship to the rate of inflation is usually the result of government attempts to control economic activity or inflation itself. This is important because real estate prices are sensitive to long-term inflation trends. It is an historical fact that major fluctuations in real estate prices have been in response to the inflationary and deflationary cycles of our economy.

The trend of interest rates in relation to inflation is important to real estate because it indicates where investment capital is likely to be placed. For example, after a period of negative interest rates, investment capital tends to move into real estate and similar inflation hedges such as gold. Positive real interest rates tend to attract capital to debt instruments. This movement of capital between different assets is an attempt to maintain purchasing power based on expectations of inflation or deflation. This is a dynamic process. It can take years to unfold and involves monetary forces that often go beyond a single government policy initiative. The movement of interest rates from negative to positive is an early indicator of monetary policy shifts from inflationary to deflationary, and consequently point to the trend of the real estate investment cycle. These shifts in monetary policy reflected in interest rates, in part, affect market decisions as investors move funds to appropriate assets trying to protect purchasing power from inflation and deflation.

Cycles in interest rates are central to the 18-year real estate investment cycle and are possibly one of the best leading indicators of an approaching rise in real estate speculation and prices. The indicator works in the other direction just as well. High positive interest rates tend to foreshadow price deflation and trouble in the real estate market. The significant factor is the amount of the inflation-adjusted real interest rate, which is calculated as follows:

Calculating Negative Interest Rates

Nominal interest rate	8.0%
Less inflation rate	11.0%
Equals real interest rate	(3.0%)

Calculating Positive Interest Rates

Nominal interest rate:	14.0%
Less inflation rate:	8.0%
Equals real interest rate:	6.0%

The above examples approximate the rates actually available in early 1974 (negative rates) and the end of 1980 (positive rates) [1, p.165]. [Formula: 3-month Treasury Bills less GNP Deflator equals Real Interest Rate. Note: A more popular indicator is the Consumer Price Index (CPI), which is equally accepted in the real estate market.]

The two time periods used in this example are important points in the real estate cycle. In 1974 the 18-year investment cycle was completing a major bottom prior to accelerating into a cyclical peak in real estate values unprecedented in speculative frenzy, institutional participation, and public infatuation. In 1980 the cycle entered a multiyear topping process working through various regions of the economy during the next 8 years.

Accomplishing the objective of transferring purchasing power through time requires a real rate of return. This means care must be taken to protect invested funds from inflation as well as deflation. During the latter stages of the expansion phase of the long wave, inflation is the challenge; during the gaps between the expansion waves, deflation protection is the challenge.

The Role of Debt and Equity Investments in Real Estate

Inflation and deflation are primary economic forces in the competition for investment capital that exists between debt and equity assets. Positive real interest rates attract investment funds to debt instruments such as corporate and government notes and bonds of varying duration and with varying inflation and default risks. Negative real interest rates tend to force funds into equity investments such as gold and real estate.

Bond prices drop under inflationary conditions to discount the value in an attempt to increase the yield and thus offset purchasing power lost to inflation. This drop in value is a direct loss to bond holders. The longer inflationary conditions last, the greater the drop in bond prices necessary to increase yields as investors build past trends into expectations for the future. The extremes of inflation tend to appear as the long wave peaks.

Fluctuation in real estate investment activity is directly related to the flow of investment funds from debt to equity in the ongoing attempt to generate real wealth. Cycles record this flow through time. Consequently, cycles are especially useful in understanding past real estate market activity and what future market activity is likely to hold for prices.

During the gaps between long waves called *depressions* or *deflationary contractions*, funds tend to flow from overvalued equity investments to bonds and interest-paying instruments. As the transition phase progresses with decreasing interest rates, demand for bonds drives up their value while the demand for inflation protection diminishes, causing a drop in gold and real estate values.

The Economic Function of Real Estate

The market fluctuations we see as price appreciation and sometimes foreclosure have a connection to the broader trends within our economy. Real estate occupies such a fundamental place in economic activity that it is routinely accepted and rarely examined.

Our lives are so closely tied to real estate that we take its role in business for granted. But real estate has an economic function that goes beyond the buildings and structures we see everyday. Real estate construction is a major contributor to the health of our economy. It is a major factor in the long wave expansion and the depressions that follow. It seems that depressions are the time period needed for the overbuilding of the long wave to be absorbed and the structures to wear out so the next wave can begin [3, p.6].

Real estate is also a major contributor to the recovery phase of the business cycle as construction leads the way to increased employment and end of recession. The role of real estate in the economy is probably more important than is commonly acknowledged. In fact, it may be more central to national prosperity than is given credit in standard economic thinking.

Functionally, real estate is the support system for production and distribution of goods and services in our economy. This capital sector of the economy serves as the foundation for distribution of technology and realization of the improved quality of life that flows from employment growth.

Technological progress means jobs and demand for real estate. And of course the need for real estate means construction jobs. In the long-term cyclical march of our economy, real estate serves as a link in the distribution of technology to people in the form of a higher standard of living and quality of life.

For example, farms and ranches are support systems for production and distribution of new technology in food production and improved nutrition. Offices are support systems for the processing and distribution of information. Shopping centers are support systems for the distribution of consumer goods. Homes are support systems for living and personal security. Each type of real estate is a link in the distribution of new technology and the improved quality of life that has gradually followed technology-based employment.

The process of bringing new technology to the marketplace is the foundation of our employment base and the primary source of our historical national prosperity. Extended cycles of expansion and contraction in our economy have a direct effect on real estate in its function of distributing technology. The economic insight that defines real estate as a link in the distribution of technology provides new understanding of the effects of the long wave cycle on real estate investment [5].

Viewed with this new insight, real estate becomes a dynamic element of the economy. Office buildings are no longer just bricks and mortar, steel and glass. They are support systems for the production, processing, and distribution of information. Lawyers produce and process information about laws and distribute that information to clients. Accountants produce and process information about taxes and accounting standards and distribute it to clients and the IRS. Each type of office use focuses on the production, processing, and distribution of information. Even doctors performing operations are distributing information in the form of technological advances in health care and are therefore delivering the improved quality of life that is the central objective of our economy.

Notice the expansion of urgent health care distribution systems (buildings) on the busy intersections near residential neighborhoods. This real estate distribution network took health care from the central hospital and doctors' offices virtually to the front door of the people on a 24-hour basis. Real estate provided the support system for implementation of the growing technological advances in health care and provided an essential link in the economy necessary for distribution of those advances to the people.

Nowhere is the distribution of an improved quality of life using real estate as a support system more apparent than in our retail outlets. Here shopping centers and discount superstores serve as distribution centers for technical innovations embodied in new products [5].

Technical innovations in residences are one of the most direct manifestations of improved quality of life distributed through real estate. Home building standards have improved as advances in creature comforts work through the real estate distribution system to the life support system we call a house. New advances fast become standards of the industry. Improvements in electrical wiring, heating, air conditioning, and insulation routinely establish new minimum building standards. As time passes we have difficulty remembering when air conditioning was unheard of and central heating was something new. Our homes have so efficiently distributed technological advances that the level of comfort they provide is now taken for granted.

Every type of building functions in some way as a link in the distribution of technology, whether in the form of new products or information services. As our standard of living has changed so have our needs for real estate. Fast food restaurants and self-service gas stations are examples of the changing use of real estate as a link in the distribution of innovations in our economy.

New technology is naturally distributed throughout our economy as market activity unfolds. The connection between new technology and the distribution function of real estate is the key to understanding the role of real estate in the economy and the potential for wealth that it holds [for more on the role of innovation and wealth, see Pilzer (6)].

2
Applying Cycles to Real Estate Financial Analysis

Real estate cycles track the expansion and contraction of market activity—the sum total of buying, selling, leasing, and new construction. Cycles provide a sense of the future based on the market activity of the past. They embody experience and provide a framework for anticipating future cash flows.

Investing in the present for a higher quality of life in the future is one way of viewing the purpose of building real wealth. Transferring purchasing power through time is, on the other hand, simply an attempt to maintain the status quo, which is the first prerequisite of protecting investment capital from inflation and deflation.

The success of the task, whether accidental or intentional, hinges on the investment response to the cycles of activity that comprise the real estate market. It is this response that determines the timing and the amount of the cash flows generated by an investment.

We have a tendency to focus on the great waves of inflation and deflation that remain in the foreground of our planning long after their effects have been absorbed and the shorter term cycles deserve our attention. The expectation that inflation will never end is itself an expression of a fundamental element of the real estate market and provides an unexamined basis for risk acceptance. It continued to dominate the thinking of market participants through the 1980s even after the trend had been decisively turned by high interest rates and overbuilding.

The fear that real estate sales will remain subdued and the appreciation of past cycles will never be seen again is also an element of the natural adjustment process. This risk-aversive mindset is likely to dominate the market during the 1990s as we work our way through the gap between the fourth and fifth Kondratieff waves. Focusing on the events of the immediate past to form expectations for the future is part of the natural thought process. But it is an incomplete and limiting perspective when considering a long-term investment like real estate.

The real estate market is a dynamic segment of the national economy. It has several elements that interact concurrently. We see an active market as a whirlwind of buying and selling activity that hinges on credit availability and the need for rental space. We also see price changes that appear sudden and random, if not secret and known only to those who are in the middle of the daily negotiations. And eventually we see periods of inactivity and stagnation, all of which are part of the long-term cyclical nature of real estate.

Behind the apparent turmoil of activity and inactivity there are fundamental factors that give energy to the market and consistency to the cycles. These supporting elements are market forces that drive real estate activity and adjust prices while shaping the phases of cycles into trends and time periods.

Using Fundamental Factors to Monitor the Real Estate Market

Cycles directly affect financial performance by influencing market rents and the ability to sell for a satisfactory price, if at all. This influence can be traced to the fundamental factors of capital availability, supply and demand, and expectations. Each has a different role in the expansion and contraction phases of market cycles.

During an expansion phase, the trend of activity and prices is upward. Higher prices attract more supply to meet the obvious demand. An expansion is the high investment, high demand, optimistic phase of a cycle, generally referred to as an *active market*. Low activity characterizes the contraction phase. It is the low investment, low demand, pessimistic phase when it is difficult to rent space and sell real estate.

During the expansion phase of the real estate cycle, sales are frequent, new construction is underway, credit is available, land prices are rising, and optimism is growing. This expansion of activity is usually the result of an expanding employment base, increasing income, and a growing population, which create demand for real estate.

In the final stages of an expansion, the cycle typically goes to an extreme, providing too much capital and in doing so creating too much supply in the spirit of excessive optimism of both lenders and developers. In the final stages of the contraction phase, the extremes are also reached before the trend changes. But at the bottom of the cycle, credit is restricted, excess supply hangs over the market, and pessimism dominates investment thinking.

The expansion phase of the real estate investment cycle depends on credit availability. Credit means liquidity for real estate. And liquidity is the one thing that can push the real estate cycle to an extreme top, as occurred in the early 1980s when cash poured from the savings and loans (S&Ls) into real estate, putting a top on the market right on schedule for completion of the fourth Kondratieff long wave. As a result, the government has been forced to establish what amounts to a real estate holding company in the form of the Resolution Trust Corporation (RTC) to warehouse the excess supply of real estate.

When the market is out of balance and burdened with excess real estate, leasing and sales are slow, new construction grinds to a standstill, credit is tight, land prices are flat or falling, and there is growing pessimism that money will be lost by investing in real estate. And inevitably, unemployment becomes a local concern as construction jobs disappear.

Contractions in real estate activity are carried to extremes in proportion to the extremes of the prior expansion as if an equal and opposite reaction were mandatory. Price deflation is the expected consequence of a reversal of inflation. But with real estate prices, deflation tends to appear as a last resort after a lender has foreclosed.

The loan balance at foreclosure becomes the market price. Appraisals are meaningless even while lenders grasp at them in the hope that the property they just bought for their loan balance is by some miracle worth more than the bid they just made for it on the courthouse steps. Foreclosure comparables monitor the drop in real estate values and become the quotation system of inactive real estate markets.

For example, the S&L fiasco of the late 1980s and early 1990s is in part a deflationary reaction to the inflationary extremes of the combined long wave and real estate cycle peaks of the 1980s. The foreclosures, debt liquidation, and price reductions mirror the extreme expansion of activity that preceded the contraction. When an expansion reaches such an extreme it is likely that the inevitable contraction will also reach an extreme of equal magnitude.

The important point to keep in mind is that any one of the fundamental elements of the cycle can dominate and push the market into expansion or contraction. An overabundance of credit can create supply beyond the actual demand. Excessive speculative demand for small investment properties can take supply off the market and drive prices beyond reasonable expectations. And even faster, investors' expectations can turn on a dime, and the once optimistic visions of the future can turn to pessimism overnight. Any one of the fundamental factors can change the trend of activity and prices.

Cycles track this market-adjustment process as capital investment, supply and demand, and investor expectations work their way through the real estate market. Each factor has a direct effect on financial performance, as the pricing system reacts naturally and somewhat predictably to changes in these fundamental elements, expressed in the trend and timing of a cycle.

The long-term nature of real estate cycles seems to ensure their perpetuation. The experience of those who go through a complete cycle is often lost on new participants. The unrecorded and unknown experience of past real estate cycles is ultimately damaging to lenders and more recently to those who through the good graces of the government insure the loans—the taxpayers. Somewhere in our recent business and economic education, as mathematical formulas struggled to prove new theories, we neglected to review the history of the damage possible to real people who invest real money in real markets.

The message of long-term real estate cycles is that past fluctuations will continue to repeat in the future. One possible reason for this is the length of the long wave. People who experience this major cycle of overbuilding have died or retired by the time the subsequent long wave reaches a danger point. Consequently, we must rely on the recorded history of real estate cycles to alert the market participants to these fluctuations [9, p.177]. But even then it is an uphill battle of changing ingrained expectations, whether overly optimistic or overly pessimistic.

Each cycle continues to bring new participants without experience. This is especially dangerous for lenders who put hard cash into projects as well as the passive investors with equity capital who look to bankers for approval of the soundness of a project. Both are vulnerable to making decisions with no understanding of the position they will hold in the history of real estate cycles. So they look to the appraisal industry for support, but there, value has meaning only for a day.

The depressions of the 1890s and 1930s were both preceded by extreme oversupply of real estate. During the 1880s there was a considerable building effort in a generally deflationary environment of falling commodity prices. By the first part of the 1890s there was an oversupply of buildings [9, p.173], and the depression between the second and third Kondratieff waves began, ending in 1898. Overbuilding occurred again in the 1920s as the third Kondratieff topped, leading into the 1930s depression with an oversupply of real estate from 1925 to 1933 [9, p.174]. In the early 1990s, 100 years from the end of the second Kondratieff, the oversupply of real estate is so large that only the federal government can absorb the losses. And again, as preceded the 1890 and the 1925–1933 glut, the current overbuilding occurred in a deflationary environment of falling commodity prices. Commodity price tops occurred in 1920 and 1980, providing one of the best timing indicators of the inflation-deflation relationship.

Why are there such extremes in real estate market activity? And why do they recur with cyclical regularity every 50 to 60 years? We are fortunate to have recent econometric verification by Forrester [3] of what Schumpeter [4] recorded so thoroughly. The only answer and the only protection we may have is awareness of the day-to-day events that almost imperceptibly build on one another and interact in a causal relationship.

Certainly, real estate cannot be analyzed independently of the economy and of the general business activity of which it is such an important part. Once this is recognized, the best we can hope to do is modify our own real estate investment strategy based on an understanding of cycles and the fundamental and governmental factors that appear to be at least partial causes of the fluctuations in today's market.

The interrelationship between capital availability, supply-demand dynamics, and investor expectations drives the real estate market. Imposed on these fundamental factors is the relatively unpredictable impact of political expediency. These governmental factors, which include frequent changes in the tax laws, regulations, and monetary policy are growing in importance. Their role seems to be one of a trigger mechanism for major changes in the cycle as they exert growing influence on the real estate market.

Yet nothing so far has modified the tendency for the real estate market to fluctuate in approximately regular cycles. Consequently, from a practical standpoint we can integrate both the fundamental and governmental factors into real estate investment planning with an understanding of their historical and recent roles in the market. This can be done with an alert eye on the possible financial effects they contribute to and are likely to cause in the future.

Financial performance is the bottom line of the real estate industry, but it does not occur in a vacuum. It occurs in a market. The market has components that we have specified as fundamental and governmental forces which drive the real estate industry. History demonstrates and computer modeling has verified that very long-term cycles occur in the economy as the real estate industry reaches overcapacity. These waves of expansion are punctuated by gaps in activity as the oversupply is absorbed or worn out and a new wave of building and prosperity can begin, bringing new technical innovations and a better standard of life to the country.

How Governmental Factors Can Trigger Market Change

Although insurance companies and pension funds were major loan participants, S&Ls led the way in the excessive lending that resulted in the debt liquidation cycle of the late 1980s and 1990s. Changes in the regulation of the S&L industry and tax laws related to real estate contributed to the excess. But the foundation for the excess was laid by the inflationary policies of the late 1960s and early 1970s (the Great Society and Vietnam War, monetary inflation in the 1970s). This is when the printing presses started rolling. The increase in prices in the late 1970s was a natural consequence.

The rise in prices changed expectations. Formerly reluctant and conservative investors began seeing real estate in a new and more accepting frame of mind. Possibly by now that view has reverted to the original more conservative approach, illustrating the effect of a complete cycle.

Government policy and changes in the tax laws often mark turning points in the real estate cycle. Usually accidentally, politically based change can send the market into volatile fluctuation in price and activity. A well-defined example of the effect of tax law change is the reduction in depreciation term in the 1981 Tax Reform Act and the subsequent flip-flop in the 1986 Tax Reform Act that not only lengthened the depreciation of real estate but also greatly complicated and restricted the tax benefits. The 1981 law increased the tax-related cash flow benefits of real estate, working in concert with the deregulation of the S&Ls to produce an oversupply. The 1986 change terminated the tax benefits and triggered the inevitable real estate depression.

Government influence continued to complicate the bottoming process as capital markets were invaded by banking regulators who discovered they might have a degree of negligent responsibility in the S&L fiasco and the creeping insolvency of the banking industry. About mid-1990, banking regulators unilaterally clamped down on lending contrary to federal policy. Bank examiners instigated highly restrictive and unreasonable capital requirements and borrower qualification and loan security prerequisites; again, slightly behind unfolding events and afraid of blame for not doing their job long after it was too late to correct their perceived negligent inaction.

This regulatory initiative triggered the longest national recession since the 1930s. It has the dangerous distinction of being the first regulatory recession, and more seriously, it shows that the control of a bureaucracy goes beyond limits of economic policy thought to rest with elected politicians. With the irony that balances the scales of the marketplace, in 1991 the federal government, through foreclosures and bank failures became the second largest owner of hotels in the United States (Hilton is first). Clearly, there was an excess of real estate as the last decade of the twentieth century began, as was the case in 1890, 100 years earlier.

Therefore, we can see the impact of governmental factors on the real estate market in three areas with examples from recent history to illustrate the consequences.

1. Changes in tax law.

   Example: The Tax Reform Act of 1981 increased the tax savings cash flow of real estate, attracting equity capital and encouraging new construction.

   Example: The Tax Reform Act of 1986 took away the tax savings cash flow of the 1981 Act and fundamentally changed and complicated the tax treatment of real estate, discouraging real estate investment, greatly reducing the yield possible on real estate investments and thus assuring an immediate drop in values. (One common estimate of the decrease in value is 30 percent.)

2. Changes in regulation.

   Example: The S&Ls were deregulated as the 1980s began while deposits remained insured by the federal government. Government insured loans without regulation and provided a source of capital for real estate loans and acquisitions, helping to produce an oversupply of real estate.

   Example: In the mid-1990s bank examiners, seeing the S&L debacle, decided to clamp down beyond the limits of prudence on all banks, thus restricting credit and triggering the longest recession since the Great Depression. For 2 years the executive branch of the government has been trying to convince the bureaucrats to lighten up.

3. Changes in monetary policy.

   Example: In the beginning of the 1970s the government tried to get the country out of recession by printing money, laying the foundation for price increases during the rest of the decade.

   Example: The Carter Administration capped the 1970s with an almost schizoid monetary policy that sent inflation through the roof and the general public to real estate as a refuge.

Obviously, these fundamental and governmental factors exist only in relationship to each other. Consequently, their impact on the real estate market is likely to be in some way exacerbated or muted by the interrelationship. Modify one variable and the other variables and the consequences change. But with the accuracy of hindsight we don't need a computer to tell us what common sense and the experiences of the last 20 years has driven home. Sometimes just understanding the pricing system of the market is all that is needed to figure out the consequences of the changes underway. For example, the relationship between cash flow and real estate value is tightly linked. Cut off the cash flow and the value will fall. The value of real estate is ultimately determined by cash flows, regardless of the source of origin.

The Effect of Capital Availability on Real Estate Markets

There are two forms of capital investment in real estate—debt and equity. During the beginning of the acceleration of the great inflation in the 1970s, low-interest loans were assumable at rates less than the rate of inflation. These loans were a windfall for equity investors and a true loss of purchasing power for debt investors.

For example, a real estate investor acquires an apartment complex in 1972 by assuming an existing 7 percent loan. The lender approves the assumption locking in a low interest rate protected by a high equity first-mortgage position. The terms of acquisition include a second mortgage bearing an interest rate of 8 percent and a 20 percent down payment. About 3 years into the ownership life of the apartments, inflation crosses 7 percent, and the cost of the first mortgage is suddenly zero. A year later inflation crosses 8 percent, and the cost of debt capital for the entire apartment complex is eliminated. The apartment complex value is growing at the rate of inflation, maintaining purchasing power for the equity investor and in fact, because of the leverage, returning a profit beyond inflation.

The leverage that provides a profit for the equity investor does so in this case at the expense of the debt investor. The loaned funds are not providing a return after inflation to the debt investor. The utility of the borrowed funds for the equity investor far exceeds the utility of the funds to the debt investor. The equity investor is getting far more satisfaction from the loan than the debt investor. The use of the funds to meet the objective of transferring purchasing power through time works for the equity investor but not for the debt investor.

In this example, inflation is approaching 10 percent and fast cutting into the purchasing power of the capital that was loaned to acquire the property. The equity investor is making money with the borrowed funds because the loans on the property are at an interest rate less than the inflation rate. Had the equity investor paid all cash he or she would simply be keeping up with inflation, but now the investor is picking up the spread on the difference between the inflation rate and the interest rate on the loans. It is a very expensive loan for the debt investor, however, because each year of inflation cuts deeper into the purchasing power of the unpaid balance of the loans.

This is just the type of inflationary scenario that created adjustable rate loans and legislation allowing banks and S&Ls to invest in a broad range of business activities. It is also the inflationary spiral that produced an uncritical expectation of real estate appreciation in the national mindset.

The real estate market depends on reasonably priced credit. Neither residential nor nonresidential construction can exist in their present form without long-term financing. This link to the credit markets is one reason the business cycle closely tracks the housing cycle. As interest rates fall during a recession, housing sales increase, and new construction gears up. Housing sales ripple through the durable goods sector of the economy as appliances, furniture, and carpets are purchased for new homes, often leading the economy to recovery. Just as high interest rates trigger recessions in the business cycle, low interest rates provide the capital to lead the economy to recovery.

There are other sides to the fundamental factor of capital availability in real estate cycles. Builders do tend to keep on building if they can get the funds and there is even the remotest chance that there will be a market for their product. The office building market has a long history of extreme overbuilding.

During the early 1980s when money was hemorrhaging from the S&Ls, there was a point where it became obvious in Texas that the see-through (completely vacant) office buildings were going to remain so for years. One developer was asked why he was starting a new project when it was fast becoming apparent that new office space could not be absorbed in a reasonable time period. He said in reply, "I know what's happening here, but I can't stop—I have a job for at least 2 more years. If they will loan me the money I'll build. If I stop I'll be unemployed." This motivation and basis for risk acceptance is somewhat different than that of a banker sitting behind a desk trying to figure out what to do with all the money he has on deposit.

During this time period, loans for real estate projects (debt investments) were more easily obtainable than ever before in history. This availability of debt capital combined with favorable tax laws to fuel an oversupply of property in certain segments of the real estate market. It almost appeared that lending institutions had suddenly discovered investment real estate and were playing catch-up with equity investors without regard for the reality of the supply-demand balance.

Again the lenders were just behind the learning curve. They were buying when they should have been selling into the peak of the cycle. Yes, they were buying real estate because it was the security for the loans they made. And to make a loan is to accept the risk of eventually owning the property in case of default at the price set by the remaining loan balance.

Each lender who properly evaluates a loan must ask whether he or she would buy the property for that loan amount. Too often the question does not consider the real estate cycle and the supply-demand relationship that is likely to exist during the time period a foreclosure is likely to occur.

The availability of capital is inadvertently controlled by government policy and directly controlled by the Federal Reserve Board and regulatory system. Directly, the Federal Reserve action is seen through the fluctuations of the business cycle as short-term interest rates are increased to avoid inflation and lowered to pull the economy out of recessions; clearly, a major element of the real estate cycle.

As the role of government in the capital markets illustrates, when the conversion of debt investments to equity investments (the foreclosure process) begins, it is too often due to market influences extending far beyond the past and future performance of the property itself. Consequently, the appraisal tradition that establishes property values for loan purposes out of the context of cycle phases is of little comfort or practical utility to the lender.

Loan policy is normally based on the acceptance of risks based on perceptions and expectations that go far beyond the specific performance of the property serving as security. But lenders are as subject to hope and optimism and fear and pessimism as are equity investors. Motivated by fear and greed, lenders are subject to speculative frenzy no less than owners.

The foreclosure process is the debt liquidation stage of the cycle. When it is complete, usually taking years, the market will be prepared for a new expansion and the new creation of credit that will occur with the new generation of both debt and equity investors. And no doubt, new tax laws and lending policies will be introduced by a new generation of political leaders to "reform" the old and provide a new prosperity.

Home equity loans present a unique collision of tax law and real estate lending with potentially disastrous consequences. The elimination of the deduction of personal interest implemented by the Tax Reform Act of 1986 spawned borrowing against home equity for consumer purchases to maintain interest deductibility. Why a government that wants to stimulate demand would eliminate interest deduction on consumer purchases is the first question. But let's just write that off to political bargaining within the old boy network and deal with the end result of encouraging excess debt on personal residences. The market took steps to protect against the tax increase by borrowing against appraised equity. The government didn't get the increase in revenue projected by the House Ways and Means Committee staff, but a lending industry was born as banks discovered the benefits of second mortgages on appreciated real estate.

In 1933 there existed a situation commonly referred to as the *mortgage crisis.* Cash was in short supply, and banks were foreclosing on houses to obtain cash. Home loans were short term then, and after 4 or so years when they came due the banks could renew or foreclose. Because of the lack of money, banks were demanding payment, which took more money out of the economy. Not only had the government tightened up on the money supply, but banks were pulling money out of the economy that could have purchased consumer goods. These two factors added to unemployment [10, p.575].

Home equity loans are now jeopardizing the perceived wealth of the nation with the burden of high interest loans. Home equity is the American savings account, and these loans are withdrawals with mandatory payback provisions. The effect of this tax-law-induced borrowing binge is more likely to result in diminished perceived and actual individual wealth and damage to confident expectations. It leaves a cash flow requirement that will remain long after the satisfaction provided by the borrowed funds has been forgotten. Is it possible that home equity loans will become the mortgage crisis of the current long-term cycle? Or, will a crisis be caused by the recent adjustable rate mortgages obtained at low teaser rates accepted on the faith that interest rates will never reach the unreasonably high levels again?

The availability of capital is central to the financial performance of real estate. There would be no liquidity and no market without borrowed funds. The 1930s demonstrated that. Nevertheless, the creative loans of today's market present a challenge that requires that we maintain high enough income levels to maintain debt service.

Supply-Demand Characteristics of Real Estate Cycles

Although investment capital is a prerequisite, the supply-demand adjustment process of real estate is the most basic force of the market cycle. The oversupply that accumulates throughout the economy during the expansion phase of the long wave is difficult to see because the time period is so long, but effects of supply-demand changes show clearly in the housing cycle with its 7-year peaks.

During the expansion phase of the housing cycle, builders acquire lots for new construction. The majority of the lots are inventoried at the peak of the cycle when demand is highest but approaching an end. Interest costs to hold land are highest at this time. The increase in interest rates, in part because of demand for credit, works to reduce housing demand while increasing the carrying cost of land.

Eventually, the added cost of houses combines with the gradual balancing of the supply-demand relationship to choke off home purchases. The struggle to survive during the following contraction in housing activity is often more than new builders and their banks can endure. Yet this burden is too often unnecessarily accepted as part of being in the construction business. Builders and lenders who are unaware that they are part of predictable, repetitive cycles tend to increase debt exposure when the cycle seems strongest at market tops. This tendency to increase risk based on the length of time the expansion phase has been in force can be avoided by recognizing the time regularity of the housing cycle.

Forecasting based on cycles applies the lessons of real estate history to present trends. Computerized accuracy of an engineer is not required. Simple awareness is sufficient for caution in the face of expansions that are on the verge of running their course.

Both expansions and contractions end, and the change that follows requires a change of investment strategy.

The implication of an approaching cycle top is that demand is soon to be less than supply. Conversely, the implication of a cycle bottom is that supply is soon to be less than demand. The approximately regular time period between peaks and bottoms in market activity provides a simple guideline for changing strategy.

Overbuilding is typical of the momentum generated during the expansion phase of the real estate investment cycle. The construction of office buildings and retail centers reflects this tendency to create excessive supply, stopping only when loans for new construction are no longer available. The natural supply-demand adjustment process can be made worse by outside interference, which can extend the cycle to extremes that otherwise would not have occurred.

Government tax incentives for real estate investment play a large role in stimulating supply through artificially created cash flows—that is, cash flows that do not come directly from the operation of the property, but from the indirect source of sheltered outside income. This unreliable cash flow from tax benefits causes instability in the real estate market and dependency on the unpredictable nature of next year's tax law change.

The Tax Reform Act of 1981 created very favorable depreciation for real estate, which stimulated building to take advantage of the tax incentive. Tax benefits combined with easily available credit to produce an extreme oversupply of office buildings, commercial centers, and hotels during the 1980s.

The influence of the tax incentives triggered an expansion in real estate construction that could only end in a major contraction. As the new supply reached the market, the tax incentives were retracted in 1986. This sequence reinforced the truth that tax incentives are as unpredictable as the politicians who dream them up. At best they destabilize the supply-demand balancing efforts of the market. At worst they create artificial demand for unneeded supply and ultimately create oversupply that adds to the absorption time necessary for the cycle to complete the bottoming process.

The supply-demand element of the real estate cycle provides an unarguable definition of overbuilding: Overbuilding exists when the rent produced by a property is insufficient to cover operating expenses and meet debt service. Property that does not meet this basic cash flow criteria shifts the problem to different owners, whether investors who buy negative cash flow properties or lenders who are forced to foreclose.

Eventually, the demand for cash flow to meet expenses and debt service catches the largest promoter, the largest bank, the largest insurance company, and the largest government. There can be too much real estate when it is understood in terms of the cash flow necessary to support operations and service debt. This is the characteristic of a long wave top that ends in collapse when the cash flow can't support debt service.

Moving from one extreme to another both satisfies demand and reduces leasing activity as tenants settle into new properties. The eventual lack of activity due to excess supply forces rents lower as owners compete for fewer tenants. Typically, new owners (due to foreclosure) with lowered expectations (due to time) adjust to the contraction by lowering rents and writing down loan balances. Then, as if completing the circle, excessive supply is absorbed. Tenants must then compete for the diminishing supply of space, forcing rents higher and eventually stimulating new construction and a higher level of activity.

This type of rhythmic price change and competitive interaction is how the market adapts to variations in supply and demand. It is truly a competitive process that requires adjustment in price (downward) to stimulate demand and absorb existing property followed by a different price adjustment (higher) to attract new supply to meet demand after the old supply is absorbed.

Balance between supply and demand is provided by the pricing mechanism. When demand is high relative to supply, rising prices check demand and, consequently, serve to ration supply. When supply is high, falling prices serve to attract demand and help the market absorb existing supply.

This cyclical ebb and flow of supply and demand, regulated by price change, is the core of the real estate industry. Investing in real estate is an attempt to capture a portion of the natural price adjustment process during a specific time period. The important thing to keep in mind is that cycles can help you time investment transactions for the most advantageous price as the supply-demand balance changes. Also, watch the outside influence of the capital markets and government policy. They can be clues to the timing of the turning points in the direction of a cycle.

Working Expectations into Real Estate Analysis

Both equity and debt investors base decisions on expectations that are heavily weighted by perceptions of the present. Cycles go to extremes in part because perceptions of the present tend to be projected as the expectations of the future. Present conditions are too readily expected to continue without change, regardless of whether conditions are favorable or unfavorable. This is the human side of risk that produces confidence in the real estate market, and that confidence level determines our willingness to accept risk.

Consequently, it is understandable that confidence tends to be high when markets are active and prices are rising. Risk is perceived as low because there appears to be sufficient activity to sustain the trend in prices and sufficient liquidity to sell an investment if the trend turns. Of course, that is the catch. If the trend does turn from expansion to contraction, the high activity which provided the initial confidence will vanish in a relatively short time [12].

Perceptions about real estate reach deep into the economy and touch consumer confidence and perceptions of wealth and expectations for future security. Housing prices are the basis of perceived if not actual financial security for most families. Buying a house is the single largest investment of a lifetime for most people, and a substitute for a cash savings account. Any perceived loss of home value can have a direct impact on feelings of financial security and willingness to spend on other consumer items. This reluctance to spend can have far-reaching negative effects on businesses that are not directly related to housing. Confidence in the sustained value of our housing plays a large role in our national feeling of well being. It is probably second only to job security in molding our expectations for a safe financial future.

Unfortunately, perceptions that are slow to adapt to changes in the cycle also affect the competitive pricing of rents for commercial and office space. Investment real estate is a competitive business that requires adaptation to changes in the supply-demand balance. Perceptions that lag the cycle and cling to expectations of the prior phase increase the risk of vacancies and the loss of tenants to competitive space. Competitive adaptation is the rule of survival during a contraction.

The challenge of investing in real estate is to develop perceptions that are based on change and expectations that recognize the cyclical regularity of the real estate market. The challenge is thus to adapt quickly to the changes in the cycle; to meet the competitive environment of a contracting real estate market with competitive rents that attract tenants in a slow market; to raise rents when the market allows; to sell fast if you need to, before the market turns down; to buy fast as the market turns up; to face the need to lower rents without clinging to expectations that the market will come back before the lender forecloses.

How you adapt to the cyclical nature of the real estate industry can have a direct effect on how successful you are in transferring purchasing power through time. Risk perception and the expectations you have affect the strategy you implement.

Ultimately, the events of the real estate market produce expectations that tend to be optimistic or pessimistic. Extreme optimism combined with easy credit and rising prices produces speculative markets. Extreme pessimism can terminate a market overnight. This psychological climate is a major cause of the tendency of real estate to overshoot logical supply-demand balance points. Hope and optimism tend to be greatest at the top; fear and pessimism tend to be greatest at the bottom.

Extremes in expectations are warnings of turning points in the cycle. They are red flags to watch for changes that are likely to trigger a new trend and a move to the next phase. Events that trigger moves to a new phase in the cycle tend to be sudden and significant. They are usually effects on the psychological climate, changing a long-established perception and turning expectations in a new direction.

It is difficult to remember the investment difficulties of a long-past contraction in real estate investment when you are in the middle of a topping process. But the property that was acquired at the beginning of the great inflation of the 1970s was the basis of the profits at the inflationary top that formed during the early 1980s.

During the first half of the 1970s we were well into the volatile inflationary environment characteristic of a long wave top. But real estate investment activity had not gained popular acceptance with the public. Public infatuation with real estate did not begin until after the mid-1970s recession. Real estate investment was perceived as a high-risk venture and ignored by popular investment wisdom. The Real Estate Investment Trust (REIT) securities debacle was fresh in the public perception. Expectations for the future of real estate were less than enthusiastic if not basically pessimistic, which created a strong investment base for change and rising prices. All that was needed was public awareness of inflation, which hit the market after the recession.

By 1980 real estate was viewed in a different light by the public at large and the major lending institutions. Credit availability and deregulation was nudging the S&Ls into real estate. Buying small rental properties was the topic of party conversation and the subject of seminars, best selling books, and investment clubs that approached the emotional intensity of a religious belief system. These are all clear warning signs of an extreme top in activity. Risk was not a popular consideration. In fact, it was unpopular not to invest in real estate and an act of stupidity to question the wisdom of going into debt to purchase property that was not producing enough income to pay debt service. If there can be such a thing as a buying panic in real estate, the 10 years between 1976 and 1986 would probably be a good time period for researching its characteristics.

Negative cash flow was accepted without question as part of the investment orthodoxy, and seminars on how inflation would appreciate buyers out of the hole were commonplace. The increase in public acceptance of real estate fueled market activity. There were more buyers both large and small, increasing the depth and liquidity of the market. Expectations of never-ending inflation seemed to put the old concerns about real estate being liquid in the background. High market activity made it easier to participate without thoughtful analysis of the consequences. There seemed to be plenty of buyers, and because of the popularity expectations changed. Real estate became the new investment vehicle to financial security.

Clearly the investing public had changed its perception of real estate. This change coincided with the trend of rising inflation, readily available credit for real estate, and a surge in new development—all fundamental elements of a cycle top.

By the end of the 1970s . . .

1. Capital was racing to real estate—both debt and equity. Loans were easy to get, and buyers were willing to invest cash as real estate investment became a national pastime.

2. Demand was outpacing supply, and developers were accelerating new construction. New products were heading for the market as never before during the first half of the 1980s.

3. Perception of real estate as a high-risk investment was lost in anticipation of the wealth that was sure to come. Public expectations locked in the belief that real estate would provide a safe haven for investment funds against the dangers of inflation. Yet the rate of inflation had peaked in 1980 and steadily decreased during the first half of the 1980s.

The fundamentals of the market all pointed to an approaching top in real estate activity during the 1980s, but real estate is a regional industry and becoming more so as pockets of employment become increasingly independent in different regions of the country. Consequently, the topping process takes years to work through the whole country as the rolling recessions of this long wave gradually work out of the economic system.

Understandably, moving through the expansion phase of a cycle with the high degree of activity that it involves creates a momentum of its own. There is a security in group behavior and excitement that anticipates continued profits from a highly active real estate market.

The perception of high activity and a secure market trend fosters expectation of continued high activity and profits. Consequently, pro formas for projects tend to assume there is no such thing as a real estate cycle or a business cycle or a long wave cycle. The short-term view tends to be the only view. The risk or reward perceived during the most recent phase of the cycle becomes the expectation for the immediate future.

When the cycle turns and real estate activity slows to a relative stop and reality creeps unavoidably into expectations for the future, pro formas are probably not seen as worth writing because the project is not likely to get a loan anyway. Low activity means no demand and no loans. It may mean a real estate market flooded with supply, low prices, and few if any buyers. And again, the short-term view is the popular view.

There is false safety in establishing a belief system around an investment vehicle. It is dangerous because it removes the uncertainty (the necessary questioning) of making a decision that might prove to be wrong. Excessive popularity is a warning sign. Group consensus provides false security—it is the safety net used by investment committees of large companies as well as the investing public.

It doesn't have to be this way—simple questions can help provide perspective. For example, are the expectations of easy cash flow distorting the possibility of not being able to make debt service? Is the hope that the market is about to turn and enter a new and profitable rent increase phase interfering with the reality of a very competitive market that requires competitive rents today?

Expectations play such an important role because they can produce investment decisions that are based more on optimism or pessimism than realistic cash flow projections.

Using Activity Trends to Define Cycle Timing

Focusing on market activity (the intensity of buying and selling, leasing, and construction) is the clearest way to visualize the real estate investment cycle. Market activity is the core of the cycle. It encompasses more than fluctuations in rental and sales prices. Activity includes speculative investment, the sum total of new construction, leasing activity, and the general buying and selling of real estate in response to supply and demand. Real estate activity as defined here is the volume of money flowing into real estate of all kinds. Therefore, high activity requires a high degree of capital availability. In commercial real estate, especially offices, the availability of credit seems to be the dominant force in the boom-to-bust cycle. In the housing market the availability of credit and investment volume can be traced to fluctuation in the cost of capital, or interest rates, which drives the normal business cycle.

Activity is the expression of the total real estate market and can be separated into trends within the real estate investment cycle, which are best described as the stages of the cycle.

1. *Basing*—low activity at the bottom, contracting
2. *Rising*—expanding activity
3. *Topping*—high activity, expanding
4. *Falling*—contracting activity

These cycle stages reflect the activity of the fundamental elements of the cycle—capital investment, supply-demand, and expectations. Changes in the trend, or the transition from one stage to another, are often triggered by governmental factors such as tax laws, regulations, and monetary policy. Cycle stages reflect the momentum of market activity that occurs as the cycle unfolds.

The sequence of cycle stages, the expansion-contraction relationship, and the timing of a cycle are all clues to the condition of the market that is likely to occur in the future. Often the transition is difficult to anticipate, but it does eventually happen to some degree in every region of the country.

Although real estate cycles do tend to have similar time periods between peaks, the timing of expansions and contractions are at best averages reflecting the unfolding of events that can last for several years. Precision and certainty as to timing are not necessary. It is important, though, to recognize that the trends within the cycle occur in sequence and that each has its own activity pattern related to capital availability, supply and demand, and investor expectations.

For example, a basing stage calls for a different investment strategy concerning debt commitment and risk exposure than when the trend is topping. Consequently, the ability to rent space, obtain financing, and sell can be easier or more difficult depending on the trend of the cycle. Knowing the sequence of the stages of a cycle provides an opportunity to adapt to the approaching change in trend and the different market conditions that constitute the pattern of activity during that stage.

Therefore, each stage of the cycle requires a different set of assumptions. Each set of assumptions results in a different financial scenario. And each scenario is a different set of cash flows with a different contribution to the likelihood of meeting the investment objective of transferring purchasing power through time and building wealth. The cyclical effect on cash flow links market conditions and financial performance.

There is a structure to the real estate cycle, even though the variations in timing and regional occurrence are almost too complicated to monitor. There is substance and reason behind the events of the real estate market that we see unfolding in the daily news. There *are* causes, and they can be understood and used in daily analysis to develop investment strategy.

Classifying Activity Patterns in the Real Estate Market

The activity patterns that tend to recur during different stages of the real estate investment cycle are well known to market professionals who are involved in the market on a daily basis. But even with this high degree of familiarity, or possibly because of it, the same rhythm repeats over the years. The tendency to overbuild and the tendency for shortages to develop is not some mistake or error. It is just the way the market works in an attempt to adapt to human needs as best we understand how.

Activity patterns can be classified by cycle stages and the characteristics typical during each stage.

Activity Patterns of the Real Estate Cycle

Cycle stage: Basing—contraction ending

Activity: low
 Capital availability: credit tight, cash equivalent preferred
 Supply-demand balance: vacancies decreasing
 Expectations: pessimistic

Cycle stage: Rising—expansion starting

Activity: picking up
 Capital availability: credit starting to loosen, some buying
 Supply-demand balance: demand for space becoming apparent
 Expectations: pessimism ending

Cycle Stage: Topping—expansion ending

Activity: high
 Capital availability: credit easy, buyers active
 Supply-demand balance: demand stronger, supply increasing
 Expectations: excessive optimism

Cycle Stage: Falling—contraction starting

Activity: slowing
 Capital availability: credit tightens, sellers look for disappearing buyers
 Supply-demand balance: supply everywhere, demand drops off
 Expectations: optimism ending

There are two obvious points in the ownership of real estate when cycle considerations are especially important. One is when measuring the success of a past investment and the advisability of selling in the present. The other is in forecasting the likely future performance when considering the possibility of making a new real estate investment. The first requires that the cash flow received over the holding period of the investment be measured to determine the real purchasing power earned. The second requires that the likely cash flows be projected into the future and the potential change in purchasing power be estimated. In both cases the timing guidelines provided by cycles can be helpful in the decision process.

Cycles reflect the change that occurs in market conditions over time. Clearly, market conditions have a strong influence on whether an investment meets its objective of transferring purchasing power and building wealth from the time of initial investment in the past to the present, and from the present to the future.

The accuracy of a pro forma depends on the accuracy of the underlying assumptions. And the accuracy of any set of assumptions depends on the awareness of the person deciding what to put in the pro forma. Cycles are helpful in real estate analysis because cycles provide a sequential time structure for choosing assumptions based on a history of recurring activity patterns of past markets. They record and monitor the repetitive events of the market, as conditions change with regularity and a degree of predictability. Cycles are both a history and a hint of the future. They are the inescapable reality of past real estate market activity and a knowing guide to the markets of the future.

Searching for the 18-Year Real Estate Investment Cycle

Although timing of real estate cycles may be less important than the patterns of activity they reflect, there is a history of investment in real estate including construction, investment, and general activity that exhibits timing that is distinct from the housing cycle. This longer term cycle appears to combine with cycles in interest rates, inflation, and construction activity of all types.

Consequently, major peaks in housing activity occur at the approximate 18-year periods with general real estate investment, encompassing three 7-year single-family home cycles. The last of the 7-year housing cycles occurs around the high point of the 18-year cycle. This is where the general flow of activity is more important than the precise timing of a cycle.

The 18-year cycle may not be noticed until an extreme brings it to the attention of market participants. The topping stage in the first half of the 1980s appears to be one of these extremes.

Peaks and Troughs in the 18-year Cycle

Peaks	Troughs
1834.3	1843.5
1852.6	1861.8
1871.0	1880.2
1889.3	1898.5
1907.6	1916.8
1926.0	1935.2
1944.3	1953.5
1962.6	(1971.8)
(1980.9)	(1990.1)
(1999.2)	(2008.4)

Note: Parentheses are (projections) of 18.3-year cycle data in Dewey [13, p. 344].

This time series has use if you can live with the necessary lack of exactitude typical of real estate market activity. The cycle in this table is described as an 18.33-year rhythm. In the real world of current markets we know that the ideal times are useful guidelines for processes that may in fact take years to complete, running longer and sometimes shorter than the ideal projection.

For example, the topping process in the first half of the 1980s took years to unfold, and became obvious only when the 1986 tax law triggered a real estate watershed. Additional complications existed because the cycle was peaking at slightly different times in different regions of the country.

Major tops take longer to complete, and this does appear to be a major top, coinciding with the 54-year long wave top. Conversely, the bottoming process to follow is likely to be a major and difficult cycle phase, as indicated by the foreclosures and government bailout programs.

The long wave cycle is a capital investment cycle. The 18-year cycle is a capital investment cycle. The housing cycle is a capital investment cycle. Certainly they are also construction cycles, but what is construction if not investment in real estate?

Past studies of time series emphasized the rhythm of regularity that defined the cycle. From a pragmatic point of view there is more to a cycle than the approximate times of the peaks and troughs. When you know the timing, what use is it unless you know the market implications as well?

The most important aspect of real estate cycles is the internal, fundamental characteristics of the activity pattern; that is, the pattern of activity typical of the stage of the cycle that is currently underway and the stage that is yet to follow. Also, the sequence of the stages can be useful because they provide some indication of what is likely to follow after the current stage is complete.

Cycles contain the real-life ups and downs of investment life in real estate. They are not just archaic academic studies of prices and time series popular in the past, before computer modeling and statistical analysis reached its current maturity. Cycles contain the life dreams and hopes and fears and losses of the entrepreneurial and investment activity that sustains our economy. While the population has grown and the number of government programs designed to prevent the panics of past cycles has increased, cycles are still very much with us. And there is growing evidence that the major element of a cycle expansion is the level of capital investment involved, which of course is largely real estate related. And the major element of a contraction may be the inability of the capital of the prior expansion to generate a market rate of return on the investment: Because of the oversupply, rents are insufficient to cover expenses and debt service.

3
Specifying Real Estate Cash Flows

Cycles are fluctuations in market conditions. Cash flow is, in part, the financial consequence of market conditions. We see fluctuations in the economy and know intuitively that the end result is likely to show in the market value of our property, the rent we are able to charge, the financing we can obtain, and even the taxes we pay.

The availability of capital, supply-demand adjustments, and investor expectations are the fundamental elements of market conditions. As these elements change they influence rental rates and when and for how much we can buy and sell. They also contribute to our perception of risk and expectations of financial well-being. Together, these fundamental elements affect the real estate market and help direct the trend of prices both up and down.

Eventually, changes in real estate prices reflect new market conditions, which require new investment decisions. These are the daily decisions, made in response to changing market conditions, that reflect the ongoing investment process—the attempt to transfer purchasing power through time and build real wealth.

The Competitive Importance of Property Characteristics

Cycles monitor changes in market conditions in the context of time. Cash flows are the financial consequences of those changes. But market conditions are not the only factors influencing cash flows. Individual property characteristics, such as the architectural style of a building, the availability of parking, the ease of ingress and egress, the location, professional management, and the competitiveness of rental rates, also affect cash flows. Property characteristics tend to become secondary considerations during expanding markets when demand is strong, but they are the last refuge of owners and the major contributing factors to cash flow when the cycle turns down and market conditions are unfavorable. A slow market tests property on an individual basis, and its competitive strength largely determines the outcome.

During periods of low activity when the cycle is falling or basing, speculative sales opportunities evaporate, and with them goes the risk insurance of an active and liquid market that permits selling underperforming property based on expectations of future profit. When the cycle turns down, individual property stands alone on its own characteristics without the backup of a sale to someone who has expectations of ever rising rents and sales prices.

Consequently, when market conditions turn negative, property characteristics are left to take up the slack in financial performance. Competitive property characteristics are the best protection against price risk in a downward trending cycle. In fact, the competitive structure of the individual characteristics of a property can make the difference between ownership survival or failure during severe real estate contractions.

The financial performance of real estate is the result of both market conditions and property characteristics. Active demand and favorable market conditions tend to offset noncompetitive property characteristics. Conversely, advantageous property characteristics tend to offset the low demand of inactive, unfavorable market conditions.

Unfortunately, this relationship is not easy to see when the emotions of ownership are involved. Expectations for continued strong demand tend to cloud awareness of the negative attributes of favored property. Nevertheless, when demand slows, the less competitive properties are hit first. Certainly, the unique characteristics of a property contribute to value in all types of market conditions, but specific property characteristics become competitively crucial under poor market conditions. It is a matter of basic value inherent in the free market. Buyers will seek out the best value in an attempt to obtain the maximum utility of their money.

For example, in a contracting market:

1. Tenants move to equivalent or better space to take advantage of lower rents.

2. Consequently, owners who understand competitive negotiation attract the available tenants.

3. The few tenants in the market for rental space are not new demand, they are simply switching from other buildings to get a better deal and improve their own cash flow.

4. Eventually, poor market conditions break down owner expectations entrenched during the preceding favorable cycle.

5. As the cycle trends down, the competition to maintain cash flow increases, rents drop, foreclosures become routine, and property values drop as lenders write down loans.

Under poor market conditions, individual property characteristics can sustain financial performance or accelerate the down trend. Conversely, when market conditions begin to improve, well-managed property leads the way, commanding higher rents and generating an overall improved financial performance.

Using Foreclosures to Monitor Price Declines

Real estate prices do fall. The cause can usually be traced directly to unemployment or a reduction of the level of discretionary income in the region. In the case of farm land, the cause is often falling commodity prices. Usually, the process shows first with increased apartment vacancies as people leave or move in with relatives to save money. As a result rents are reduced, and because of the lower cash flows, property values decline.

Price change in real estate is sometimes a slow process and is often difficult to see. Unfortunately, it becomes apparent that prices are falling only well after the fact and then only because of the increase in the number of foreclosures. They are the one indicator of a downward trend in prices that can't be argued with. The foreclosure process also illustrates the importance of the debt-equity capital relationship to real estate.

When a property is foreclosed, the minimum price reduction can be calculated by erasing the equity of the former owner. Usually this figure is 20 percent to 30 percent of the value of the property at the time of the loan. For example:

Appraised value at construction	100%
Initial loan	70%
Developer's equity	30%

At foreclosure the developer's equity portion of the appraised value disappears. The lender buys the property for the amount outstanding on the loan plus interest and attorney's fees on the courthouse steps in the county where the property is located. This bidding process is open to anyone who wants to make an offer. Usually the lender bids for the property at a price equal to the loan plus legal costs. That bid establishes the new market value. It is the price of the market on that date as determined at public auction. And it is usually a reduction of the value by a minimum of 20 percent to 30 percent that often does not reflect the full extent of the market weakness. Lenders are virtually forced to bid for their loan amount and may have to carry the property for years, waiting for the market to improve.

When lenders make loans they expect a certain cash flow to follow over a specific time period—the payoff for the debt investment. When owners invest in real estate they also expect a certain cash flow over a specific time period—the payoff for the equity investment. In a contracting real estate market owners are the first line of defense in trying to protect cash flow. If this fails, lenders are second in line, trying to protect cash flow, often through foreclosure.

Competition is always part of the investment real estate market as it is with any business. But real estate has no national quotation system; consequently, price changes are unknown until a transfer occurs, which is relatively seldom during the low activity of poor market conditions; and then, the transfer is often by foreclosure. Regardless of the trend of prices or the state of market conditions, real estate investment activity is ultimately a competition for cash flows.

Therefore, the first cash flow consideration is whether the market is active and expanding to the degree necessary to provide sufficient rental income to meet expenses and debt service. If not, then the reality of cash needs will not support the price of the project, and without an additional capital infusion the price will fall, possibly resulting in foreclosure. Real estate has always been a risky business. Despite the recent popular attraction during the last 15 years it remains a risky business.

Distinguishing between Real Estate Benefits and Cash Flows

Real estate cash flows come from several sources. Sometimes these sources are referred to as the *benefits of ownership*. This appropriately describes the positive expectations of real estate owners. There is an acronym popularly used from time to time that is intended to keep the benefits of real estate investment in mind. It forms a word from the first letters of the benefits of ownership.

R ... Rent

A ... Appreciation

T ... Tax shelter

E ... Equity buildup

Usually these are the benefits that are perceived to be affected positively of negatively by changes in market conditions or property characteristics. Anticipated benefits are the reason to invest in real estate for both individuals and corporations. But they are only fuzzy expectations and far from beneficial until the moment they are realized as cash flow in hand. The popular impression reflected in RATE can't be quantified and realistically measured until converted to cash flows received at a specific point in time. RATE describes the benefits, but in reality cash flow is the only tangible benefit.

Benefits	Cash flows	Received
Rental income	Net rental income	Monthly
Appreciation	Sales proceeds	Disposition
Tax shelter	Tax savings	Annual
Equity buildup	Sales proceeds	Disposition

Appreciation and equity buildup can also be realized as cash flow when property is refinanced, providing possibly the best tax-free way to realize real estate cash flows.

One of the challenges facing the real estate industry after the end of World War II was convincing the investing public of the benefits of real estate ownership. It was a battle until the market peak of the 1980s. Then with the false comfort of inflationary expectations, the public, the pension funds, and the savings and loans (S&Ls) all jumped headfirst into a market that collapsed under the collective weight of excess popularity. As late as the recession in the mid-1970s, the sale of investment real estate was a difficult process. Explaining the benefits of ownership was the common way to convey the concepts of investment real estate.

One attempt to clarify why everyone should own real estate materialized as a form that appears to have been developed in California. If nothing else it was a clear expression and a move toward reducing benefits to cash flows.

Property Analysis

Name: Lincoln Apartments   *Down payment:* $240,000

Rental Income	$12,000	
Estimated net rental income after expenses and debt service for an annual return of		5%
Appreciation	$47,925	
Property values in this area increase at about 5% per year for an annual return of		19.97%
Tax Shelter	$11,155	
First year tax loss of $22,310 in the 50% tax bracket for a return of		4.6%
Equity Buildup	$ 4,030	
Annual loan payments of $74,080 less interest of $70,050		1.7%
Total return on investment	$75,110	
		31.3%

This format is more an expression of potential than reality. Its primary purpose is to specify the benefits of investing in real estate so that anyone can understand them. Clear explanation requires separating the factors that contribute to income into manageable units. Therefore, the first step in specifying real estate cash flows is to isolate the sources.

Unfortunately, the preceding presentation does not take the process to the next step, but it does represent a clarification in thinking. At the time of its popularity it went a long way toward explaining the financial structure of income property.

Nevertheless, all the benefits of ownership are simply expectations until they are received as cash flows. Before that time the classic benefits of real estate ownership represent only descriptions of potential. They remain, therefore, once removed from the true measure of financial performance—cash flow received at a specific time. Cash flow and time comprise the financial reality of real estate ownership.

The Role of Expectations in Analyzing Ownership Benefits

The concept of expectation is central to understanding investment decisions and the timing of those decisions. It is also important in understanding the movement of prices beyond rational limits. In most investment markets there is a time period in the cycle of activity when the price moves to an irrational extreme. The real estate market is not exempt from this tendency. Extremes in the real estate market require the optimistic expectations of investors (usually involving inflation) and sufficient equity or debt capital to fuel acquisition, which may continue for years.

Conversely, the move down can occur more quickly. A sudden change in investor expectations can cause buyers to withdraw from a real estate market overnight. Waiting too long to sell can mean a drop in price, eliminating the expectation of appreciation and the cash flow that would have been realized at the anticipated sales price. Expected appreciation is not cash flow.

The probability that the popularly expected benefits of real estate will be converted to cash flow changes as the market cycle changes. Vacancies occur and rental income decreases. Tax laws change and tax savings diminish. Inflation rates decrease and price appreciation stops at some invisible ceiling. And in all cases you can't measure a benefit that hasn't been converted to cash flow. It is only at refinance or at a sale, for example, that the benefit of appreciation can be realistically measured. And, as illustrated in the following example, rental cash flow only exists after expenses and debt service are paid.

Office Plaza Acquisition Structure	
Purchase price	$1,120,000
Debt	$ 896,000
Equity	$ 224,000

Operating performance	Monthly	Annual
Scheduled rental income	$19,600	$235,200
Vacancy	1,960	23,520
Gross income	17,640	211,680
Expenses	8,114	97,368
Debt service	7,828	93,936
Net rental cash flow	$ 1,698	$ 20,376

The only financially relevant factor in the preceding operating statement is the amount of the net rental cash flow. There are other benefits such as tax savings, but they are not reflected in the operating statement. Appreciation can't be specified as a cash flow unless it is actually realized when the property is sold or refinanced. The same holds true for equity buildup due to loan reduction. It is not realized as a cash flow until a sale or refinance occurs. All benefits must make it to cash flows in order to be measured financially.

The tax shelter benefit of real estate is not a cash flow either unless it is realized as savings when taxes are due. A market that depends on the tax laws for price support is looking to a vulnerable source of cash flow. The unpredictability of the tax laws provides an ongoing lesson that tax benefits should not be relied on for the cash flow necessary to support a specific property much less an entire market, as occurred in the early 1980s.

When the depreciation benefits of the Tax Reform Act of 1981 were withdrawn and replaced by the extreme complexity and other disincentives for owning real estate contained in the Tax Reform Act of 1986, many investors, large and small, saw why real estate is a risky business. Ironically, this occurred after a prolonged period of price increases and new construction and triggered a change in expectations when the real estate market was overbuilt. Thus, the tax benefits and the appreciation component of real estate suffered a simultaneous blow at a time when the market was fundamentally in danger because of oversupply in many regions.

The tax benefits of real estate must make the trip to actual cash flow. So must the appreciation benefit. Changes in market conditions resulting from fundamental or governmental factors have a direct effect on cash flow. Benefits contribute to cash flows only when they exist. Appreciation is a benefit, but sales proceeds is the cash flow. Tax shelter is a benefit, but a reduced income tax payment is the cash flow. Rental income is a benefit, but the cash flow occurs only after vacancy, operating expenses, and possibly reserves for capital replacement, and debt service are subtracted. Benefits describe potential cash flows but remain unrealized unless converted to cash.

Risk Factors Affecting Real Estate Benefits

As national economic cycles affect regional market conditions, the different benefits of real estate ownership are viewed with varying degrees of importance. During periods of high inflation, appreciation tends to be valued as an offset to low rents. When tax shelter benefits generate significant cash flow they can also be perceived as an offset to rental income. Strong benefits tend to offset weak benefits in the attempt to achieve a high total cash flow from a property.

Because of the varied sources of real estate cash flows, much of the market risk can be balanced by individual property characteristics. For example, a solid combination of appealing property characteristics can outweigh poor market conditions. Competitive rents, a well-designed building, and a good location all work to increase the likelihood of maintaining cash flow from operations when the market cycle turns down.

Competitive advantage is the most reliable way to offset risk because it is attached to the property itself. Tax shelter for a high-bracket investor can contribute to total cash flows under certain tax and market conditions and offset an operating loss. Tax shelter and appreciation from speculation have offset negative rental cash flows during expanding market cycles. Props under the market that mask lack of solid demand from a growing population and income level illustrate the type of risk normal to real estate. External, indirect factors certainly affect values, but income property that cannot meet expenses and debt service without outside help usually has a limited period of potential. The props could be removed without warning.

It is all too easy during the boom years of real estate to think in terms of benefits and ignore the financial necessity of making the transition to cash flows. For example, analyzing a real estate market in broad generalizations of continued appreciation due to expectations of inflation is much easier than considering the historical impact of supply-demand cycles that might prevent the sale of a property for enough even to pay the debt balance. Risk tends to be ignored when the cycle is favorable, and every investor is subject to the tendency—large development companies as well as beginning investors.

The benefits of real estate ownership are only relevant to the extent that they actually produce cash flows at certain points in time. Consequently, cash flows must be specified in a time frame and in an amount before they can be measured. This is the case because the financial worth of any real estate investment is the present value of the cash flows it generates during its entire holding period. In fact, this is the value even when we don't know the exact cash flows or the time periods they are received. It is the value even when the cash flows are not the cash flows we want. And it is the value even though we may never know the actual present value amount.

Applying Cash Flow Analysis to Real Estate

Real estate investment is a dynamic process. From the moment funds are committed, market forces begin to act, changing the value of the invested funds in subtle and sometimes drastic ways. These changes can be quantified and measured and the results can be used to help make investment decisions.

Cash flow today and the expectation of cash flow in the future reflect this dynamic market activity. All real estate investments are expected to produce cash eventually. Income property produces rental income; limited partnerships produce (tax) losses; land investments produce capital gains.

In all types of real estate it is the total amount of money received after expenses and taxes during the complete holding period that comprises the cash flows, whether from rents, tax savings, sales proceeds, or refinance proceeds.

Cash flows two ways. It flows into an investment when you make a downpayment and when you make monthly payments to cover debt service and taxes on land, or an operating loss on income property and capital improvements paid for from funds not generated by the property. Cash outflows such as these, including the downpayment, are appropriately referred to as *negative cash flows*. Negative cash flows are funds that flow from outside the property into the property. These cash flows represent money invested in the property and can come at any time during ownership. Realistically, the downpayment is usually not the only investment made in a real estate project. This is a complicating fact of analysis that many traditional methods of valuation ignore.

Cash also flows from the property to you. These cash flows are usually referred to as *positive cash flows*. These are the cash flows that offset the invested or negative cash flows and are the basic expectations of most persons who choose to invest in real estate.

As a rough gage, positive cash flow should be more than negative cash flow over the entire holding period of the investment. Although this may seem obvious, it is not always the subject of thorough analysis, even by investors who should know better. A simple statement of total cash flows, negative and positive, can reveal a lot of information about a property.

Financially, the present value of the positive cash flows should exceed the present value of the negative cash flows from the beginning to the end of the investment when discounted at an appropriate interest rate. If the net present value is not positive, the property lost money. This is how you can measure the true financial value of a real estate investment based on the dollar amount and the time value of the cash flows.

The first step in the process of measuring cash flows is to specify the amounts and the times they are paid or received over the holding period of the investment. In our example the annual cash flows are negative until the end of the third year when the land is sold. There are three sources of negative cash flows during that period: (1) the downpayment when the land is purchased; (2) the interest on the loan during ownership; and (3) the property taxes during ownership. The only positive cash occurs in the last year when the property is sold.

Cash Flow Analysis

Project: Commercial lot

Acquisition price: $75,000

Terms: 20 percent down; 12.5 percent interest only, payable annually with a balloon payment at the end of the third year.

Sales price: $150,000

	Year 0	Year 1	Year 2	Year 3
Cash Received				
Sale proceeds				$150,000
Cash Paid				
Downpayment	($15,000)			
Interest		($7,500)	($7,500)	($ 7,500)
Property taxes		($2,000)	($2,000)	($ 2,000)
Balloon payment				($ 60,000)
Cost of sales				($ 11,000)
Net Cash Flows	($15,000)	($9,500)	($9,500)	$ 69,500

The amount of the cash flows and the time they are received are of equal importance to financial analysis. A sale in the fifth year for the same price would not be as valuable as the sale in the third year for a couple of reasons. First, the $60,000 balloon payment would require a capital infusion from sources outside the investment proceeds. Second, the combination of the additional investment for the balloon payment plus the two-year time delay in the positive cash flow would reduce the present value received from the only positive cash flow, which in this case is proceeds of sale.

Cash flow is concrete. The money you pay and the money you receive can be specified in time and amount even with the most intricate investments. It is only by specifying cash flows that you can measure whether an investment is transferring purchasing power through time and increasing wealth. Cash flows are the product of the benefits and must be accounted for to avoid the dangerous comfort of relying on vague expectations of inflation, tax shelter, and popular infatuation with real estate to support an investment decision. To have financial meaning, the benefits of ownership must be quantified in terms of the contribution they are likely to make to cash flow.

Specifying Cash Flow from Rental Income

Each real estate benefit can be expressed as measurable cash flow by netting the positive and negative figures attributable to the benefit. The most familiar example of this is the operating statement for income-producing property. Its purpose is to arrive at the cash flow from rental income. The same process can be followed to specify cash flows from the other benefits of ownership, including appreciation, tax shelter, loan reduction, and finance proceeds.

This netting of cash outflows and inflows to determine the net cash flow can be done with any cash flow regardless of the benefit of ownership that generates the income or expense. Then the cash flows from each source can be combined in summary form to specify the total after-tax cash flows for the time period analyzed. For example, the following operating statement accounts for the internal cash flows related to rental income. The purpose is to display the cash flows that affect the bottom-line cash flow from rent. The objective is to calculate the actual rental cash flow.

	Cash Flow Analysis Rental Income		
	Year 1	Year 2	Year 3
Scheduled rental income	$37,440	$38,400	$39,360
Less vacancy	(1,872)	(1,920)	(1,968)
Effective rental income	35,568	36,480	37,392
Less operating expenses	(16,874)	(17,262)	(17,640)
Net operating income	18,694	19,218	19,752
Less debt service	(16,903)	(16,903)	(16,903)
Cash flow from rent	$ 1,791	$ 2,315	$ 2,849

This analysis is an operating statement before income taxes and possible allocation of overhead charges that might be appropriate in a large organization. But the purpose goes beyond the typical operating statement to emphasize the net cash flow for financial analysis rather than accounting purposes. Notice that this statement does not account for depreciation, which in real estate investment is another potential cash flow.

Financially, cash flow is the only measure that accurately reflects investment performance. Consequently, the accounting profession has gradually given more importance to cash flow statements in an attempt to accurately reflect the performance of a business while providing information to management necessary for effective financial decisions. To a large degree this trend appears to have grown out of recognition of the importance of present value analysis. The appraising and investment analysis fields are gradually accepting cash flow as the basic measure of financial performance.

This evolving view of cash flow as the measure of investment performance is a necessary step toward recognizing the essential requirement of accounting for the time value of money. Specifying cash flows is the first step toward recognizing that the worth of any venture is the present value of the cash flows it generates discounted to the present value.

Calculating Cash Flow from Tax Savings

Real estate ownership is a business. As a business it has certain financial factors in common with all businesses. The jargon used in various business fields may be different, but the underlying meaning is often the same when reduced to cash flows and the time value of their receipt. Most businesses and investments generate income from operations or as a return on invested capital. And from time to time capital assets are sold and a gain is realized. Also, every business has tax consequences that must be accounted for. In this regard real estate is historically somewhat different.

Tax-shelter incentives for real estate investment have a long tradition in the United States. Manufacturing, retail, and office structures to support employment and affordable housing are all major contributing factors to the relative political stability of the country. Tax laws have facilitated this with incentives for capital investment in real estate, usually with the intent of providing homes, jobs, and the prosperity that follows. Although tax incentives are subject to change with each session of Congress, they have survived in one form or another through the years, increasing and decreasing the tax benefits of capital investment based on the political vision at the time.

Tax shelter is not some mysterious benefit of real estate. Financially, it is just one other source of cash flow. As such, it can be specified in amount and time, and its contribution to present value can be measured.

Sheltered income occurs when depreciation exceeds net cash flow from rent. There are a few steps in the calculation of tax savings. First, depreciation of the property improvements is calculated. Second, depreciation is offset against rental cash flow. Third, when depreciation exists in excess of net rental cash flow that amount is treated as a tax loss, not an economic loss, which is deducted from ordinary income, creating a tax savings. It is a savings because without the tax deduction this amount would have been paid in tax.

Since only improvements can be depreciated, the value of income property must be allocated between land and improvements. A commonly accepted method of allocating value to improvements is to use the percentage relationship of building to land on the property tax valuation.

Determining Building-to-Land Ratio

Land value	$ 45,000	15%
Improvements	$255,000	85%
Total value	$300,000	100%

In this example the dollar amount is not important. Only the percentage is necessary. It can then be applied to the purchase price to determine the dollar allocation for depreciation purposes.

Allocating Value to Improvements

Purchase price	$275,000
Times percentage allocation	× 85%
Allocation to improvements	$233,750

Therefore, the portion of the property value that can be depreciated is established as $233,750. Depending on the tax laws in effect at the time you may be able to deduct the annual depreciation from rental cash flow and any excess loss from ordinary income. The amount of deductible loss varies frequently with changes in the tax laws so the following is for illustration purposes only. The current year's tax law should always be consulted for actual guidelines. What is important now is to understand the transition from tax shelter to cash flow.

To calculate depreciation you first determine the number of years over which the property can be depreciated. This changes from time to time. For now, as an illustration we can use 27½ years for residential income property and 31½ years for nonresidential income property. The amount of depreciation is calculated by establishing a rate and applying it to the depreciable basis. The rate in this example for residential real estate is 0.0364 (1/27.5).

Calculating Depreciation

Depreciable basis	$233,750
Times depreciation rate	× 0.0364
Depreciation deduction	$ 8,509

The annual depreciation amount is subtracted from the basis at the end of each year of ownership to adjust the basis.

Calculating Adjusted Basis

Depreciable basis	$233,750
Less depreciation	(8,509)
Plus land value	41,250
Adjusted basis	$266,491

Each year depreciation is deducted to offset the wearing out of the improvements. The portion that wears out should be deducted from the value, and the amount necessary to replace it is deducted from taxable income. This aspect of the tax laws allows replacement of capital structures without diminishing investment capital by taxes. Consequently, money stays in the economy where it has a chance of doing productive work.

Depreciation is, in effect, an offset to net rental cash flow plus the principal portion of debt service. Since only the interest portion of debt service is deductible, the portion which goes to loan amortization must be added to rental cash flow prior to the deduction. This step generates the taxable income amount as a result of rental operations adjusting for the depreciation amount that is not accounted for on the operating statement.

Computing Taxable Rental Income

Rental cash flow	$1,791
Plus loan principal	$1,152
Taxable rental income	$2,943

This is the amount of annual rental income that is taxable and therefore can be offset by depreciation of the improvements. Even though loan principal is not received as cash flow it is taxable income.

The next calculation establishes the figure commonly referred to as *tax shelter.* It is calculated by netting the amount of depreciation for that year with the taxable rental income to produce the tax loss, which is then deducted from ordinary income.

Calculating Tax Loss

Taxable rental income	$2,943
Less depreciation	($8,509)
Tax loss (shelter)	($5,566)

The tax loss from this calculation is deducted from ordinary income, resulting in tax savings. There are limits to this type of deduction, and it is restricted under certain conditions. But for now the method of calculating cash flow from tax savings is the important aspect in this example.

Actual tax saved is calculated by multiplying the loss by the tax bracket amount. The higher the tax bracket the more valuable the tax loss as actual cash flow. The implication, of course, is that high tax rates increase cash flow from tax savings. This is one example of how tax laws can influence public interest in real estate.

Calculating Tax Savings

Tax loss	$5,566
Times tax bracket	× 0.33
Tax savings	$1,837

The cash flow represented by tax savings in this example is $1,837 for a 33 percent tax-bracket taxpayer. If the marginal tax bracket were 50 percent the cash flow from tax savings would be about $2,783. Cash flows from tax savings are highly unpredictable because of frequent modification of the tax laws. Nevertheless, tax shelter can be a meaningful source of cash flow under the proper circumstances and must be accounted for in order to accurately measure the tax shelter benefit of real estate.

Cash Flow from Tax Savings			
	Year 1	Year 2	Year 3
Cash flow from rent	$1,791	$2,315	$2,849
Plus principal	1,152	1,256	1,369
Taxable income	2,943	3,571	4,218
Less depreciation	(8,509)	(8,509)	(8,509)
Equals tax loss	(5,566)	(4,938)	(4,291)
Times tax bracket	× 0.33	× 0.33	× 0.33
Cash flow from tax savings	$1,837	$1,630	$1,416

The principle applied to convert a tax loss to cash flow is the same regardless of the amounts involved or the tax laws in effect at the time. The important point is to recognize that tax shelter can be specified as a cash flow. It does not have to remain some vague and unmeasurable figure. In fact, cash flow from tax savings is the reason shelters of the past have attracted many to investment real estate.

As indicated in this example the income from rent is fully sheltered from tax because of the depreciation of improvements. The additional tax savings provides a loss, which generates tax savings and thus a positive cash flow from property ownership.

The purpose of this illustration is to explain the cash flow that results from the real estate tax shelter benefit. The Tax Reform Act of 1986 put severe restrictions on the use of this benefit. These restrictions are much too intricate to be included in this discussion; furthermore, they are likely to be relaxed in time. However, the fundamental requirement of translating the new tax laws into positive or negative cash flows will remain a requirement for the financial analysis of real estate.

Through the years real estate investment professionals have argued that the unique tax benefits of real estate make it difficult to compare with other types of investments. The reasoning is that the only accurate financial comparison is an after-tax comparison.

Investments other than income real estate are not routinely evaluated on an after-tax basis, which automatically overstates the return. Few popular investments even present additional tax shelter opportunities. Consequently, the added income from tax savings on a real estate investment should properly be compared with other investments after subtracting the tax paid. In fact, the only complete way to view financial performance is on an after-tax basis. To ignore the tax consequences of any investment is to ignore a cash flow. To ignore tax calculations with income property is to ignore potential income from the investment.

Complete financial analysis requires that all cash flows generated by an investment be considered, including positive cash flows from taxes saved, and negative cash flows from taxes paid. Most investments create an income tax liability or negative cash flow. From an investment standpoint, taxes are an expense of doing business. Consequently, the tax that is paid reduces the net income generated by the investment and must be accounted for to correctly evaluate the performance of the investment.

From a strictly financial view, either positive or negative net cash flows can result from the tax laws. For example, the depreciation that provides cash flow from tax savings also reduces the basis that will likely add to the capital gain realized when the property is sold, thus increasing the tax paid at that time.

Real estate investment produces tax consequences. And tax consequences produce either positive or negative cash flows, which must be included in the financial analysis of an investment.

Calculating Cash Flow from Sale Proceeds

Appreciation and equity buildup (loan reduction) are converted to cash flow when property is sold or refinanced. Refinancing, when possible, may be the single most advantageous source of after-tax cash flow from real estate ownership.

Cash flow from sales proceeds is the final measure of the combined benefits of appreciation and equity buildup. The first step in this calculation is to determine the equity realized from the sale, which constitutes before-tax sale proceeds.

Calculating Before-Tax Sale Proceeds

Sale price	$360,000
Loan	(172,000)
Cost of sale	(27,000)
Before-tax sale proceeds	$161,000

The next step is to calculate the tax due and net it to determine the after-tax sale proceeds. This step requires a series of calculations.

Calculating Realized Gain

Sale price	$360,000
Adjusted basis	(249,473)
Realized gain	$110,527

Realized gain represents the taxable profit or capital gain made on the sale. The amount of tax due is then calculated by multiplying the realized gain by the tax rate.

Calculating Tax Due

Realized gain	$110,527
Times tax rate	× 0.28
Tax due	$ 30,948

Income tax is a cost of investment activity, which reduces cash flow from sale proceeds. Consequently, the capital gains tax due must be subtracted from the sale proceeds.

Calculating After-Tax Sale Proceeds

Before-tax sale proceeds	$161,000
Tax due	(30,948)
After-tax sale proceeds	$130,052

This series of calculations represents a simple accounting process necessary to determine a cash flow. The cash flow from sale proceeds forms a major part of the attraction of real estate. This is the cash flow that embodies the benefits of appreciation and equity buildup, both of which cannot be measured financially until they are expressed as a cash flow.

Building a Cash Flow Summary

The degree to which a real estate investment transfers purchasing power through time and increases real wealth is a function of the amount and timing of the combined after-tax cash flows of the property. When the cash flow is received can be as important as the amount of the cash flow.

All cash flows received over the holding period of the investment count—whether negative or positive. Therefore, the negative cash flows must be netted with the positive cash flows for each source, annually. Both negative and positive rental cash flows must be netted to determine the net rental cash flow. The same procedure is followed with the cash flows from tax savings, sale proceeds, and refinancing. When the specification process is complete in each cash flow area for each year, the cash flows can then be summarized.

When the principle of specifying cash flows is fully understood, there may be other areas of positive and negative cash flows that become apparent. For example, a cash infusion for capital improvements such as a new roof or new furniture or remodeling that can't be paid out of rental income can be specified as a separate negative cash flow during the year it occurs. The down payment is a negative cash flow that occurs at acquisition and can be specified as such. Refinancing proceeds are a positive cash flow. There are other possibilities. The amount and the time of occurrence is all that is needed to specify a cash flow.

The guideline is simple. If you invest or pay money into a project or property it is negative cash flow. If you receive money from a property it is a positive cash flow. The source doesn't matter. The challenge is to not overlook a cash flow. Each is important.

The following summary combines the cash flows and the time of occurrence in our example.

	Cash Flow Summary			
	Year 0	Year 1	Year 2	Year 3
Downpayment	($100,000)			
Rental income		$1,791	$2,315	$ 2,849
Tax savings		$1,837	$1,630	$ 1,416
Sale proceeds				$130,052
Total cash flow	($100,000)	$3,628	$3,945	$134,317

Depending on your experience with the cycles of the real estate market you might think the return represented by this cash flow summary is high or low. Keeping in mind that this is an after-tax cash flow summary, can you find another in the market that provides a 12.76 percent return? That is the compounded rate represented by the cash flows in this example.

Financial analysis goes beyond the traditional market analysis that determines price, rents, and expenses. The objective of financial analysis is to calculate the worth of an investment in the context of time.

Money has a time value. Financial analysis is a process of measuring how time changes the value of money. This change may, in part, occur through the gradual reduction of purchasing power due to inflation. An inflationary loss in purchasing power represents as real a financial loss as a drop in market price due to lack of demand. Both reduce the amount you can purchase with the funds generated by the investment.

How to Adjust Sale Proceeds for Taxes on Inflationary Gains

One of the greatest barriers to transferring purchasing power through time is the tax paid on the portion of appreciation resulting from inflation. This is a major reason refinancing can increase a return so significantly. Since there is no tax payable on loan proceeds, the appreciation attributed to inflation is not taxed when you refinance. Current tax law does not divide capital gains into real wealth gains (in purchasing power) and inflationary gains (the worthless portion). As a result, real wealth gains are taxed at a higher rate than revealed by marginal rates.

For example, a land investment made 10 years ago for $100,000 is sold today for $500,000. Over that 10-year period cumulative inflation has been 50 percent. Therefore, half of the gain represents inflation and is not an increase in purchasing power. But tax is paid on the inflationary gain and the real gain. Consequently, tax paid must be deducted from gross sale proceeds to determine the net sale proceeds. The net figure is then reduced by the cumulative increase due to inflation. The purpose is to determine the after-tax gain in real wealth. The following is a simple way to make this adjustment:

Calculate the Tax Due

Sale Price	$500,000
Less basis	(100,000)
Gain	400,000
Times tax rate	× 0.28
Tax due	$112,000

Calculate the After-Tax Cash Flow

Sale proceeds	$500,000
Tax paid	(112,000)
After-tax cash flow	$388,000

Adjusting After-Tax Cash Flow for Inflation

After-tax cash flow	$388,000
Less inflation (50%)	(194,000)
Real after-tax cash	$194,000

The before-tax nominal cash flow of $500,000 is reduced 61.2 percent by taxes and inflation. From a financial analysis viewpoint, the increase in purchasing power over and above the initial investment is $194,000 in real after-tax wealth. In this example the compounded rate of return is 6.85 percent.

Comparing the tax paid and the actual increase in real wealth provides a picture of the high tax rate that results from taxing inflationary gains. This calculation is made by dividing the tax paid by the real gain.

Calculating the Real Tax Rate

Tax paid	$\dfrac{\$112,000}{\$200,000}$	$= 56\%$ real tax rate
Real gain		

The insidious erosion of wealth by inflation and taxes reduces the productive capital base of the country and contributes to unemployment. Inflation does it by eroding purchasing power. Taxes do it by removing purchasing power from productive use. To remain competitive we must keep job-producing capital in the economy and protect it from inflation and taxes.

This example illustrates why inflation is so damaging and how taxing inflationary gains increases the tax rate beyond stated percentages. Although the specifics of inflationary damage vary from cycle to cycle, the principle remains constant. Inflation and taxes decrease purchasing power, thereby reducing the uses to which you can put money, the satisfaction it can provide, and the amount of capital remaining for new investment in the economy that will generate employment and a high standard of living.

4

Standard Measures of Real Estate Performance

Time and money are the two components of investment return. Traditionally, the annual rate of return has been the most routinely used method of analyzing the relationship between time and money. The usefulness of the annual percentage for comparing different investment yields is inescapable. It is the most basic expression of investment return and has worked well in practice; but it tells only part of the story.

Through the years the methods used to measure real estate performance have evolved, with expanded understanding of the time value of money. Use of rules of thumb, averages, and annual rates of return have gradually given way to discounted cash flow analysis. After-tax evaluation of seemingly incomparable cash flows on an equal basis has now become readily accessible as a result of inexpensive computer technology. Financial understanding is progressing toward wide application of the basic principle of financial analysis: all investments can be measured and compared fairly based on the time value of the cash flows they produce.

Even with recent advances in application of financial analysis, progress is incomplete, and the tendency to view real estate out of the context of cyclical changes remains a common barrier to market understanding. The highly cyclical nature of the real estate industry tends to be ignored by the recent participants and many industry professionals. Coping with the uncertainty of an increasingly volatile market is an uncomfortable exercise for many who entered the real estate business looking for a stable investment arena. This is understandable when you recognize how real estate investment analysis grew from the appraisal process, which is limited to specifying a market value on a given date.

The customary appraisal procedure used by banks and lenders (debt investors) serves its purpose when real estate prices are steady or appreciating. But the limits of this practice become obvious when the market turns downward. Appraisals made at the top of a cycle are meaningless curiosities and no comfort for lenders when the market stops expanding and begins a prolonged contraction.

Evaluating the cyclical risk associated with real estate loans is not part of the usual appraisal assignment. Risk evaluation is, of course, the responsibility of the lender, who participates in the rewards of a debt investment secured by real estate. Ironically, lenders tend to rely heavily on property appraisals without recognizing the history of cycle extremes typical of real estate. There is nothing new about booms and busts in real estate markets.

Nevertheless, as the foreclosure process and debt liquidation of the 1980s accelerated, the first question was how an appraisal could be so far off. During the initial stage of the decline in real estate values it was not yet widely acknowledged that real estate prices could fall. Consequently, the tendency was to blame the appraisal. And when that didn't explain what was happening, the premise of the appraisal procedure was challenged, and the underlying rationale was redefined.

When news is bad, some people tend to first blame the messenger, and in this case the appraiser was the messenger of market value for banks and savings and loans (S&Ls). If the value today was less than the value a year or two earlier, clearly the messenger brought the wrong message; or so it seemed. This was the initial reaction of lenders and federal regulators when the real estate contraction began.

Apparently, the entire lending industry and the government agency that regulates it never knew that the real estate industry is not only risky but also cyclical. Try as they may to find scapegoats, the ultimate causes reflect natural market tendencies carried to extremes by the excess capital availability of deregulation.

Distinguishing Between Appraisal and Financial Analysis

Appraised value is not necessarily the price paid or received for a property, although it might be. Certainly, there is nothing absolute or guaranteed by an appraisal, especially the price set by the market. Appraised value is more often an informed opinion backed by experience and the educational credentials of an appraiser.

Lenders use appraisals to support the value of real estate used as security for a loan. An appraisal also provides evidence that the property can be liquidated for a price sufficient to pay off that loan. If lenders didn't require appraisals for their files the custom would likely end, and prices would be solely determined between buyer and seller. At the very least the appraisal industry would shrink in size without the demand for appraisals from lenders.

Ironically, when Resolution Trust Corporation (RTC) took over the real estate of failed S&Ls in Texas, the appraisal business boomed because of the regulation requiring yearly appraisals. By the 1990s this questionable documentation became so expensive that the requirement was reduced to appraisals every two years. The change caused widespread unemployment among Texas appraisers.

Usefulness of the real estate appraisal process is the price-reporting service it provides. Appraisals are price quotes, and from a pragmatic standpoint that's about all they are. The appraisal process provides an accredited method of gathering price data and reporting it to the market participants. Appraisers fill the real estate industry's need for a price quotation system by monitoring actual sales, construction costs, and rents. It is a service of limited scope and to expect more than it is designed to provide, or capable of providing, is dangerous. Responsibility for risk remains with the investor (debt or equity) and can never be removed by an appraisal.

Appraisals do venture slightly into the future and qualify the opinion of value with the reservation that the appraised price is what a buyer would pay in a reasonable time period to a seller who is not under duress. But no statement can fully warn against a slow real estate market where credit is nonexistent and demand is a vague memory of past markets.

There are several other qualifying assumptions, which unfortunately tend to acquire unwarranted significance. For example, "highest and best use" (translation: the use that makes the most money); "a willing buyer" (translation: the real estate market still exists); "a reasonable time period" (translation: six months). These old cliches have been unexamined and overly comforting for too long.

Recent requirements have tried to move the appraisal custom closer to the reality of market dynamics by introducing consideration of the most probable sales price within a specific time period. But this may also be asking too much of a process that is actually a price-reporting system. Viewing it otherwise is to burden appraisers with forecasting the market, which is the task of investment analysis and the responsibility of investors who are compensated for the risks and bear the losses.

Every lender, big and small, probably needs an in-house real estate risk analysis department to take the investment decision beyond appraised value—the current price quote. The false security provided by the established customs of the appraisal industry are little comfort to owners in a seriously contracting market where prices fall and buyers withdraw from the market.

Under these market conditions appraisers are at a serious disadvantage because so few transactions close; consequently there are no prices to report and compare or to use to estimate current market value.

The distinction between the appraisal process and investment analysis is crucial to understanding the risk of real estate ownership over time. An appraisal that is a price quote on a certain date cannot remove the decision responsibility of an investor who may plan to hold real estate debt or equity through several stages of the cycle.

More goes into the decision to make an investment than the market value at the time of investment. For example, the potential for profit is primary and depends in part on the future strength of the local market, including employment growth, income level, and population growth. This dependence of investment decisions on future market activity stands in stark contrast to the dependence on past market activity relied on for appraisals.

Nevertheless, the appraisal process forms the historical foundation for the analysis of real estate. For example, an appraisal is designed to answer the following question: What is the market value of this property as of the date of the appraisal? The answer provided by an appraisal depends on the ability to report transactions of the past, which support the appraised value as of the appraisal date. Although the recent pricing information in an appraisal can be very useful, it is only part of the information needed for financial analysis.

Financial analysis is designed to answer a different question: How likely is this property to transfer purchasing power through time and build real wealth? Answering this question requires historical data and more. Also, the answer will be qualified by a degree of probability necessary in any forecast.

Appraised value is, by design, a price fixed in time. Financial analysis is a dynamic process, involving cycles, probability, and the time value of money. Investing based on an appraisal is often necessary, but it is rarely a sufficient foundation for anticipating market fluctuations and the resulting risks that are characteristic of the cyclical real estate market.

Applying the Three Basic Appraisal Methods

The tendency to confuse the appraisal process with investment analysis is one reason real estate cycles go to extremes and lenders get in trouble. A static appraised value fosters a static view of a dynamic and changing real estate market.

In its most basic form, an appraisal employs three methods of comparing property values. Historically, the methods used to analyze real estate evolved out of these three appraisal approaches. Use of the word *approach* refers to the methods approaching an opinion of value, which are (1) comparing sale prices, (2) calculating replacement costs, and (3) capitalizing rental income. Consequently, the three appraisal methods are named for the methods used to estimate value:

1. Comparable sales approach

2. Cost approach

3. Income approach

The comparable sales method of appraisal establishes an opinion of value by comparing recent sale prices of properties that are similar in location, use, and income to the property being appraised. It is a very efficient method in highly active markets with frequent sales. But it stops short in a contracting market when sales slow and the frequency of transactions needed for a relatively accurate estimate simply don't exist.

In a contracting market the time span between closed transactions is so lengthy that it is a source of frustration for appraisers. To be valid the data must be relatively recent. In a serious real estate contraction it is common for sales to actually stop. Since an appraisal is, in effect, a market price quotation, an active market is somewhat of a necessity to generate the necessary raw data.

The comparable sales approach to market value compares recent sales data on an equal basis, attempting to match size, location, and quality. To accomplish this, the price of property is reduced to a common basis of measure by comparing sales in terms of price per square foot rather than the gross dollar amount. The following example of land prices illustrates the procedure.

Comparable Sales Data

Date	Zoning	Size (ft^2)	Price	Price per ft^2
1x9x	C-1	40,000	$200,000	$5.00
2x9x	C-1	32,000	$250,000	$7.81
3x9x	C-1	55,000	$350,000	$5.91
4x9x	C-1	38,000	$225,000	$5.92
5x9x	C-1	60,000	$405,000	$6.75

Averaging these prices produces an estimate of $6.28 per ft^2. Occasionally, the highest and lowest prices in the comparable sales data are eliminated, and the middle range of prices is averaged. This procedure produces an estimate of $6.19 per ft^2.

Various adjustments can be made based on the judgment of the appraiser. For example, the details of the financing arrangements with certain comparable property may require an adjustment. Sometimes favorable financing by the seller can command a higher sales price. Occasionally it is necessary to weight the data to adjust for large size differences.

Raw price data is just one component of the appraisal process and possibly the most important component because it reflects actual transactions. Closed transactions are the end result of market activity and the final determinant of market price.

The farther an appraiser must move from actual sales the less reliable the opinion of value. In contracting markets appraisers are sometimes forced to rely on the asking prices of would-be sellers, thus reducing the accuracy of the market price estimate. The comparable sales approach attempts to answer the following question: What are the sales prices of similar properties in similar locations?

The cost approach to appraisal uses the cost of new construction and land prices to estimate market value, reasoning that the money required to replace land and structures represents today's value. This approach is based on the premise that new construction competes with sales of existing property. New construction is an alternative to investing in an existing building. As an alternative it provides a source of additional price data on market activity.

Sellers of existing buildings compete with the possibility open to buyers of purchasing land and constructing a new building. This alternative checks price increases of existing property by bringing new supply on market when prices of existing buildings exceed new construction costs. This is one way the pricing system referees the supply-demand relationship.

The cost approach answers the following question: What does it cost to replace this land and building? Answering this question requires an estimate of the depreciation of the structure—not for tax purposes, but actual repair costs necessary to bring the building to current new standards. In other words, for appraisal purposes the value today is the cost to buy the land plus construction costs, less the remodeling costs necessary to bring the building to new condition.

Determining the replacement costs of property can be extremely detailed if warranted, but the basic procedure is not complicated. First, the estimate of land value is part of the appraisal data inventory. Second, construction costs are readily available from estimates provided by contractors who build similar buildings. Therefore, if land costs are running about $6.25 per ft^2 and construction costs are running about $65 per ft^2, a 12,000 ft^2 building on a 50,000 ft^2 lot would be calculated as follows:

Land (50,000 ft^2 × $6.25/ft^2)	$ 312,500
Building (12,000 ft^2 × $65/ft^2)	$ 780,000
Total replacement cost	$1,092,500

The cost approach is simply a different formula for arriving at a price quote of the market value on a certain date. In reality, the market is constantly changing in varying degrees of expansion and contraction and rising and falling prices. As land and construction costs fluctuate, the cost of replacing existing buildings also fluctuates. Each component of construction costs from material prices to labor, interest rates, and insurance costs are subject to change without notice. Consequently, the cost approach emphasizes the composite price structure of real estate and the close relationship between the real estate market and construction activity.

The income approach to appraisal is the most closely related of the three to investment analysis. Here rental income is used to estimate market value. It is this tradition that formed the basis of the early methods of analyzing real estate investments.

The income approach starts with a survey of the rents, vacancy, and operating expenses of similar property. The net operating income from the survey is then capitalized at typical capitalization rates to arrive at a market value estimate. For example:

Scheduled rental income	$1,000,000
Less vacancy	100,000
Effective rental income	$ 900,000
Less expenses	350,000
Net operating income	$ 550,000

To capitalize the value of the income in this example divide $550,000 by the annual percentage return available in the market for competing investments. This percentage is referred to as the *capitalization rate* or *cap rate*. It is usually chosen by looking at cap rates of comparable real estate sales, which of course makes it a comparable sales method based on income. Cap rates can also be selected by looking at other long-term investment opportunities. For example, if we use low risk treasury bonds that are, for purposes of example, yielding 8.5 percent, the value would be calculated as follows:

$550,000 divided by 8.5% equals $6,470,588

$$\left(\frac{550,000}{0.085} = 6,470,588 \right)$$

In other words, if you paid $6,470,588 cash for this property with no debt, the initial annual percentage rate of return would be 8.5 percent, and the dollar return would be $550,000.

$$\begin{array}{r} \$6,470,588 \\ \times\,0.085 \\ \hline \$\ \ 550,000 \end{array}$$

Capitalizing income to arrive at the price of real estate is a relatively sensitive gauge of market values. When based on net operating income (NOI) it is an annual rate of return before debt service and income taxes. Furthermore, it is directly tied to cash flow and the returns available from competing investments.

For example, assume that an 8.5 percent free and clear rate of return does not meet your decision criteria for real estate investment. A higher return may seem more appropriate, say a 10.5 percent cap rate.

$550,000 divided by 10.5% equals $5,238,095

$$\left(\frac{550,000}{0.105} \;=\; 5,238,095\right)$$

Increasing the capitalization rate by two percentage points reduces the estimated value or potential sale price of the property by about 1.2 million dollars. This illustrates how important the capitalization process is to the appraisal of investment real estate. It expresses the relationship between income and price and is one of the links between real estate and interest rates or yields on competing investments. In a sense, cap rates reflect the cost of capital for real estate equity investment. Obviously, this yield should be higher than the cost of capital (interest rate) paid to attract debt investment to the same property.

Capitalization is the first step toward measuring the relationship between the funds invested and the cash flow produced. It is nothing more than the reverse application of the basic rate of return concept. Rather than dividing the net operating income by the price to solve for the annual percentage rate of return, we divide the net operating income (NOI) by the desired rate of return to determine the price, or capital value. Keeping in mind that net operating income is rental income reduced by vacancy and operating expenses, but not reduced by debt service, the concepts can be summarized as follows:

1. Net operating income divided by price equals cap rate, which is sometimes referred to as the *free and clear return*, and sometimes as the *overall rate*.

$$\frac{\text{NOI}}{\text{Price}} \quad \frac{\$\ 550,000}{\$5,750,000} = 9.57\% \text{ cap rate}$$

$$\left(\frac{\$\ 550,000}{\$5,750,000} = 0.095652\right)$$

2. Net operating income divided by cap rate equals price, which for appraisal purposes is determined by income and market rates.

$$\frac{\text{NOI}}{\text{Cap rate}} \quad \frac{\$550,000}{9.57\%} = 5,750,000 \text{ price}$$

$$\left(\frac{\$550,000}{9.5652\%} = \$5,750,000\right)$$

Capitalization is the process of using income to determine capital value. If a 9.5 percent rate of return on the capital value, or price, of income property is the market return then it makes sense to use that rate as a factor to determine the market value of the property. This is how rental income relates directly to the price of real estate in traditional analysis methods. The procedure is almost automatic and unconscious for many in the real estate business who use 10 percent for ease of mental calculation.

The cap rate is applied to determine market value without reference to the debt on the property. In other words, it is applied as if the property were free and clear of loans, although it can and is sometimes adjusted for the debt on the property. There are also more advanced applications of capitalizing income that consider the time value of money. But the basic capitalization procedure forms the foundation for the early investment analysis techniques used in real estate.

Adapting Appraisal Methods to Investment Analysis

At first glance it would seem that a direct relationship exists between the appraised value of property and its worth as an investment. This assumed connection is dangerous. When you recognize the fact that real estate is a highly cyclical industry and that an appraisal is a price quote for a particular day you can see the potential for trouble by attributing undue significance to an appraisal. This of course is what happens in the lending industry and with government agencies who seem to look for ways to transfer responsibility when the market makes a natural cyclical contraction. Acting as if overbuilding never happened before, an appraisal becomes a statement of truth and absolute, almost moral, value rather than the estimate intended by industry standards. In the real world, values are prices of properties that have sold, nothing more.

Appraisals are not normally projections of future price performance or a guarantee of a stable price for an individual property in a dynamic market. Furthermore, there is no real estate market in the world that guarantees the price today will be the price tomorrow. This is probably one of the lessons of the 1980s when high appraisals made at the cycle top fueled additional lending because the "value" justified the loan and formed a floor under the price, or so it may have seemed.

In the 1960s the National Association of Realtors adopted what was to become the transition document between appraisal and investment analysis. The title of this form was "Property Analysis," popularly referred to as *Form B*. It combined the three approaches to value used by appraisers in a one-page attempt to address every aspect viewed then as important about a specific property. It was a crowded document, but it did isolate certain important cash flows.

There is something magic about forms that organize vast amounts of important information. They can provide security for the user who assumes that all the necessary information is at hand and nothing has been overlooked. Furthermore, good forms solve problems and answer a number of questions. They guide the user through the analysis process and lock on to the raw data, processing the smallest detail into usable format. The following sequence of terms is used in the income statement section of this early form:

Scheduled gross income	$100,000
Less vacancy	10,000
Gross operating income	90,000
Less operating expenses	38,000
Net Operating Income	52,000
Less loan payment	32,400
Gross spendable income	19,600
Plus principal payment	4,400
Gross equity income	24,000
Less depreciation	16,000
Real estate taxable income	$ 8,000

Obviously one of the purposes of this form is to illustrate the tax savings of an investment in real estate. This tax advantage sets real estate apart from other investments and can make it difficult to compare on an equal basis. Much of the effort of real estate investment analysis has been directed toward overcoming the confusion involved in computing the cash flows that result from the multiple benefits of real estate ownership. Form B was an early attempt to accomplish that objective.

One purpose of Form B was to clarify the rate of return available on equity after debt service. This percentage indicator of financial performance took the capitalization process a step further than net operating income by adjusting the rate of return after debt service on the property. Rather than relying on the net operating income of a debt-free property to establish value, attention focuses on the rate generated by rental income after payment of both expenses and debt service.

To arrive at the rate Form B specified market value:

Market value	$547,000
Less loans	335,000
Market value equity	$212,000

And it reduced NOI by debt service:

Net operating income	$52,000
Less loan payment	32,400
Gross spendable income	$19,600

To determine return on equity:

Rate: 9.25%
Gross spendable income divided by market value equity

$$\left(\frac{\$\ 19,600}{\$212,000} = 9.25\% \right)$$

The "rate" here represents the percentage rate of return on equity (market value less loan balance). In actual usage Form B was a sales tool, and the market value figure was often a price set by the owner who was attempting to sell. Therefore, a purchase with a down payment of $212,000 cash would generate a return of 9.25 percent based on spendable income. Of course, in negotiating a purchase it is likely that an attempt would be made to obtain a lower price, which would result in a higher rate of return on the cash investment.

Conditioned as we are to think in percentage terms, it is understandable that in actual practice the rule of thumb for this form was to focus on the rate of return provided by a cash down payment for the equity. Consequently, the value of the property was automatically determined based on the capitalized value of the gross spendable income added to the loan balance. Therefore, if the expected rate of return in the market is 6 percent, the price of the property could be increased by capitalizing the gross spendable income at the lower rate.

For example, when the income of $19,600 is divided by a rate of 0.06, the result is an equity value of $326,667, which when added to the loans of $335,000, results in an estimated value of $661,667.

$$\frac{\text{Spendable income}}{\text{Cap rate}} \quad \frac{\$19,600}{0.06} = \$326,667.00 \text{ equity}$$

Reducing the cap rate has the effect of increasing the price on the property. This implies, mistakenly, that if rates of return in the market are lower, real estate is worth more. A more accurate way of viewing the relationship between market value and rates of return is in the context of investor expectations and cycles.

This interpretation would say that investors expect continued additional cash flow from price appreciation or tax savings and are therefore willing to accept a lower return from rents while waiting for a sale at a higher price because of appreciation. As a result, a lower discount rate is applied to the expected future value. This is a typical inflationary market expectation. Note that the deflationary scenario is increasing bond prices as interest rates fall. Consequently, the inflation premium gradually works out of real estate, as investors apply a higher discount rate to future values.

In addition to the financial accounting sequence, Form B also contains a series of blanks designed to determine market value based on the appraisal guidelines, using the income, replacement costs, and comparable sales methods. These three appraisal methods parallel the basic model of real estate investment analysis: financial performance is the combined result of the characteristics of the property and market conditions. The thread of consistency in the analysis of property embodied in Form B, which grew out of the appraisal tradition, is applicable today. Although the methods of measurement have changed, the core concepts remain a representation of the historical progression of real estate investment analysis.

Form B was replaced in the 1970s by a new form for the analysis of real estate entitled "Annual Property Operating Data" (APOD). This change in presentation eliminated the appraisal summary used on the old form and only provided information on operating cash flows and the financing on the property.

The APOD form started the transition to discounted cash flow analysis in popular usage by focusing on cash flows with no reference to traditional appraisal methods. And in an almost prophetic move this form also removed the calculation of tax benefits as a financial contribution of the property, emphasizing operating performance instead. Virtual elimination of much of the tax benefits of real estate took place over 10 years later with the passage of the Tax Reform Act of 1986.

The APOD form also changed the labels for income and expense items to conform to current usage and expanded the list of expense items. The purpose of this form was to accurately specify the cash flow from rental income. In this regard it was a progressive step in gathering the cash flows necessary to do a thorough financial analysis.

Furthermore, the APOD form marked separation of investment analysis from appraisal methods. This breakaway from evaluating investment property based on a static market appraisal moved the industry closer to the dynamics of time value-based financial analysis used in business and the lending industry. Concurrently with the introduction of this form, the National Association of Realtors introduced its members to discounted cash flow analysis using the internal rate of return. This was a first step toward the use of the dollar amount present value criteria more widely recognized today.

The sequence of the Annual Property Operating Data form follows in summary form:

Scheduled Rental Income	$200,000
Less vacancy	20,000
Effective Rental Income	180,000
Plus other income	0
Gross Operating Income	180,000
Less operating expenses	76,000
Net Operating Income	104,000
Less annual debt service	64,800
Cash Flow before Taxes	$ 39,200

Although both the annual rate of return and the one-year capitalization of income used to establish value in Form B were virtually eliminated with this new form, they still held on in actual practice. Conceptualizing investment performance on the basis of annual returns is embedded in the way we think. The APOD form attempted to move conventional analysis toward discounted cash flow analysis over the investment period, which typically involved several years.

Applying Annual Return Measures of Investment Performance

Cash returned as a measure of real estate investment performance is a logical outgrowth of the yearly view typically applied to most investments. You make an investment, and each year a percentage of that amount is returned to you as interest, dividend, yield, or rent. Meanwhile the capital you invest remains safe (or in danger) within the investment vehicle until it is converted back to cash; or so the reasoning goes.

Current financial analysis theory does not separate annual cash flow from invested capital; nevertheless, the practice is widely used and important to the evolution and understanding of the methods used today.

Much of investment analysis is a process of determining various percentage relationships between cash invested and cash received. Percentage measures allow comparison and choice of the optimum investment; that is, the investment that returns the most cash in relation to the amount invested during a one-year period.

For example, a 25 percent rate of return on invested capital is a faster and larger cash return than a 15 percent return over the same time period of one year. The rate of return, therefore, expresses quantity and speed of cash flow in relation to the initial investment. Conventional thinking reasons that the greater the risk, the faster you should expect your capital to be returned to you—that is, the higher the rate of return should be. A higher rate of return is conventionally required where the risk is high because the faster and larger the cash return the quicker you reduce the amount of capital at risk.

Although there are logical problems connected to this older way of viewing risk and return, it does help express our intuitive understanding of the utility concept of money and time value.

Calculating Payback Period

Payback period analysis, popular among real estate investors at one time, was a crude measure of performance based on time value. During the late 1950s and 1960s, payback period was used to analyze real estate investments. One criterion was to try to negotiate a transaction so the down payment would pay back in three years out of rental income. At the time, a three-year payback was considered a good deal, but five-year paybacks were more common.

Those low inflation years did produce high rental income returns. A 25 percent return was an expectation among some hard negotiators. This method of analyzing investment real estate placed it in the category of high profit businesses with earnings from rental operations.

Since much of the investment property was older, and inflation was not ingrained in expectations, a high discount rate was intuitively applied to future values, which resulted in lower present values. An inflation premium simply wasn't yet built into prices; consequently, the rental returns were higher in relation to the down payment amounts.

As a result, rental income was often high enough to use payback period as a criterion for choosing between real estate acquisitions. These returns are far from the negative cash flows typical at the cycle peak during the 1980s when price speculation and tax shelter offset other cash flow sources. Calculation of payback period follows.

Calculating Payback Period

Price	$150,000
Less loan	135,000
Equity	$ 15,000

Down payment: $15,000
Net rental income: $3,000 per year
Payback period: 5 years (5 × $3,000 = $15,000)

As the long wave cycle progressed and prices increased after the 1970s recession, rental cash flow returns decreased in response to the inflation premium and high debt on new property. Eventually, analyzing real estate in terms of the payback period was little used because the returns from rents became so small that payback was not a consideration.

Payback period was an expression of the theory that the return *of* an investment and the return *on* investment can be separated in time. Its application viewed cash flows during the initial years as the return *of* investment. This mindset was the result of a risk-aversive investment climate and expectations for deflation that still existed into the late 1960s. Getting your money out of an investment made common sense, because if you lost the property you at least had your money back.

As the nature of the long wave economic cycle changed from deflationary to inflationary in the 1970s, price appreciation became the dominant expectation and in some markets the sole decision criterion. In a sense, expectation of price increases was an inverse application of the payback analysis criteria. Now the payback came with the last cash flow from sale proceeds. And during the holding period operating losses and negative cash flows were accepted as the investment practice necessary to participate in the speculative bonanza of real estate appreciation.

One of the problems with entrenched expectations such as these is that prior experience either doesn't exist because there is a new generation of investors, or it is ignored because the potential reward is worth the potential for risk. Both contribute to the boom-bust scenario that occurs again and again in real estate.

Using Rate of Return Measures

Rate of return measures are the second half of the theory that an investment must provide a return *of* the capital (payback) and a return *on* the capital (annual percentage). Similar theories come and go as our understanding of real estate investment analysis progresses. But such theories are not isolated concepts. Each inch of progress in understanding is built on the experience of the past and what we have learned as a result. Relating past thinking to present analysis techniques may help avoid some of the conceptual confusion that can occur when applying the newer analysis methods.

Clearly, there are two components to investment return. In common usage the phrase *rate of return* refers both to the dollar amount and the percentage relationship. The percentage expression is the annual rate represented by the cash received relative to the initial investment amount. One use of the word *return* is the dollar amount. The other use is the percentage relationship of the annual dollar amount to the down payment.

The rate of return measures how fast invested capital is returned to the investor (10 percent a year, 12 percent a year) and is calculated by comparing the known dollar amounts of down payment and net rental income. A high rate of return reflects a fast payback. For example, the five-year payback in the earlier example is a 20 percent return. A 33 percent rate of return would represent a three-year payback.

Rate of return calculations are basic to the investment world and easy to calculate. For example, net rental income divided by down payment equals the rate of return on invested funds.

Calculating Rate of Return

Net rental cash flow	$\dfrac{\$\ \ 5,000}{\$100,000}$ = 5% rate of return
Down payment	

This quick method of evaluating the financial performance of property is a natural way to view any investment. You can apply the calculation in reverse to capitalize the annual income. Capitalization in this application is a simple method to determine the down payment appropriate for the property based on the net rental cash flow it produces.

Using Rate of Return to Calculate Value

Net rental income	$\dfrac{\$5,000}{5\%}$ = $100,000 down payment
Rate of return	

Annual rate of return methods for evaluating investment real estate are so ingrained in our thinking they will probably always be with us. Even though they are inadequate to measure the total life performance of an investment, custom dictates that we at least in part view the investment world within the context of annual performance. For example, the annual percentage rate is the legal disclosure amount under the truth-in-lending laws. It is also the time frame for measuring yield on savings accounts, bonds, and stock dividends and interest rates in general. But with debt investments such as these, unlike real estate, the interest rate is known so the dollar return must be calculated by applying the percentage rate to the investment amount.

Applying Cash-on-Cash Return

Cash-on-cash return expresses the relationship between the initial cash investment or down payment and the yearly cash "thrown off." This measure is closest to the savings account model that forms the basis of yearly cash returns. Its advantage is clarity and simplicity, avoiding any confusion of meaning in negotiations.

Cash-on-cash return expresses the rate of return measure in a manner designed to prevent confusion with other measures of performance such as the cap rate, which does not usually consider debt service and the rate of return which could involve tax accounting. The point in stating that the return under consideration is cash on cash is to clarify that the return generated by the property refers to cash items only, including both expenses and debt service, but not depreciation.

Calculating Cash-on-Cash Return

Price	$595,000
Less loan	350,000
Down payment	$245,000

Cash flow from rent (after debt service): $19,600

Cash-on-cash return: 8% $\left(\dfrac{\$\ 19{,}600}{\$245{,}000}\right)$

In practice, cash-on-cash return is used to refer both to the dollar amount and the annual percentage relationship between net rental income and the investment (down payment). To clarify this relationship, the term *cash thrown off* or *cash throw-off* is used to unmistakably clarify that the subject of discussion is dollars, not a percentage or rate of return relationship to the down payment.

Cash-on-cash return clears away any misunderstanding of the calculation used to reach the number; that is, no factors are part of the equation other than the cash relationships—the cash down payment and the cash flow generated from operation of the property. The use of cash-on-cash return was another move in the transition to establish a cash flow-based view of investment real estate.

Cash-on-cash return moved real estate closer to using pure cash flow analysis. From there it was a small step to expand the application of cash flow to include tax savings and sale proceeds and any other benefit that could be quantified as cash. Once that insight was accomplished, the addition of time value followed.

Calculating Return on Equity

Return on equity takes the concept of annual return a step further and measures the relationship between net rental income and the current market value of the property. This performance measure is intended to monitor appreciation and loan reduction in relation to operating income with the purpose of selling or exchanging when the percentage return on equity gets low. Unlike most rate of return measures, which focus on analysis for determining purchase value, this application monitors property performance during ownership. Return on equity is not a measure of actual cash flow because the equity is not yet realized as cash when the evaluation is made, but it does measure the relationship between income and market value. This technique seems to have grown out of high activity, rapidly appreciating real estate markets.

The assumption of this analysis technique is that return on equity should stay within market guidelines. Monitoring return on equity provides an analysis method designed for market conditions which exhibit appreciation and the availability of underperforming property.

For example, when prices rise faster than rents increase, there is a point where the rate of return based on potential equity is very low. The property is more valuable than the return on rental income seems to warrant. This is the time to move equity to another property with a smaller equity-to-price relationship and therefore a higher return on equity from rental cash flow, providing more upside potential for appreciation.

| | Original property | | New acquisition |
	Year 1	Year 5	First year
Price	$200,000	$480,000	$1,700,000
Less loan	150,000	140,000	1,360,000
Equity	$ 50,000	$340,000	$ 340,000
Rental cash flow	$ 3,000	$ 7,000	$ 20,000
Return on equity	6%	2%	5.88%

The objective is to use the increase in equity due to appreciation and loan reduction to acquire property of a higher value and thereby increase overall wealth. With property of higher value, the annual percentage appreciation will be larger, thus increasing the amount of overall wealth. Eventually, it will be time to repeat the process and acquire an even larger property. Obviously, this acquisition-oriented analysis method requires use of a tax-deferred exchange, because tax on the gain would unnecessarily reduce purchasing power of the equity. It is easy to see why return on equity can be a useful analysis tool, but it does require a certain kind of market for implementation.

Return on equity is designed to be used as a decision criterion for acquiring larger property with increased equity of the original property. It is founded on the premise that every investment should maximize cash flow as a percentage of equity.

During cycle phases when price increases outpace rent increases, the challenge is to find property that has appreciation potential relative to rental income greater than the current investment. Carried to the logical extreme, investors accept smaller rates of return from rents as the search for price appreciation becomes the central investment goal. Ultimately, negative rental cash flow becomes acceptable as long as the market is active and prices continue to increase. Markets that accept negative cash flows in the hope of future resale or higher rents have limited lives. Eventually, the cycle turns.

Customary methods of measuring the financial performance of real estate have proven inadequate for analyzing the total performance during the entire holding period of the property. At best, annual rates of return on the cash invested or the current equity of property are snapshots of performance and in some cases completely irrelevant to the dynamics of the real estate cycle. Nevertheless, it is understandable that the annual rate of return and related methods form the historical basis of investment performance measures.

Applying Breakeven Analysis to Real Estate

To a large degree, standard real estate analysis methods represent the struggle of real estate investors to acquire and retain wealth in a dynamic and fluctuating market. Focusing on cash flow represents a leap of progress in the effort. The risk of investing in real estate is that the property will not generate the cash flow needed to pay operating expenses and debt service and eventually will be repossessed by the lender. Breakeven analysis is a recognition of that possibility.

Unfortunately, breakeven analysis has become a lost concept in recent real estate investment activity. It was crowded out by expectations of appreciation and assumptions of inflation as the cycle peaked in the 1980s. Subsequently, the destruction of those expectations was so rapid that the concept was again lost in the watershed of foreclosures.

Traditionally, breakeven analysis is used in business to specify the future date and income or unit sales level at which continued capital investment will no longer be needed to carry a new investment venture. The usefulness of breakeven analysis lies in the fact that it is a reality-based challenge to the acceptance of negative cash flows. In real estate, breakeven is the point in rental operation when positive cash flows exceed negative cash flows. Breakeven normally refers to rental cash flows only but may include income from tax savings.

Breakeven analysis is in part a measure of cash flows over time. Instead of asking what the return is, it asks when the negative cash flow will stop and the positive cash flow start. It is both a question of time and money. Determining when the property will break even is the operations correlate to determining the payback period. Breakeven analysis is easy to do and appropriate with any negative cash flow property. It forces consideration of whether future income levels will cover expenses and debt service.

	Year 1	Year 2	Year 3
Effective rental income	$20,000	$25,000	$30,000
Less operating expenses	10,000	10,000	10,000
Net operating income	10,000	15,000	20,000
Less debt service	(20,000)	(20,000)	(20,000)
Cash flow before taxes	($10,000)	($ 5,000)	$ 0

Breakeven analysis requires consideration of whether the market will support a specific real estate investment, and it forces the investor to consider whether support of the property is an appropriate alternative. Because breakeven has a time element to it, the possibility of not covering negative operational cash flows must be considered. Breakeven analysis requires specific consideration of income, expense, and debt service requirements over the term of ownership. Since the property is not carrying itself when it is acquired, breakeven forces calculation of the amount and the time of additional capital investment, then forces a choice of whether it is worth it.

How Analysis Techniques Reflect Inflationary Expectations

The traditional real estate analysis techniques contain an implicit gauge of perceived risk and market expectations. For example, it is only by offering a higher quantity return (cash) that a property of low quality (physical condition) can attract investment capital. The cash-on-cash return offered by low quality property must generally be higher in order to make up for the lack of potential for rent increases and appreciation.

In contrast, expectations of price appreciation can offset low rents and make negative cash flow tolerable when market conditions and the quality of the property warrant. Ultimately, much of the value of real estate for transferring purchasing power through time is in the price. Furthermore, price appreciation is the primary consideration for broad public participation.

To a large extent the demand for investment real estate depends on expectations for the future of the market. When expectations of high inflation control market decisions the anticipated future cash flows are discounted at a lower rate, resulting in higher prices. When high inflation is not part of expectations, future values are discounted at a higher rate, resulting in lower real estate prices. Price discounting plays a large role in the real estate cycle, reflecting market expectations at the time.

Before the 1970s there was no way to measure negative rental cash flow property, because the market did not accept operational losses as a viable investment possibility. It was intuitively unreasonable to consider a way to measure negative cash flow from rents because such property made no sense. Inflation had not hit the market yet. In fact, when such property started changing hands, many old-timers simply couldn't figure out why anyone in his or her right mind would buy property that didn't carry its own weight. At first, during the 1970s when inflation started creeping up, this type of property was referred to as *overfinanced property* because of the high leverage. Although the term *overfinanced* was a criticism, it was the best possible strategy at the time because of low real interest rates.

Acceptance by the market of negative cash flow property was one of the first signs of a major market adjustment to high inflation and a speculative real estate cycle. As it turned out, in these early stages the high leverage of overfinanced property was a smart strategy for equity investors. The debt investors who financed acquisitions at low rates were the losers during the inflationary spiral.

After the peak of inflation in the 1980–1981 period and prior to 1986, much of the rental-income risk associated with real estate was covered by the return available from tax savings. During the early 1980s prices were too high and rents were too low, so tax savings had to carry the cash flow burden. With the passage of the Tax Reform Act of 1986, the tax benefit source of cash flow terminated and with it a major support of real estate prices. The consequences gave new meaning to the concept of market risk. This removal of tax savings cash flow changed investor expectations for real estate almost overnight. Real estate supply was extremely high as a result of the favorable depreciation rules passed five years earlier. Consequently, the impact on prices was greater. Oversupply and the new tax law combined with reality to remove the inflationary premium built up in real estate during the previous several years.

It is implicit in real estate investment that a positive return must come from somewhere for the property to survive expenses and debt service. Real estate prices and market activity are to a large degree subject to changes in public sentiment without warning. Consequently, viewing the return generated on a property in the context of the risk specific to that return is essential for thorough analysis. This guideline applies to the return from appreciation, which is subject to sudden withdrawal of buyers; it applies to rental income which is always in competition with other property; and, it applies to tax savings which is subject to the unpredictable moves of the federal government, which are inconsistent, accident prone, and just as likely to provide an incentive one year and a disincentive four years later.

5
Discounted Cash Flow Analysis: The Comprehensive Measure

Both compounding and discounting measure the value of money in relation to time, but they determine value in different time directions. Discounting measures from the future back in time; compounding measures from the present forward in time. Therefore, compounding calculates future value, and discounting calculates present value.

Discounting is used in many investment fields; consequently, the percentage expression has different names common to the financial specialty. But the process is always the same regardless of the name used to describe it. For example, *yield to maturity* used in the bond market is the same percentage as the popular *internal rate of return* (IRR) used in real estate and business. They are both percentage expressions of the discounting procedure.

Discounting is particularly useful in real estate analysis when the cash flows are known or can be reasonably projected and you want to determine the compounded interest rate they represent. The internal rate of return can be used to accomplish the calculation. It begins with cash flows and solves for the interest rate.

Discounting can also be used to solve for the present value of a series of cash flows. In this application the discount rate (interest rate) you choose is applied to future cash flows to determine the net present value (NPV). This is a dollar amount rather than a percentage. It calculates the net relationship between the money invested and the money received from an investment. A positive NPV indicates that the present value of the cash received is greater than the present value of the cash invested.

Therefore, discounting is used both to solve for the interest rate (IRR) at which invested funds grow when only the amount and time periods are known, and to calculate the net present value of the positive and negative cash flows (NPV) generated by a project.

The following illustrates the relationship between compounding and discounting and the financial functions they perform.

Compounding calculates forward in time by multiplication:
| Percentage: | Dollar amount: |
| Interest rate | Future value |

Discounting calculates backward in time by division:
Percentage:	Dollar Amount:
Discount rate	Present value
Applied as IRR	Applied as NPV

If you understand compounding you understand discounting. One way of visualizing these time value calculations is to think of discounting moving backward in time from the future (value) to the present (value). Conversely, think of compounding moving forward in time from the present (value) to the future (value).

Discounting is the inverse of compounding. Mathematically, this means that the formula for compounding, which solves by multiplication, can be inverted to create the formula for discounting, which solves by division.

The usefulness of discounted cash flow analysis to real estate lies in the fact that IRR and NPV allow comparison of totally different investments on an equal basis. These two time value calculations provide a common denominator for all cash flows—time value.

Applying the Time Value of Money

Money has a certain utility. Its value is in what it can be used for, and the satisfaction that use provides. The marginal utility of money refers to the demand for cash and the satisfaction each extra dollar provides [15, p.87].

Cash has a lower marginal utility during inflationary spirals than the equity of the appreciating assets it can be invested in. Consequently, negative rental cash flows are more easily accepted by the market in the present because of high expectations of future appreciation. But during deflationary recessions, cash liquidity is in high demand. For most, this is when cash is tight just to meet the basic needs of life. Therefore, cash has a high marginal utility because each extra dollar is important for financial survival and security. During serious contractions the demand for cash is high relative to supply because so much cash flow is redirected to paying debts built up during the previous expansion. During tight money cycles, cash has a high marginal utility, which means each extra dollar is extremely valuable, in part because it is in short supply.

But when the cycle is expanding with easy credit, the marginal utility of cash is lower. In this type of market each extra dollar provides less satisfaction. Cash is not as highly valued in the present, in part because the supply is plentiful and expectations for the future are comfortably optimistic.

There is also a time preference for money. We prefer to get money sooner than later. If we get it sooner we can use it sooner. We can invest it to earn more money or we can spend it on what we choose. Time preference also varies depending on the market cycle.

Time preference affects real estate values in a direct way during different stages of the market cycle. For example, the greater the time preference for cash the higher the discount rate applied to prices and therefore future cash flows from sales proceeds. This is one reason you can buy real estate at a discount during recessions: There is both an increased time preference for cash and a higher marginal utility. People prefer to get cash now because the use they have for it puts a high value on each available dollar. The preference for cash liquidity is high during contractions, often out of fear and the need for financial security. The demand for each additional dollar is high because during this stage of the cycle cash is crucial to survival. Sales at relatively bargain prices occur just to get cash. This is the reason that a higher discount rate is applied to future real estate prices. The demand for cash is high, and the expectation for real estate appreciation is low.

During high inflation there is a low time preference for cash in relation to appreciating assets. Cash is not in high demand relative to supply because there is a large supply of cash under inflationary monetary conditions. Under these market conditions cash loses purchasing power as time passes; consequently, it is viewed as best left invested in inflation hedge assets that appreciate, such as real estate.

Expectations for continued inflation eventually become so entrenched in public thinking that it takes years for them to work through the economy. This is the stage of the cycle when cash has a lower marginal utility because each additional dollar beyond basic needs provides less satisfaction. Furthermore, there is so much cash in the market that demand relative to supply is low. This of course is the time to sell property that you don't want to hold during the approaching turn in the cycle.

But from a financial viewpoint there is a cash management purpose underlying the time preference for money. Cash received sooner is more valuable in time. Money can only be invested if you have it. And the sooner you have it the sooner it can be put to work earning interest or participating in the appreciation of property. In this sense the sooner you earn money the faster you can put it to work earning interest or invest it in a project of your choice.

Dynamic market forces work to shape the direction of the market cycle which in turn changes the time preference for money and the marginal utility attributed to it. We see this as the interaction of governmental factors and the fundamental factors of capital availability, supply-demand, and expectations working together to affect time preference and marginal utility, which in turn affect real estate rents and prices.

For example, during regional depressions the high demand for cash and a high time preference cause sellers to discount future values at a higher rate, producing lower present values (prices). As the process continues inflationary expectations are eventually washed out of the market and price appreciation is no longer of concern. These are the stages of the cycle during which sellers finally give up and are no longer willing to wait for a higher price because higher prices are not part of expectations anymore.

This mindset is the opposite of that which exists during times of high inflation or in regions where speculation is active. Here, low demand for cash relative to supply and a low time preference for cash forces prices higher, as sellers expect rising prices and are, therefore, willing to wait to sell and receive appreciation and more cash later. Consequently, the discount rate applied to real estate prices is lower, resulting in higher prices or present values.

This process occurs in mirror image with bond prices, which tend to move in the opposite direction of real estate during long-term fluctuations of inflation and deflation. Bond prices fall with high inflation as the purchasing power of cash erodes. Therefore, a higher discount rate is applied to their expected future value, lowering the present price. Since bonds are long-term liquid cash equivalent instruments, prices drop because the expected loss in purchasing power forces the market to discount future cash values at a higher rate. When inflation ends, the discount rate on bonds is lowered and prices begin rising.

During inflation, real estate prices increase as the market discounts the future value of appreciating assets at a lower rate; and bond prices fall as the market discounts the future value of cash assets at a higher rate. During inflationary spirals cash loses purchasing power, and debt is readily placed on assets with expectations that it can be paid back with inflated, less valuable dollars. More debt puts more strain on current cash flows until debt cannot be serviced, resulting in bankruptcies and foreclosures.

When rental cash flows can't support debt service, the end of the expansion is here and the beginning of debt liquidation starts. The resulting depression in economic activity lasts until enough debt is liquidated, one way or another, for rental cash flows to catch up with debt service.

During extended contractions, a high time preference for cash develops. It is needed to service high debt payments and meet current needs, but difficult to obtain due to relatively tight credit conditions of low levels of market activity. Demand for cash in the present outweighs anticipated future cash flows from appreciation that no longer seems to exist. As pessimism grows, liquidity becomes more valued simply by eliminating the risk that future cash flows may not be received. Money received sooner eliminates the chance of never receiving it. This intuitive understanding of risk is the basis for the desire to sell when prices are falling, occasionally causing panics when the public realizes the cycle is turning.

Although the causes underlying the degree of time preference for money differ depending on market conditions, the ultimate financial aim in both inflationary and deflationary cycles is to gain the utility of money as quickly as possible. Financially, the time preference for cash is due to the marginal utility of each additional dollar, which can be measured by the real interest rate it can earn.

The relationship among invested capital, future cash flows, and time forms the basis for measuring the financial performance of real estate. Since investing is a process of transferring purchasing power through time and increasing real wealth, it is essential to include the effects of time on cash flows. Time value is the common denominator of all cash flows; consequently, to accurately measure different cash flows they must be reduced to a common time value. Discounting accomplishes this requirement.

Understanding the Internal Rate of Return

The internal rate of return (IRR) is the same as the common interest rate familiar to all who have deposited cash in a savings account, money market fund, or other interest-paying account. IRR is simply a different name for the familiar process of calculating interest earned on invested capital over time. It is nothing more than the interest rate at which invested funds compound or grow. From a traditional real estate analysis view, IRR is the rate of return earned by an investment during the entire ownership period of the property.

Technically, the IRR is a discount rate because of the method of application: Instead of applying a percentage to the initial investment to determine the future cash flows (compounding), the future cash flows are compared with the invested funds to determine the percentage (at which the invested funds compound). Consequently, when searching for the IRR, we are solving for the unknown interest rate at which a known series of cash flows has grown.

The word *internal* is added to the standard phrase *rate of return* to indicate that the interest rate applies only to the cash flows of the specific project or investment being analyzed; that is, cash flows that occur internally and not from external sources. Internal is intended to clarify. It should not be interpreted as implying some different meaning than the familiar interest rate that it is— an interest rate determined by the discounting process.

The internal rate of return is the interest rate at which the present value of the cash flows receive equal the present value of the cash flows invested. It is the discount rate at which the net present value is zero.

For example, an investor bought a commercial lot for $100,000 five years ago. She currently has an offer from a retail shoe store chain to buy the lot for $225,000. What rate of return does this offer represent? In other words, what is the IRR of this investment?

Year 0	($100,000)
Year 1	0
Year 2	0
Year 3	0
Year 4	0
Year 5	$225,000
Internal rate of return . . . 17.61%	

The most practical way to solve a simple one-payment IRR problem is to use the present value keys on a business calculator. It can also be calculated with the present value tables using trial and error and interpolation, which clearly demonstrates the relationship between IRR and NPV.

In this example the $100,000 investment compounded at 17.61 percent. Or, stated another way, the IRR was 17.61 percent. This IRR is the interest rate earned by the investment. But rather than starting with the initial investment and applying the interest rate, IRR starts with the cash flows produced by the investment and solves for the interest rate at which the investment compounded. The meaning of IRR in this illustration is that $225,000 when discounted at 17.61 percent over five years will produce a present value of $100,000.

The internal rate of return is conceptually important because it links the traditional annual rate of return measurement to the typical multiple-year holding period characteristic of real estate.

Using the discounting formula to determine the compounded growth rate of an investment is a requirement of the marketplace. In real estate the only data we have are the cash flows and the time periods in which they occur. Consequently, to determine the interest rate at which cash flows compound, we must discount them to the present value of the invested funds.

Understanding Net Present Value

Net present value (NPV) is the dollar expression of the discounting process. Internal rate of return (IRR) is the percentage expression. The two are related conceptually and mathematically even though the formulas are different. IRR is the discount rate at which an investment's positive and negative cash flows have the same present value, resulting in an NPV of zero.

This, of course, means that the present value of the invested funds is the same amount as the present value of the money received from the investment, when compared on the common basis of equal time value. Consequently, when positive and negative cash flows of equal present value are netted together, the result is a net present value of zero. IRR and NPV level varying cash flow amounts to a common time value denominator by discounting.

Although both IRR and NPV are conceptually related discounted cash flow analysis techniques, the mathematics of the formulas put restrictions on IRR that do not exist for NPV. Central to this difference is that IRR must solve for a percentage figure which depends on the relationship in time and amount of all the cash flows in the series. In contrast, NPV chooses an appropriate discount rate and solves for the net dollar amount of both positive and negative cash flows.

NPV is a much simpler calculation and does not produce the errors and multiple answers common to IRR calculations under complex cash flow conditions. Probably because of this, NPV has slowly grown in popularity as an investment decision criterion while IRR has taken a second position in practical usage.

Rather than generating an interest rate as with the IRR, net present value calculates either a positive or negative cash flow amount. To accomplish this, NPV discounts all cash flows to the present value and nets cash flows paid against cash flows received, including the initial investment.

Applying the Mathematics of IRR and NPV

The best way to demonstrate the relationship between IRR and NPV is to discount a series of cash flows without using the present value tables, a business calculator, or computer. Fortunately, the math formula for present value is very simple. Since the IRR is defined by NPV it can also be understood using the more simple NPV calculation.

In the following example an interest rate or discount rate of 10 percent is used to calculate the net present value of the future cash flows. Since the NPV is zero, this discount rate is also the IRR [16, p.6].

Calculating NPV and IRR Using a 10% Discount Rate

			Present value $= \dfrac{\text{Future value}}{(1+i)^n}$		
Year n	Future value	(divided by)	1.10^n	$=$	Present value
0	–$10,000		1.0		–$10,000.00
1	$ 1,000		1.1		$ 909.10
2	$ 1,000		1.21		$ 826.45
3	$ 1,000		1.331		$ 751.31
4	$ 1,000		1.4641		$ 683.01
5	$11,000		1.61051		$ 6,830.13
			Net present value		0

The discount rate used in this example is 10 percent, and because the NPV is zero, 10 percent is also the IRR. A NPV of zero defines the IRR. In this example the discount rate is the internal rate of return because the present value of the positive and negative cash flows are equal.

This formula also illustrates the inverse relationship between compounding and discounting. In the above example the factors used were actually compound interest factors, which is why present value was determined by division. Had we multiplied rather than divided we would have produced the compounded growth amount or future value, rather than the discounted present value. Consequently, we can write the formula to reflect the correlation between compounding and discounting.

Compounding
Future value = Present value $\times (1+i)^n$

Discounting
Present value = Future value $/ (1+i)^n$

The present value formula can be adjusted to calculate present value factors, which allow the use of multiplication to discount a series of cash flows.

Usually, present value is calculated by multiplying cash flows by the present value factor obtained from a table provided at the end of many books on finance. But you can determine these factors without using tables and calculate any present value amount at any rate you choose. For example, the divisors in the above example can be converted to factors by dividing them into 1.

Computing Present Value Factors

Present value factor		=	$1 / (1 + i)^n$		
	PV factor	×	Future value	=	Present value
1/1.0	= 1	×	−$10,000		−$10,000.00
1/1.1	= 0.909091	×	$ 1,000		$ 909.10
1/1.21	= 0.826446	×	$ 1,000		$ 826.45
1/1.331	= 0.751315	×	$ 1,000		$ 751.31
1/1.4641	= 0.683013	×	$ 1,000		$ 683.01
1/1.61051	= 0.620921	×	$11,000		$ 6,830.13
			Present value		0

Using the examples as a guide you can compute present value factors for any interest rate (discount rate) you like. For example, what are the present value factors needed to calculate the present value of cash flows received over five years, discounted at 8 percent?

Calculating Present Value Factors for an 8% Discount Rate

PV factor = $1 / 1.08^n$	
Year	Factor
0 . . . since no time has passed	1
1 . . . 1/1.08	0.925926
2 . . . 1/(1.08 × 1.08)	0.857339
3 . . . 1/(1.08 × 1.08 × 1.08)	0.793832
4 . . . 1/(1.08 × 1.08 × 1.08 × 1.08)	0.735030
5 . . . 1/(1.08 × 1.08 × 1.08 × 1.08 × 1.08)	0.680583

Calculating Present Value Factors for a 7% Discount Rate

PV factor = $1 / 1.07^n$	
Year	Factor
0	1
1 . . . 1/1.07	0.934579
2 . . . 1/(1.07 × 1.07)	0.873439
3 . . . 1/(1.07 × 1.07 × 1.07)	0.816298
4 . . . 1/(1.07 × 1.07 × 1.07 × 1.07)	0.762895
5 . . . 1/(1.07 × 1.07 × 1.07 × 1.07 × 1.07)	0.712986

If you have a series of cash flows that occur monthly, the present value factor for monthly discounting can be calculated by dividing the annual rate by 12. If you want to discount cash flows that occur quarterly, the annual rate can be divided by four. For example, the discount factor for cash flows received monthly can be calculated as follows:

Monthly PV factor = $1 / (1 + (i / 12))^n$
Using an 8% factor: $1 / (1 + (0.08 / 12))^n = 1 / 1.006667^n$

Therefore:

Month	Monthly factor
1 ... 1/1.006667	0.993377
2 ... 1/(1.006667 × 1.006667)	0.986798
3 ... 1/(1.006667 × 1.006667 × 1.006667)	0.980263

It can be useful to know how to calculate present value factors for several reasons. Knowing the steps of the calculation takes the mystery out of the math and reduces the possible intimidation factor that occasionally accompanies anything beyond four function safety. But more importantly, it is not always possible to locate tables for the interest rate you want to use as a discount factor. Furthermore, you may not have a computer handy with the functions programmed into the software. When you understand the mechanics of calculating discount factors all you need is a calculator to determine net present value for any time period and any interest rate you want.

Net present value is the first calculation needed to determine internal rate of return. Most applications do not neatly produce the internal rate of return as a result of the net present value calculation like the first example (page 109). Trial and error are necessary to determine the discount rate which closely approximates a NPV of zero. The exact rate can then be specified by interpolation. This calculation illustrates the link between NPV and IRR.

Year	Cash Flows	8% factor	Present value
0	($10,000)	1	($10,000.00)
1	$ 700	0.925926	$ 648.15
2	$ 800	0.857339	$ 685.87
3	$ 850	0.793832	$ 674.76
4	$ 900	0.735030	$ 661.53
5	$10,500	0.680583	$ 7,146.12
		Net present value	($ 183.57)

This first trial indicates that the IRR is less than 8 percent because the NPV is negative. Consequently, we must use a lower discount rate to try to find a positive NPV. The objective of this process is to determine the discount percentages that will produce one positive and one negative NPV. Then we can solve for the exact rate that lies between the two. Therefore the following series uses a 7 percent discount rate.

Year	Cash flows	7% factor	Present value
0	($10,000)	1	($10,000.00)
1	$ 700	0.934579	$ 654.21
2	$ 800	0.873439	$ 698.75
3	$ 850	0.816298	$ 693.85
4	$ 900	0.762895	$ 686.61
5	$10,500	0.712986	$ 7,486.35
		Net present value	$ 219.77

Since the NPV is positive we know the IRR is more than 7 percent but less than 8 percent. Therefore, we can solve for the exact rate as follows:

$$IRR = R + \frac{NPV}{(NPV + NPV)}$$

$$IRR = 7\% + \frac{219.77}{(183.57 + 219.77)}$$

$$IRR = 7.544875\%$$

The important thing to notice here is the link between the math of NPV and IRR. Understanding the relationship can help keep the two concepts simple and useful within the limits of their applications.

From time to time through the years, various analysts have complicated and confused interpretation of these simple concepts, reading more into financial analysis than necessary to reduce cash flows to equal time value amounts. But these basic time value calculations have stood the test of time while the more complicated variations drop from use, a reminder that academic complexity is no guarantee of usefulness or of market survival.

Expanding the Use of Net Present Value

The discount rate used to determine NPV is usually chosen as the minimum acceptable rate of return needed to make a decision to proceed with the investment. For example, a corporation may use the cost of capital (prime rate, commercial paper rate) as the discount factor, or possibly its actual borrowing costs. The reasoning here is that, at a minimum, a corporate (or individual) investment should generate cash flows sufficient to offset the cost of investment funds.

As an alternative the discount rate may be established based on an analysis of the risks involved in the project; or, it may be established based on the company objective for a return necessary to commit to the project after considering capital cost, return on equity, and overhead.

Therefore, net present value as typically used is a decision criterion for the allocation of capital between equally acceptable investment opportunities; and also, as a cutoff decision criterion as to whether to proceed with a chosen project at all. This is its historical use in finance, but the current use in real estate has much broader application.

The investment criterion rule is simple: If the net present value is positive the investment decision is affirmative. If the net present value is negative the investment decision is negative because it does not generate the minimum return needed to proceed.

As a decision tool, net present value determines whether the total of the present values of the cash inflows, when discounted at a desired interest rate, is larger than the total of the present values of the cash outflows. This is why it is called "net" present value, because all negative cash flows are netted against all positive cash flows. NPV immediately determines whether an investment makes or loses money in real terms adjusted for time value.

If the present value of the cash invested is less than the present value of the cash received, NPV indicates that the investment is losing money on a time value basis. One of the more important aspects of NPV is that it equalizes all cash flows based on the common denominator of time value.

This aspect of NPV has facilitated its widespread use in the office leasing segment of the real estate industry. Owners can readily determine whether the tenant improvements (invested cash flows) will be offset by the cash flows received from lease income. Also, tenants can determine which leasing package (rental rate, rent concessions, improvements) offered by competing buildings is the best value. Furthermore, a prospective purchaser can use NPV analysis to determine the value of the building based on the cash flows generated by the leases.

Discounting reduces all cash flows—negative and positive, initial and subsequent—to a present value amount allowing comparison of investment alternatives on an equal money and time measurement scale. This is accomplished regardless of whether the cash flows are negative (investments) or positive (income) and regardless of the time period at which they occur. Net present value provides a fair financial basis for comparison of cash flows that differ in amount and time.

For example, which of the following two sets of cash flows provides the greater increase in purchasing power?

		Alternative 1	Alternative 2
YEAR 0:	Down payment	−$100,000	−$100,000
EOY 1:	Net rent	5,000	4,000
EOY 2:	Net rent	5,000	−4,500
EOY 3:	Net rent	−4,500	5,000
EOY 4:	Net rent	4,000	5,000
EOY 5:	Rent plus sale	175,000	175,000
	Net total	$ 84,500	$ 84,500

Both sets of cash flows have the same nominal investment amount ($104,500 in negative cash flows) and the same nominal income ($189,000 in positive cash flows). And both have the same nominal net income ($189,000 minus $104,500 equals $84,500). But when adjusted for time value, the two income streams have different values:

	Alternative 1	Alternative 2
NPV at 13%	$2,658	$1,531
IRR	13.63%	13.35%

Although the nominal amounts of both cash flow streams are the same, the net present value of each is different. This difference is due to the effects of compound growth, which give the edge to alternative 1 because higher rents were received in the early years of the investment.

Analysis of these two cash flow streams also indicates the inability of IRR to provide a meaningful decision criterion, or measure of the transfer of purchasing power and accumulation of wealth. In fact, the percentage rate of growth is virtually incidental information to any investment decision when compared with the real dollar amounts involved. Anyone involved in the high leverage real estate business has experienced this realization when acquiring property with borrowed money that generates high cash flow. In this common situation, there is no way to measure the actual rate of return because there is no money invested by the person or company that receives the cash flow. Clearly, in many real-life situations the amount of money generated by an investment is more informative investment management information than the compounded rate of growth.

In the above example the net present value amounts are significantly different but the internal rates of return are not.

NPV 1:	$2,658	IRR 1:	13.63
NPV 2:	$1,531	IRR 2:	13.35
Difference	1127		0.28

$1,127 / $1,531 = 73.61%   0.28 / 13.35 = 2.1%

The NPV of alternative 1 is 73.61 percent larger than the NPV of alternative 2 when both are discounted at 13 percent. But the IRR of alternative 1 is only 2.1 percent higher than the IRR of alternative 2, which represents the discount rate at which both NPVs are equal. At first glance, looking at the IRRs alone would indicate an insignificant difference between the two alternatives. A look at the NPV reveals that the two are quite different in the real world of cash flows.

This illustrates one of many dangers of relying solely on rates of return for investment decisions. They are often meaningless and misleading, but accepted without question.

The effect of inflation on the purchasing power of money has placed present value analysis in the position of importance it deserves. The challenge is to determine the suitable discount rate to use for calculation of net present value and to expand the application of this useful technique to its full potential.

Using Opportunity Cost to Determine a Discount Rate

Opportunity cost establishes a conceptual floor under the selection of a discount rate. At the least, opportunity cost represents the alternative use of capital available through investment in low-risk government securities. Money that sits in a non-interest-bearing account for a year represents a year of lost investment opportunity in no-risk U.S. Government Treasury Bills.

A year that passes without meeting the minimum return opportunity available through Treasury Bills is a year of purchasing power lost to inflation. If Treasury Bills are paying 6 percent and inflation is 4.5 percent and income taxes are about 33 percent of earned income, you will not quite break even with a 6 percent return.

After-tax purchasing power at a 6% rate of return on $100,000

Treasury Bill rate	6%	$6,000
Less inflation (4.5% × $106,000)	4.5%	(4,770)
Less income tax (33% of 6%)	2%	(1,574)
Change in after-tax real wealth	−0.5%	($ 344)

There are three factors in this simple example. A slight change in any one of them and you move toward a gain or an increased loss in purchasing power. For example, what would happen if marginal tax rates were at 50 percent as they have been from time to time in the past, or if inflation moved to 6 percent?

Capital must first be protected from losses due to market risk and inflation, income taxes, and operating expenses. Only then can it begin building real wealth.

Clearly, investment funds should be managed with understanding of the opportunity cost of not earning the minimum cash flow available from relatively risk-free, liquid investments. These rates tend to at least encompass current inflation concerns. Not obtaining this minimum return opportunity means watching inflation cut into the body of your investment funds. For example:

Investment capital available	$100,000
Less inflation at 4%	4,000
Remaining purchasing power	$ 96,000

Obviously, the opportunity to invest money today is worth something. There is a measurable cost in terms of purchasing power when capital is committed to a project that does not generate a return.

Purchasing power diminishes with the passage of time. No investment action is required to generate this loss to time. Add market risk and the requirement to run faster to stay even increases.

Maintaining after-tax purchasing power is the first priority of investment activity. Only then can wealth be created.

Applying Present and Future Value Analysis to Real Estate

Future value is calculated by compounding. Present value is calculated by discounting. Compounding is the procedure for determining the future value (or amount) that cash will grow to when invested in the present. Discounting is the procedure for determining the present value (or amount) of cash to be received in the future.

The relationship between compounding, discounting, and present value is illustrated in the following example, which also demonstrates how you can make an investment decision based on financial analysis rather than responding to market forces.

For example, a real estate broker presents you with a land investment opportunity consisting of a commercial lot which can only be bought for cash. The owner is flexible on the price, provided he receives all cash. After checking the growth potential of the local market you determine that the lot will probably sell in three years for $175,000 net to you. What should you pay for the property today to ensure that your minimum rate of return is 25 percent after holding costs and sales expenses?

In other words, what amount invested today will compound annually to generate $175,000 pretax at the end of three years? This question can be answered by multiplying the estimated sales price by the three-year 25 percent discount factor.

Present Value of Estimated Sales Price

Future value	$175,000
PV factor	× 0.511999
Present value	$ 89,600

The purchasing power gained by this investment will be reduced by capital gains tax. Since there is no way of telling what the current tax rate is until Congress adjourns for the year in question, let's just pick a 33 percent rate for purposes of illustration. But the first step in calculating the tax consequences is to determine the realized gain. This is the profit on the transaction and is calculated by subtracting the adjusted basis or cost of the property from the sales price.

Calculating Realized Gain

Sale price	$175,000
Less basis	(89,600)
Gain	$ 85,400

Tax liability is then calculated by multiplying the gain by the estimated tax rate. For this example we can calculate the tax liability as follows.

Calculating Tax Liability

Gain	$85,400
Tax rate	× 0.33
Tax due	$28,182

Real purchasing power is the money that ends up in your pocket, not in the federal government's coffers. Consequently, all investments available in the marketplace are best compared on an after-tax basis when possible, to determine the true increase in real wealth under the tax circumstances of the owner.

Ignoring the tax cost is the same as ignoring operating expenses. Under certain conditions the tax savings from depreciation of improved real estate can result in a positive cash flow. But in this example the tax on the sale of the land reduces the cash flow.

Calculating After-Tax Cash Flow

Sale price	$175,000
Less tax paid	(28,182)
After-tax cash flow	$146,818

This after-tax cash flow should also be adjusted for inflation, say three years at 5 percent each to get a real inflation adjusted amount.

Calculating Real After-Tax Cash Flow

After-tax cash flow	$146,818
Present value factor	× 0.863838
Real after-tax cash flow	$126,827

The amount of $126,827 is the benefit of sales proceeds reduced to actual purchasing power. It is the after-tax present value adjusted for inflation. Notice that the inflation adjusted amount after three years at 5 percent is roughly 85 percent of the original amount as approximately reflected by the 0.863838 present value factor.

Using a standard business calculator you can see that $89,600 invested for three years that returns $126,827 after inflation and taxes represents an annual compounded rate of 12.28 percent—about half of the nominal 25 percent rate.

The purpose of investing is to transfer purchasing power through time and thus increase real wealth. Time value analysis, encompassing the relationship between compounding and discounting and present and future value, is the only way to measure the success of the effort.

Using the Internal Rate of Return

Although the internal rate of return is flawed under certain cash flow configurations, it is nevertheless popularly used as the percentage figure for discounted cash flow decisions. The internal rate of return is the compounded rate of return earned by an investment. In other words, it is the percentage rate at which funds grow while invested in a real estate project, just as they would in a savings account. The difference is that with the IRR we don't start with the rate. We know, or estimate, the cash flows and the time periods in which they occur, then we solve for the interest rate—the IRR. The fact that we must solve for the rate does not change the fact that the rate is a compound interest rate. Nor should the various names used to describe this interest rate—i.e., the internal rate of return—be allowed to imply that it is anything other than an interest rate.

In fact, the unique jargon used to describe the discounting or compounding processes in different financial fields often obscures the similarity between all financial analyses. For example, interest rate, yield, yield rate, yield to maturity, discounted rate of return, equity yield, discount rate, and internal rate of return all refer to the same percentage rate at which an investment compounds. The fact that this interest rate is solved for by discounting future cash flows does not change the concept or make this simple basic interest rate something new and complicated.

Solving for an internal rate of return requires specifying cash flows and the dates they occur. Then the formula for IRR determines the discount rate at which the cash inflows equal the outflows; that is, the rate that discounts the present value of the money received to an amount that exactly equals the present value of the money invested. This discount rate is the IRR.

One use of IRR is when the cash flows are known; for example, when an offer to purchase is under consideration or an owner is analyzing property based on past cash flow. In this set of circumstances the IRR is used to determine whether the offer to purchase represents an acceptable compounded growth rate of the invested funds. This application of IRR is preferred by some in the real estate industry because it analyzes historical cash flows and thus eliminates the forecasting error likely in projections of future cash flows.

For example, 18 years ago a farmer purchased a 40-acre parcel on the outskirts of what today is a major metropolitan area. He bought the land for $14,000 cash and grew various crops, making money some years, losing money other years, but about breaking even for the time he owned the property.

He is now considering an offer to purchase presented to him by a major subdivision developer that would net $500,000 cash after-tax and cost of sales. He wants one million dollars after-tax and has been unreasonable when confronted with the fact that his price is too high for the current market. Can this offer be put in better perspective with an understanding of the internal rate of return it represents?

Property	40 acres of farm land
Holding period	18 years
Acquisition price	$ 14,000
Purchase offer	$500,000 (net after tax)

Market conditions: Active, but slowing with indications of topping. Regional economy in expansion for over four years. Interest rates in an upward trend. Real estate development is active, rapidly filling demand for commercial space. Job opportunities have expanded steadily, the population has increased accordingly, and home construction is booming. Several new office buildings have recently been completed and are in the rent up phase.

Negotiation considerations: High interest rates are increasing development costs. The potential purchaser has the reputation of basing land acquisitions on the maximum purchase amount that he can afford and still make the project succeed financially. An after-tax net to the seller of one million dollars is above market and would make the development unfeasible. The offer that has been made is comparable to the prices of land in the area.

Question: What is the rate of return represented by this offer and how does it compare with returns from other investments?

Answer: This sale would represent an after-tax internal rate of return of 21.97%.

A counteroffer at the price wanted by the farmer of one million dollars net after tax would not be accepted, and the developer would probably not pursue the property.

The question facing this owner is whether a 21.97 percent return in hand is better than the possibility of no sale at all. Considering the rarity of a 21.97 percent after-tax rate of return and assuming that the offer to purchase is within market value parameters, there would seem to be little debate possible.

But the financial reality of the real estate market is that buyers will sometimes pay too much, and sellers will sometimes not accept a very good offer. In fact, it is common for an owner to price property just slightly higher than the market value until the market cycle ends and no sale at all is possible until the next cycle starts.

Financial analysis can help put a market decision in perspective. Considerations of personal objectives, liquidity, and alternative uses of the capital may play a role in the decision of the farmer to take the offer. But when the financial benefits are clearly superior to other returns during the holding period and the offer is within market bounds, IRR can provide a solid analytical structure for a financially based decision.

It is this added perspective that the IRR can provide. To some extent the familiarity of a percentage rate of return is the reason IRR can be helpful. Actually, if you think about it the farmer would be at a disadvantage not knowing the financial return realized by the sale. If personal objectives and market considerations are relatively neutral, knowing that the after-tax rate of return exceeds any investment available during the holding period provides crucial financial information for decision purposes.

The internal rate of return provides financial perspective by comparing alternative investment opportunities on a common percentage basis. Although IRR is often used as a sole decision criterion, its main advantage is more likely the comparison possible of real estate rates of return with other returns in the marketplace.

The internal rate of return provides a market perspective of financial performance on the equal basis of after-tax cash flows without prejudice toward the type of investment or the source of cash flows. It allows a rate of return comparison of real estate with stocks, bonds, savings instruments, business ventures, and any other cash flow-generating project.

Since we tend to think in terms of an annual percentage return on investment, the internal rate of return is a natural transition step to the analysis of property based on discounted cash flow analysis. IRR is the compounded interest rate, which is solved for when only the cash flows and the time they occur are known. It is the interest rate at which the present value of the negative cash flows equal the positive cash flows.

Using the Internal Rate of Return to Analyze a Purchase

Thinking in terms of a percentage return on investment has a natural effect on investment decisions. Buying a stock might automatically bring to mind whether the dividend history is sufficient. Investing in a bank certificate of deposit always requires a percentage rate of return comparison with money market rates and other savings instruments. Consequently, it is natural to look to the compounded rate of return of a real estate venture for at least part of the decision criteria.

For example, suppose you are considering the purchase of a 20-unit apartment complex. Market analysis indicates low vacancy and increasing expectations of profit from apartment ownership. Financial analysis based on historical performance of the property indicates that the following cash flows will be likely over the next four years. The question is, what is the rate of return represented by these cash flows? And is that rate of return acceptable for the risks and management requirements that will accompany ownership?

Annual After-Tax Cash Flows

	Year 1	Year 2	Year 3	Year 4
Down payment	($60,000)			
Net rent	$ 3,000	$3,500	$4,000	$ 4,500
Tax savings	$ 1,000	$1,000	$1,000	$ 1,000
Sales proceeds				$88,000
Total cash flows	$ 4,000	$4,500	$5,000	$93,500
Internal rate of return				16.85%

In this example the internal rate of return is calculated for the anticipated holding period of the property. The investment project is a measurable unit consisting of cash flows and time. This contained approach (cash flows bound by time) to financial performance measurement and investment decision making does not mean that a project should not be reevaluated in light of actual performance during ownership. On the contrary, it is continuing monitoring of financial performance that serves as a guide as to whether to hold or dispose of property.

For example, as market conditions change you might find that the potential sales price has increased beyond your projections. Recognizing the cyclical nature of real estate you may decide to sell or exchange while the windfall is still available. Or, a change in the tax laws may reduce your total cash flows to an unacceptable level relative to the management headaches associated with the property and provide a reason to sell.

Knowing the rate of return represented by the cash flows of your property makes good financial sense when you buy, while you own, and when you sell.

Three Applications of IRR to Real Estate

There is a tendency to attribute greater significance to the internal rate of return than the compounded interest rate that it is. This has occasionally resulted in confusion and a misunderstanding of the useful simplicity of the concept. It seemed to some people that IRR was a new way of measuring value that went beyond the compounding of money at an annual percentage rate that we are used to, but it's not.

Technically, the IRR is the interest rate that discounts cash flows received to an amount that equals the cash flows invested. Another way of viewing IRR is to say that the cash flows invested produce the cash flows received because they are growing at the compound interest rate. But in this case we must solve for the rate with knowledge of only the time periods and the cash flows.

Three situations illustrate how the internal rate return works in practice.

1. An initial investment followed by a one-time cash flow in the future; for example, the cash purchase of a mountain lot

which carries insignificant property taxes and is sold for cash after some years of ownership, or a rental house that breaks even and is eventually sold for cash.

2. An initial investment followed by a series of equal periodic cash flows; for example, purchase of a long-term lease underlying a medical office condominium office complex, or a note and mortgage with equal periodic payments.

3. An initial investment followed by a series of cash flows which vary in amount; for example, acquisition of an office building with leases expiring and renewing at varying market rates and at different times in the future, or rental property with fluctuating occupancy.

In each of these cases the IRR calculation solves for the discount rate at which the present value of the projected cash flows equals the present value of the cash flows invested. In simple cash flow structures this involves an initial investment followed by positive cash flows, which is the structure that works best given the limits of the IRR formula. All of the calculations that follow can be made on a common business calculator.

For example:

1. An individual purchased a mountain lot 10 years ago for $5,000. He currently has an offer to sell for a price that will net $35,000 after tax. This appears to be a high offer in view of the market for mountain lots today. But how does the offer appear financially? What is the internal rate of return represented by the lot investment and purchase offer 10 years later? What is the interest rate at which the $5,000 investment grew over the 10-year period?

Property	Mountain lot
Initial investment	$ 5,000
Holding period	10 years
Purchase offer	$35,000
Internal rate of return	21.48%

The $5,000 invested at 21.48 percent grew to $35,000 in 10 years. There are four variables in the calculation: (1) the initial investment; (2) the time it remains invested; (3) the amount of cash flow received when the investment is sold; and (4) the unknown variable, the interest rate at which the investment grows—the internal rate of return.

Since the cash flow generated by the initial investment is given, it can be discounted to an amount that equals the initial investment and thus solved for the internal rate of return.

2. You are offered a note secured by a second mortgage on a house just down the street that your neighbor recently sold. Apparently, your neighbor wants to cash out his equity and take a trip around the world. Consequently, he is willing to sell the note and mortgage at a 30 percent discount off the current balance of $30,000. Ten years remain on the note with annual payments of $4,882 including 10 percent interest. What is the pretax internal rate of return represented by this investment opportunity?

Property	Second note and mortgage
Balance	$30,000
Offered price	$21,000 (30% off balance)
Cash flows	10 payments of $4,882
Internal rate of return	19.25%

The face amount of the interest on the second note is immaterial to the calculation of the rate of return at the new discounted price. All that is needed to perform the calculation is the amount invested, the cash flows, and the frequency of their occurrence. In this case there are 10 cash flows of $4,882 each for 10 years.

3. The most common application of the IRR to real estate involves determining the rate of return offered by income property with cash flows of varying amounts. Generally, this involves cash flows from the benefits of ownership. For example, appreciation and loan reduction are realized as cash flow when the property is refinanced or sold; rental income is realized each month during ownership while tax savings are realized annually.

For decision purposes cash flows must be factored in with the objectives of the owner, the risk of loss inherent in real estate, and the direction of the market cycles interacting on real estate. Given circumstances in which such nonquantifiable factors are roughly equal, the IRR calculation is applied to see if the property meets the minimum return requirements for investment; or, which alternative investment provides the highest internal rate of return.

For example, after searching for investment opportunities you have located an office building with positive cash flow, which also shows some promise of holding value and possibly appreciating over the next five years. A conservative projection indicates that the following cash flows are reasonable estimates of the potential.

Property	Office building
Down payment	$120,000
Cash flows	Projected over five years with sale at the end of the fifth year.
Year 1	$ 8,000
Year 2	$ 8,000
Year 3	$ 8,500
Year 4	$ 9,000
Year 5	$200,000
Internal rate of return:	15.67%

The internal rate of return is used as a decision tool to determine whether a proposed acquisition is likely to meet minimum rate of return criteria. For example, a conservative projection of cash flows is used to determine if a minimum rate of return is possible based on the projected cash flows. Based on the IRR, the property must indicate a likely possibility of generating a minimum return that falls within the range of rates of return available from alternative investments.

Problems with the Internal Rate of Return

There are a few problems with the mathematics of using the internal rate of return formula in complex cash flow situations. For example, IRR should not be used when doing probability distributions because the nature of the calculation can produce incorrect results. Only NPV should be used because it is a linear formula which simply increases or decreases with the addition of another cash flow. IRR is nonlinear, and one change in cash flow changes the computation of the equation [11].

Under certain cash flow conditions, sometimes involving negative cash flows, it is possible to get more than one internal rate of return or not find an IRR at all [14, p.425]. These limitations of IRR eliminate the usefulness of calculation as a decision criterion for choosing between alternative investments.

There are other problems with the misuse of IRR, which relate to the danger of applying a percentage to support investment decisions under conditions of extreme uncertainty. Here, the tendency to accept a computer printout without examination of the assumptions on which it is based creates a danger of using IRR as substitute for critical thought.

The problems with the internal rate of return can be avoided with the use of net present value as a single decision criterion. Furthermore, NPV is more meaningful from an investment analysis viewpoint. It measures the accumulation of actual wealth in dollar terms as well as actual losses. And if a percentage figure is essential, the discount rate used to arrive at NPV can be applied with careful examination of the relation to NPV. The internal rate of return can provide useful ancillary information, but it has questionable value as a sole investment criterion.

Developing a Perspective for Real Estate Projections

Cash flow projections are estimates of financial performance based on future market events that can never be known with certainty. This fact of real estate investment is often cited as one of the drawbacks of discounted cash flow analysis in general and IRR in particular. Actually, this is just a condition of investment life. Taking risk is what investment profit is all about, regardless of the financial method used to evaluate it.

Any method used to project financial performance beyond known market conditions involves subjective judgment and a willingness to bear the responsibilities of evaluating investment risk. Discounted cash flow analysis is simply one element of that process. When properly viewed as one component of the judgment process, discounted cash flow analysis can be a useful tool.

However, the farther financial projections reach into the future, the greater the likelihood of error. Forecasting error is a potential of any investment analysis process. But it can be lessened by recognizing that real estate markets move in cycles and by including a sensitivity to these fluctuations in financial projections.

The reliability of real estate cash flows in part depends on the ability of the property to adapt to changing market conditions. This adaptation in turn depends on the management decisions of the owners and the flexibility with which new market conditions are met by appropriate action.

Effective real estate investment depends on the completeness of the context in which it takes place, including the financial resources, experience, and judgment of the investor; the understanding of the owner of market price trends, cycles, and potential changes in national and regional economic conditions; as well as the physical condition, location, and financing of the property.

The internal rate of return and net present value are methods of focusing judgment on the financial outcome of these and other market factors. The practical benefits of IRR and NPV stem from the comparison and decision planning they facilitate by directing attention to cash flow. But no number can replace analytical judgment.

Financial forecasts based on estimates of changes in market conditions or the physical characteristics of property translate directly to cash flows which can be measured by IRR or NPV. They are both financial measures of how well a property is transferring the purchasing power of the invested funds through time and meeting the ultimate goal of increasing real wealth.

6

Building a Model for Real Estate Financial Analysis

The worth of a real estate investment is the present value of its cash flows. Rental income, sales and refinance proceeds, and tax savings may contribute to cash flows. In sum, they provide the raw material of financial performance.

As with many business projects, there is uncertainty that the anticipated cash flows will actually be realized. This is the risk normal to any investment activity. It is simply the environment in which we must invest and is no reason to avoid making financial projections.

Risk of forecasting error will always exist and must be dealt with just as all the other investment risks. Anyone who invests accepts risk and develops an expectation of the outcome, whether formalized in a financial forecast or ignored with vague references to our inability to predict future uncertainties. By recognizing, defining, and measuring the natural risks of real estate investment, we can take a step toward adapting to and profiting from the continuing fluctuations of the market.

But it is the nature of financial analysis to do more than determine the risks and estimate the return at the time the investment is made. Investing in real estate is a commitment to the future, the success of which depends on the potential of the property, the market, and the management effort necessary to realize that potential.

Consequently, financial analysis can be used for much more than making a decision to invest or as a method of choosing among investments. An analysis of market conditions and the competitive characteristics of a property, as reflected in cash

129

flows, can also be used to make the decision to sell property, to change management, to remodel, to refinance, or to implement any number of rental and marketing strategies. Real estate financial analysis is to a large extent a process of gathering information, projecting future events, and measuring the financial outcome. Its use goes far beyond the initial acquisition decision.

The Function of a Financial Model

A financial model is a structure for organizing known information and testing assumptions about the future in order to measure how likely an investment is to transfer purchasing power through time while building wealth. A model facilitates analysis by organizing and speeding consideration of possible financial outcomes. It provides a form that increases the understanding of the substance of real estate investment, and in the process it provides new information and reveals opportunities, risks, and choices.

For example, viewing waves of real estate investment in the context of the 18-year cycle and the rise of interest rates is a time-based inflation model for price speculation and an early warning of oversupply. It structures price movement within time and thus provides a framework for investment decisions that goes beyond current conditions. In doing so it replaces confusion with perspective, and concern about the future with historical experience. Consequently, what we refer to as *current market conditions* becomes connected to the future by awareness of the cyclical history of real estate activity. This broad perspective is one of the useful outcomes of viewing real estate investment within models that acknowledge the important influence of time on market activity.

The model for real estate analysis that we are using here has three components. Together they form the basic conceptual model for real estate analysis used in this book.

The Basic Real Estate Analysis Model

Existing	Market conditions
Plus	Property characteristics
Equals	Financial performance

Each component of this model can be organized and analyzed in extensive detail. Earlier chapters have placed emphasis on the cycle component of real estate market conditions and discounting measures of financial performance. The physical nature of individual property characteristics has been given less emphasis here because the existing literature, especially in the area of development and management, leaves little new to be said.

We have also discussed the financial performance measures used in real estate analysis with emphasis on the importance of specifying cash flows, regardless of the source. Anyone who has owned and managed real estate through a complete cycle knows well that cash flows through time are the measure of financial performance. Furthermore, the emphasis in this analysis model that has been placed on the time value of money is a necessary consequence of recognizing the purpose of investment as the transfer of purchasing power through time while building real wealth. Recognizing the cyclical fluctuation of market activity simply adds new perspective to this fundamental financial measurement method. The time value of money and the timing of cycles are an appropriate combination for real estate financial analysis. It is a fact of market activity that people discount future values at different rates based on their expectations of price change in the future. Cycles reflect price change.

The emphasis on cycles and cash flows does not imply that the physical characteristics of real estate are less important to financial performance. It provides a model for making sense out of the role of real estate in our economy and the effects of cycles on cash flows while acknowledging the important role of property characteristics. Living with real estate from day to day and making the management decisions necessary to compete in the market provides perspective on the importance of property characteristics far better than can be done here.

Property characteristics are the concrete elements of real estate that we can touch and walk on. Market conditions and financial performance are more abstract and fluid and difficult to pin down, but it can be done. That is why cash flow and cycles are important to our model. They are measurable.

Cycles are models for timing market conditions in terms of low and high activity, which provides an advance indication of risk and opportunity. High and low market activity have an effect on prices and rents and, therefore, on financial performance. This cyclical fluctuation is largely determined by fundamental factors such as capital availability, supply and demand, and investor expectations. It is also determined by governmental factors such as tax law changes, changes in banking and other regulations, and changes in monetary policy.

Specifying cash flows provides a model for organizing and measuring financial performance. We acknowledged that cash flows can come from rental income, tax savings, refinance proceeds, and sales proceeds. Each of these cash flows can be measured in amount and in time.

Building an Expanded Financial Model

The basic model can be expanded without becoming unmanageable to include the factors that are important to real estate performance. The model can then be used to establish assumptions concerning fluctuations in cash flows as the cycle progresses.

The Expanded Real Estate Analysis Model

Market Conditions: The expansion and contraction of market activity over time in response to changes in:

Fundamental factors:
1. Capital availability (debt and equity)
2. Supply-demand (absorption/employment-income)
3. Expectations (optimistic and pessimistic)

Governmental factors:
1. Changes in tax laws (incentive-disincentive)
2. Changes in regulations
3. Changes in monetary policy (inflation)

Combine with . . .

Property characteristics: Including but not limited to
1. Physical condition (age, deferred maintenance)
2. Location (stable, growing, declining)
3. Site characteristics (access, parking, security)
4. Management (professional)
5. Competitive posture (design, tenant appeal)

To produce . . .

Financial performance: In the form of cash flow from
1. Rental income
2. Tax savings
3. Refinance proceeds
4. Sales proceeds

Which is measured using . . .
Discounted cash flow analysis (IRR and NPV)

Time value measurement completes the real estate financial analysis model. This final component reduces cash flows, both negative and positive, to a net present value. With this addition we can measure the degree to which an investment accomplishes its purpose of transferring purchasing power through time and building real wealth. But the applications go beyond that objective. The basic cash flow model can be used for any set of financial circumstances that involves cash flows received over time.

The model can also be structured in several formats. In the following format the model presents a summary of money paid into the property and money received from the property. The purpose is to net cash flows paid against cash flows received.

	Year 0	Year 1	Year 2	Year 3	Year 4
Equity investment	(15)		(3)		
Rental income		1	2	2	2
Tax savings		1	2	1	1
Refinance proceeds				3	
Sales proceeds					15
NET	(15)	2	1	6	18

NPV at 8% 5.7
IRR 18.82%

This example can be expressed more simply:

	Year 0	Year 1	Year 2	Year 3	Year 4
Cash invested	(15)		(3)		
Cash received		2	4	6	18
Net	(15)	2	1	6	18

NPV at 8% 5.7
IRR 18.82%

Or, even more simply:

	Cash flows
Year 0	(15)
Year 1	2
Year 2	1
Year 3	6
Year 4	18

NPV (8%) 5.7
IRR 18.82%

Expanded financial analysis models that encompass a complete statement of operating income and expenses are often necessary. For example, expanded versions are more useful when exploring the effect of raising rents, reducing expenses, remodeling, and other management decisions. The key financial factor in all cases is the change in net present value. Net present value is the measure of financial performance. Changes in market conditions and property characteristics are important only to the extent that they change the net present value of the investment. This model is a structure for analyzing the combined financial effect of market conditions and property characteristics. For example, an economic contraction with poor market conditions can result in vacancies that require cash investment to meet operating expenses. This can turn a positive net present value negative and place increased burden on the other sources of cash flow.

During the early 1980s as rents and prices began topping out, the offset to negative operational cash flow was tax savings. Prices and debt loads had increased to the point that rental property could not provide a satisfactory return on fundamental factors alone. The extremely favorable tax treatment of the 1981 Tax Reform Act increased the demand for tax-based cash flow, drawing the general public into limited partnerships and rental property. When this governmental contribution to market conditions was taken away with the Tax Reform Act of 1986, expectations for real estate began the transition from optimistic to pessimistic as rents and prices fell to attract tenants to the oversupply. Again the cyclical wave from expansion to contraction was complete, with a push to the extremes by the political manipulation of income tax laws. It is rare that a cycle top can be so clearly framed by government action. The period between 1981 and 1986 deserves a special place in real estate history.

Acknowledging the cyclical nature of real estate can help reduce the timing risks inherent in the investment process, whether acquisition, ownership, or disposition. Not selling when the moment is at hand is as risk-filled as buying at the top of the cycle. There is always a chance to buy at a price, but there is not always a chance to sell.

Modeling expected financial performance serves as a discipline to measure the market consequences of the ever present risks and opportunities of our dynamic economy. Each risk is a risk only to the extent that it interrupts cash flow. Negative changes in the expected cash flow from real estate should be considered with equal weight as positive changes. Both are sources of opportunity. The cyclic nature of our economy with positive and negative phases creates that opportunity. A financial model facilitates analytical thinking about potential change and then measures the potential financial outcome.

This financial model is intended to be customized for individual requirements. The components of a financial model should flow naturally from the decision criteria and level of detail that you determine to be meaningful and useful for your needs. Ideally, a financial model should be flexible in order to expand or shrink in size with the amount of cash flow detail necessary to meet your decision criteria.

Analytical Guidelines for the Financial Model

Although the level of complexity dictated by specific analysis requirements may vary, there are certain basic procedures that form the structure of the analysis process. There is a structure that deals with the analysis process itself and the uncertainty reflected in the risk that possibly the future will not turn out the way you expect.

Personal computers and the widespread availability of spreadsheet software have made the financial analysis of real estate cash flows available with ease to any who understand the concepts. A financial model provides the structure for analysis of real estate investments. Computers facilitate the analysis process.

Analysis is a process of asking three questions. But there is no end to the number of possible answers.

1. What is?

2. What if?

3. What effect?

Real estate analysis by question applies to market conditions, individual property characteristics, and financial performance. It can also be applied to any other aspect of real estate you decide is appropriate for your application. The questioning process is actually the procedure we go through when analyzing anything.

First, we gather the data. Second, we modify the variables.

Third, we measure the results. Before the availability of personal computers, the modeling of financial outcomes was a laborious paper and pencil task. The alternative required computer time-sharing for those who did not have mainframe access. Now financial modeling is easily accomplished with financial functions contained in spreadsheet software. The challenge is understanding enough about the changing market to ask the right questions.

What is?

Answering this question requires gathering the facts about market conditions and the characteristics of the property, both financial and physical. What are the rents and expenses and net rental cash flow in relation to competing properties? How does the location and physical condition affect the cash flow and the potential for additional income? What are current market conditions? What is the trend of the cycle? What politically dependent factors are there currently influencing market activity?

What if?

Answering this question requires exploring alternatives and considering new possibilities and recognizing the consequences that are most likely in the future. For example, what cyclical changes are in store for the rate of inflation and the trend of real interest rates, capital availability, the supply-demand dynamics, and investor expectations? Is the market likely to permit an increase in rent in one or two years, or, is a decrease in rent called for? For how much and when is a sale likely? Are real estate values declining or increasing? What are the political winds likely to blow in this year in the way of tax, regulatory, and monetary policy changes? Will political change trigger a favorable turn in the cycle?

What effect?

Answering this question involves measuring the effect of change on financial performance. For example, what is the effect of a rent increase on the present value of the projected cash flows every year for the next five years? What is the effect of a reduction in rents? What is the effect of a sale at the end of three years or five years? What effect will an increase or decrease in rent have on the potential sale price? Will remodeling costs be offset by the possible rent increase? Will this year's tax law change increase or decrease cash flow? How will other political changes affect the economy and real estate prices?

Asking the right question is the challenge of real estate analysis. For example, during the boom years of the early 1980s when the real estate market was topping there were no questions, just answers. Every rock had a real estate guru under it with a get-rich-quick formula and the answer to financial security. Every stock brokerage company seemed to have a real estate limited partnership that was the answer to public participation in the real estate boom. Insurance companies and pension funds discovered real estate portfolio management. Deregulation of banking opened the lending flood gates. More hotels, more office buildings, and more of everything real estate was introduced to the financial markets. There was no consideration of the cyclical history of real estate; only unquestioned assumptions that the expansion would continue in the long term as it had in the short term. People weren't asking the right questions.

Questioning current market conditions is the logical outcome of recognizing the cyclical nature of real estate market activity. Asking what is?, what if?, and what effect? is facilitated by financial modeling. Each question can be factored into the financial model as a cash flow and measured by discounting.

Traditional techniques for analyzing real estate are models with limited applications. For example, the old forms that combined the core of the appraisal methods used at the time with the annual percentage return criterion in a one-page format constituted a model of sorts that covered the present. At the time it did produce a bit of order and provided a common language for property analysis and negotiation purposes, but it was useful primarily because it fit the way the world was viewed then.

Our understanding of markets and money has grown since those early days, and now we view real estate in a more complex and complete framework. Earlier analysis techniques and decision criteria such as the current rate of return were limited to answering the first question—what is? And the answer was usually limited to the property itself with little attention to the larger question of market cycles or present value calculation. Questioning was left to intuition. Little math was applied with the possible exception of the occasional investor with a computer background and time-share access.

But now with built-in financial functions such as NPV and the ease of use of software, computer application of financial analysis is routine. This frees us to further our understanding of the market and what we have done to it, how it works, how it can benefit us, and how we can avoid errors through our increased understanding.

Moving from Questions to Cash Flows

Cash flow has only two characteristics:

1. The dollar amount
2. The time it occurs

Financial value can only be measured in terms of dollars and time because money has no use unless it exists in measurable amounts and at specific times. This financial fact illustrates why markets are vulnerable to sudden change when unrealistic expectations carry market activity and prices to extremes based on abstractions such as appreciation and inflation.

Eventually, cash flow in one form or other determines the fate of a real estate investment, whether a debt payment unmet, a lost sale, or a successfully completed transaction. Real estate analysis that is grounded in reality and the decisions that follow must consider cash flows in the context of time. This requires attention to both sides of the cycle, not just the one making news today.

As with all investments that depend on future performance, there is always the question of uncertainty—will the flow of market change produce the result you anticipate? This element of uncertainty is inherent in all cash flow projections. It is a question of probability and can only be addressed within the context of degrees of likelihood.

Moving from questions to cash flows introduces another set of questions. But in this step we move from consideration of market and property scenarios to dollar amounts. This step is the content of the financial model. It involves answering three questions:

1. How much?
2. When?
3. How likely?

In other words, what is the probable amount of the cash flow and when is it likely to be received or paid? Cut through the issues that contribute to, or detract from, cash flow but tend to be given exaggerated meaning.

For example, avoid popular assumptions and generalizations that translate into equal percentage increases in cash flows or expenses. This easy way out of making financial projections typically focuses on uninterrupted inflation, as measured by the consumer price index and erroneously attaches it to real estate rents and prices, implying a causal relationship where there is none.

Look instead to the specifics of your market area. Plan for error. Capitalize for the known difficulties and build in sources of reserve for the unforeseeable. Real estate thrives or dies on the specifics of regional market dynamics, most important of which is the level of income and employment growth.

By asking How much?, When?, and How likely? you constantly challenge unexamined expectations and confront the reality of change in the real estate market, which is reflected in the cash flows of a specific property. As a result, you reduce the risk of making investment decisions based on the tendency to confuse actual cash flow with the benefits of ownership such as appreciation and tax shelter, which at best only describe the sources of potential cash flow.

For example, appreciation is not cash flow. The asking price for a property is not cash flow. The advertised rental rate of an office building is not cash flow. In fact, all may be somewhat off the mark, vague impressions of a desperate owner or an insulated corporate structure out of town and out of touch with local market reality. Cash flow is reality. Anticipated appreciation and asking prices are steps toward cash flow and should not be looked to for a sense of financial security. Change is the only sure thing about the future. How likely are your expectations of cash flow to be realized?

Recognizing market risk emphasizes the very important need to continually focus on actual cash flow and keep it separate from the irrelevant investment noise coming from the market forces that influence, but are not actual cash flow.

There is always risk that an expected benefit will not make the transition to cash flow, and consequently will fail to make an actual contribution to the transfer of purchasing power through time.

By questioning the likelihood of projected cash flows through financial modeling we address the element of risk inherent in real estate ownership. When we ask how likely a cash flow is to be realized we face the cyclical nature of the real estate market and challenge the comfort level typical at market tops and the level of fear typical at market bottoms. Introducing probability into the analysis process emphasizes that no assumption should remain unquestioned.

What we expect to happen to our investments determines the level of risk we perceive at the time we enter an investment. Consequently, sudden changes in public expectations for the future value of real estate can turn the direction of market prices practically overnight even without change in the supply or availability of capital.

Speculative markets are especially subject to such sudden changes in demand. Buyers are fully capable of walking away from a market on a moment's notice, thus reducing the probability of receiving an expected cash flow. For example, the residential market in New York City has a history of vicious buyer withdrawal. Buyers in Manhattan are astute and market sensitive, withdrawing when the least indication of falling prices is sensed, waiting and hammering on owners for a lower price.

The probability of receiving an expected rental rate or sales price and the manner in which the expected cash flow is accounted for in pro formas is central to real estate analysis. During favorable market trends we are conditioned to expect continued increases in rents and prices, which reduces our perception of risk. This is one reason cycles are helpful in keeping investment analysis grounded in the real world of market fluctuations and the risks that are always present. Awareness of cycles forces us to question our perception of risk.

The financial analysis of real estate investments is a process of asking questions and determining likely answers. A financial model simply facilitates the process by providing a framework for modeling cash flows within a range of likelihood. Thus far in our model we have introduced two sets of questions:

What is?   (Gather the data—market, property, financial.)

What if?   (Question the potential for change.)

What effect?   (Model the cash flows and measure NPV.)
  1. How Much?   (Cash flow amount)
  2. When?   (Timing of the cash flow)
  3. How Likely?   (Degree of likelihood)

The first set of questions addresses the analysis process itself. The second set of questions facilitates the answering of the last question in the first set—What effect?—by providing a structure for the modeling of cash flows and their financial measurement by discounting.

A Simple Method for Building Probability into Projections

Real estate financial performance flows from market conditions and property characteristics and is expressed in the timing and the amount of the cash flows both positive and negative. Consequently, a financial model specifies and measures the present value of cash flows under varying market conditions.

For example, a financial model can be applied to known cash flows, such as past property performance, to determine a sale price today. It can be used to project future performance in order to determine a purchase price today. It can also be applied to the known cash flows of a lease or debt instrument to structure a financially profitable transaction. A financial model can also be designed to deal with uncertainty by generating a range of possible financial outcomes.

The risk that the future will not produce the results you anticipate can be built into a financial model. There is no need to avoid uncertainty. It is just as much an opportunity as a potential loss. Asking How likely? is the first step in dealing with a range of probabilities.

A model simulates possible financial outcomes in order to make investment choices that will most likely meet specific financial objectives. Its guiding purpose is to provide consistent decision criterion under different market conditions as expressed in cash flows.

Net present value can be modeled under varying market conditions by translating those conditions to cash flows. In some cases, such as an office space lease, all of the cash flows are known. For example, the tenant improvement costs, the rental rate, the expense stop, and the ceiling on the rent increases can all be fixed and calculated for the tenant and the landlord. Since the cash flows are known by the fixed terms of the lease, the financial effect of various concessions and rent structures can be easily projected. Lease terms are a matter of negotiation, and the best financial structure can be readily determined by calculating the present value of the cash flows involved.

But without the fixed terms of a lease, the initial emphasis of the financial model becomes an attempt to determine the most likely range of possible financial outcomes under conditions of uncertainty. There are three classifications of likelihood that can help keep financial projections in perspective while acknowledging the uncertainty of the market. Scenarios that acknowledge uncertainty within degrees of likelihood help keep assumptions in perspective. And certainly no projection is worth any more than the likelihood of the assumptions on which it is based. That is why so much emphasis has been placed on the analysis of market cycles and the effect on cash flows.

The question is: How likely is a given financial projection to occur? There are various ways to answer the question. If you have access to software with Monte Carlo simulation or other random distribution capabilities you can generate a quantified statement of probability for any series of numbers you want. In the alternative and for our purposes, simply framing projections within reasoned analysis of the market trends can accomplish the goal of questioning assumptions and accounting for uncertainty within the context of cyclical change.

There is a method of establishing a range of possible outcomes that uses judgment but can still be used with statistical analysis if you wish. Consequently, it serves the need to acknowledge risk and the uncertainties of real estate investment activity.

This approach divides cash flow assumptions into three analytical categories and consequently generates three cash flow scenarios based on the possible outcomes. This portion of the model deals with the unknown by ranking uncertainty in three categories designed to facilitate questioning of financial projections by answering the question:

How likely?
1. Optimistic
2. Pessimistic
3. Most likely

This portion of the model questions whether the assumptions underlying the cash flow projections are at the high, low, or midrange of likelihood? If nothing else, just going through the analytical exercise of thinking about the probability of more than one result will prevent an unexamined real estate venture with all the risk it implies.

Financial modeling permits you to generate cash flow projections that are defined in terms of amount and time, but appropriately qualified by recognition of the uncertainty involved in any forecast. The alternatives of ignoring uncertainty or refusing to forecast are not necessary or useful. You can acknowledge uncertainty by adjusting the cash flows in the model. Each adjustment reflects a different scenario and a different degree of probability. For example, the following sets of cash flows represent the bottom line of the many different influences on market conditions and property characteristics.

	Year 0	Year 1	Year 2	Year 3	Year 4
Optimistic					
Cash Flows	(25)	2	3	7	40
NPV (8%) 14.38					
IRR 22.78%					
Pessimistic					
Cash flows	(25)	0	0	1	10
NPV (8%) (16.86)					
IRR n/a					
Most likely					
Cash flows	(25)	2	3	4	35
NPV (8%) 8.33					
IRR 17.10%					

Certainly considerable detail work is involved in isolating the cash flows for each scenario. For example, the optimistic projection may assume an upswing in the real estate cycle for several years, allowing an increase in rents, refinancing, and ultimately a sale that reflects a high rate of price appreciation. In contrast, the pessimistic scenario may assume a slow market with breakeven performance or possibly a loss from rental operations and difficulty selling, if selling at all.

The most likely scenario falls between the two but is not necessarily positive under declining market conditions. During a prolonged contraction in the real estate cycle the most likely scenario may be one of negative cash flows, and the pessimistic alternative might involve foreclosure.

The objective is to reflect the possible course of events under each scenario in terms of the most likely effect on cash flow. There are guidelines to follow that can help construct different real estate scenarios. For example, of all the contributing elements, nothing is more helpful than an awareness of the specific employment and population characteristics of your investment region. If jobs are expanding, the probability is that real estate demand will be strong. Given that base, the question becomes one of the supply-demand relationship within the specific segment of real estate, which is reflected in the absorption rate.

The entire real estate model can be understood as an interrelated whole. It is a way of looking at daily investment activity in an orderly fashion.

The Real Estate Financial Analysis Model

Market conditions
Plus property characteristics
Equals financial performance

This interrelationship is analyzed by asking . . .

What is?
What if?
What effect?

During the scenario process cash flows are modeled by asking . . .

How much?
When?
How likely?

The end result is a series of possible outcomes classified as . . .

Optimistic
Pessimistic
Most likely

Guidelines for Real Estate Market Assumptions

When market conditions are unfavorable and activity is low, the characteristics of a property become an increasingly important contribution to financial performance. When activity is high during favorable market conditions, property with poor characteristics can generate cash flow based on speculative expectations. These speculative surges have limited lives, but they are opportunities to participate in a fast increase in values. Speculative surges constitute demand-driven markets which can end suddenly at any time the buyers' expectations for future price increases change.

Consequently, it is important to try to determine market conditions as accurately as possible within the context of the flow of the cycle. Doing so is nothing more than prudent risk evaluation. As discussed, the important elements of real estate cycles consist of fundamental and governmental factors.

Fundamental Factors

1. Capital availability (both debt and equity)
2. Supply-demand (absorption, employment-income)
3. Expectations (including optimism-pessimism)

Governmental Factors

1. Tax laws (incentives and disincentives)
2. Regulations (banking and other)
3. Monetary policy (inflation)

Assumption guidelines can be effectively applied by considering each factor and its effect on the real estate market; and in turn, how change in one factor might affect the cycle and the financial performance of a specific property.

Consider the cycle: Is the real estate market in the process of:

1. Expansion (demand-driven markets—high activity)
2. Contraction (supply-driven markets—low activity)

Consider the industry segment:

1. Single family
2. Apartments
3. Offices
4. Retail
5. Industrial
6. Farms and ranches

Fundamental Factors

1. *Capital availability.* Are loans available for new construction in the market segment under consideration? If so, new supply may be on the market eventually. Is credit tight? If so, shortages may become apparent in a few years.

Example: High interest rates at the 1980 and 1981 recessions reduced money available for real estate, followed by the S&L lending spree into 1986.

2. *Supply-demand.* Are vacancies being absorbed rapidly relative to the new supply coming on the market? What is the absorption rate for your market segment? Or, are tenants moving to newer more competitively attractive space? Are new jobs moving to the region that increase the income level of the people and reflect the emerging technology of the current long wave cycle? Or are higher paying jobs leaving the region and being replaced by lower paying service jobs that don't cover living expenses?

For example, employment and income levels dropped: (1) in the rust belt in the early 1980s after farm commodity prices peaked; (2) in the oil-producing regions in the mid-1980s after the drop in oil prices and demand; (3) in New England in the late 1980s after the financial and banking contraction began; and 4) in California in the early 1990s as the rolling real estate depression arrived. Employment in manufacturing continues to suffer during this long wave adjustment due to jobs leaving the United States in the attempt to keep products competitive in the global economy.

3. *Expectations.* Are market participants overly optimistic or pessimistic about future prospects for real estate? Are prices at an extreme because of unrealistic expectations or because of employment related factors? Are you in a speculative bubble driven by hope and fear rather than economic expansion or contraction?

For example, inflationary expectations accelerated after the mid 1970s recession and became so ingrained during the early 1980s that real estate became an evangelical cause of gurus feeding on the small investor. The foreclosure and bank failures of the late 1980s and early 1990s began the long process of replacing overly positive expectations with overly negative expectations.

Governmental Factors

1. *Tax laws.* Do tax laws provide an incentive for real estate investment? Or are they a cause of reduced market activity?

Example: In 1981 real estate was given favorable tax treatment and an incentive for creating new supply. In 1986 real estate was burdened with the most complex and restrictive tax laws in history. Both are unusual and extreme examples of the power of government to stimulate and then destroy markets.

2. *Regulations.* Are the zoning regulations supportive to real estate development? Is there a major change in the banking regulation that will open up the credit markets? Or, are the regulators closing the doors?

For example, deregulation of the S&Ls flooded the market with real estate projects in the early 1980s as insured funds went to new and questionable loans. In the fall of 1990, as the full extent of the national banking crisis sunk in, the regulators put tight loan guidelines on the solvent banks and tripped the country into the longest recession in post World War II history. Both were trigger events contributing to changes in the real estate market. Neither were sole causes.

3. *Monetary policy.* Is inflation on the increase? Is the government trying to spend the country out of recession? Is the government trying to prevent an inflationary boom by raising interest rates? Are real interest rates negative? Are they positive and on the increase?

For example, in the early 1970s there was an attempt to spend our way out of a recession, followed by a boom in commodity and oil prices, leading into the recession in the mid-1970s. Interest rates were less than the rate of inflation, indicating a negative real cost of capital. After the 1974–1975 recession, inflation accelerated into the beginning of the 1980s until the Federal Reserve raised interest rates to historic levels and turned the trend.

These fundamental and governmental factors combine, interact, influence each other, and ultimately have an effect on market activity and the financial performance of real estate. The key to using them in the analysis process is awareness of the trend in market activity as indicated by the change in the four cycles of importance to real estate. For example, where are we now in the long wave, business cycle, 18-year real estate cycle, and housing cycle? How do they overlap and influence each other? If activity is expanding, is it in a steady rise or topping? If activity is contracting, is it just starting to fall or is it basing? What new trigger events are on the horizon, and which way are they likely to turn market activity?

The purpose of viewing the real estate market in this structured manner is to evaluate the level of risk and the likelihood that a property will produce the anticipated cash flow during a given time—that is, to judge its likely financial performance.

Property Characteristics

Concurrently, the contribution of the individual property characteristics can be factored into this structured view. Property characteristics are also reflected in price.

How do the characteristics of the property fit in the market?

1. Rental rate (competitive, special incentives?)
2. Management (professional?)
3. Location (stable, growing, declining?)
4. Site characteristics (access, parking, security)
5. Physical condition (age, deferred maintenance)

Which of these characteristics (and others unique to the property) contribute to or detract from financial performance? Which will offset negative market conditions? Which are inhibiting maximum financial performance now?

Poorly built property can perform well financially in high growth markets. Competitive, attractive property can perform well during contracting markets. The objective is to recognize that both types of markets have occurred and will occur again. This recognition then requires an evaluation of the likely contribution of property characteristics to financial performance of the property during expanding as well as contracting markets.

The third basic element of the model involves evaluation of the financial performance of the property. In this step the structure of the model turns to cash flow. Here we look at the sources of cash flows (both positive and negative). The financial analysis process translates market conditions and property characteristics into cash flows. This is a process of reducing market elements and property characteristics to cash flows that can be measured in amount and time. For example:

1. Rental income (sustainable? can it be increased?)
2. Expenses (high?, low?, realistic?)

3. Capital improvements (what is needed?)
4. Debt structure (interest cost, amortization term)
5. Operating income (actual loss or tax loss)
6. Refinance potential
7. Resale potential (when? with what improvements?)
8. Tax incentive income (dependent on tax benefits?)

The purpose here is to specify the likely sources of cash flow in the context of cyclical market conditions and the characteristics of the specific property.

Each element of the model can be stated as a cash flow amount, received at a designated time. All that is needed is the necessary and sufficient information to determine the timing of the cash flows within a reasonable range of likelihood. Every cost and every benefit can be stated as a cash flow—negative or positive.

Therefore, in summary:

1. The purpose of investing is to transfer purchasing power through time while increasing real wealth.

2. Real estate is a cyclical industry and part of our cyclical economy.

3. Individual property characteristics can smooth out fluctuations in financial performance caused by cycles.

4. Long-term economic trends of inflation and deflation and technical innovation impact real estate values.

5. Financial analysis is a process of measuring the amount and time value of cash flows generated periodically during the life of the investment in the property.

Investment assumptions that do not recognize these basics miss the lessons of real estate history. Certainly, an investment program that ignores the time value of money misses the meaning of increasing wealth that is central to real estate investment. And given the fluctuation of the real estate market over the last 20 years is difficult to imagine that the role of cycles would not be part of a forecast.

Nevertheless, it is understandable why real estate cycles have been lost in much of the thinking concerning financial projections. For example, growth phases that last for several years tend to obscure memories of the difficulties that follow the eventual arrival of a contraction. Expectations of ever-increasing prices become the unspoken assumption with little objection from those with doubts. Naturally, we want to expect the best, and to a large extent the real estate industry thrives on positive thinking. But it need not do so to the detriment of reality and at the expense of investing with awareness of the inherent risks.

Using Real Interest Rates as a Real Estate Indicator

Each segment of the real estate market has its own unique risk characteristics. Fundamentally, real estate investment risks relate to the supply-demand characteristics of the segment, the availability of capital, and the expectations of the participants. Of these factors the supply demand relationship based on employment, income level, and population growth is the best indicator of a healthy real estate industry.

These factors translate into general price appreciation as the result of solid economic growth without the need for inflation to provide the illusion of gain. The expectation that inflation will automatically support real estate is based on the assumption that inflation will continue without government efforts to control it. This expectation is a risky assumption on which to base real estate investment. But there is a fundamental indicator that goes beyond expectations to track the trend of inflation in the market.

Real interest rates (adjusted for inflation) provide a market-based indication of changes in demand for inflation hedges such as real estate. Speculative waves causing extreme price increases in real estate can be tied directly to negative real interest rates. Conversely, a reduction in speculative activity tends to follow high positive interest rates. Real interest rates are an indicator of the trend of inflation and the impact it is likely to have on expectations for real estate values.

The fluctuation of interest rates in relation to inflation has proven reliable as an early warning indicator of a change in speculative real estate investment. The movement to negative real interest rates is an indication of a coming increase in real estate activity. The best example of this occurred in the early 1970s when loans could be assumed at less than the rate of inflation.

One measure of negative real interest rates occurs when the consumer price indicator (CPI) is higher than the three-month

Treasury Bill rate. This indicates that the interest earned on invested capital is negated by the loss in purchasing power, and inflation is likely to cut into investment capital.

For example:

Amount invested in T-Bills	$100,000
Interest earned annually	5%
Amount received	5,000
Loss to inflation at 6%	(6,000)
Net purchasing power received	(1,000)
Balance of capital (real money)	$ 99,000

In this example inflation erased the purchasing power of the interest and diminished the real present value of the capital by $1,000. Consequently, negative real interest rates tend to force investment capital from interest-paying debt instruments to hard assets that have potential for price increases. This is, of course, a major reason real estate is viewed as an inflation hedge. Price increases in real estate tend to offset the purchasing power lost to inflation.

The opposite is also true. When real interest rates are positive, high money tends to move into interest bearing instruments. The speculative motive diminishes in the population at large when interest rates are higher than inflation. In fact, a key timing indicator is the point when the trend of interest rates crosses the trend of inflation. Extreme and extended interest rate moves above or below the rate of inflation indicate that cycle extremes for real estate are on the way.

Consequently, keeping an eye on real interest rates can provide an early indication of a potential increase (or decrease) of the capital moving in or out of real estate. This attempt to protect capital from loss in purchasing power can be monitored by observing changes in real interest rates from positive to negative.

For example:

1. Positive real interest rates

T-bill rate	5%
CPI indicator	4%
Real interest rate	1%

2. Negative real interest rates

T-bill rate	5%
CPI indicator	6%
Real interest rate	(1%)

Real interest rates provide an ongoing monitor of the potential movement of investment capital from debt instruments to equity assets that tend to increase in price with the upward trend of inflation. Assumptions that involve ever-increasing inflation should be modified to include the relationship to interest rates with an awareness of the steps that both the market (especially the bond market) and the government might take to control inflation. The point of course is that inflation alone does not tell the story. It is important for assumptions to include the relationship of inflation to interest rates and the effect on the purchasing power of investment capital.

A snapshot of negative real interest rates may not reflect the years of gathering momentum that is often required for a full cycle of inflation. This is why the recent history of the real estate cycle is helpful in determining the assumptions necessary to project financial performance.

Just as real interest rates point to the inflation trend, public attitudes point to the trend of expectations. For example, years of complacent investor attitudes toward real estate tend to precede exceptional increases in the price cycle. Conversely, years of public speculation in real estate with a long period of price increases tend to precede a severe and prolonged downturn in expectations, speculative demand, and prices.

The Modeling Function of Time Value

Analyzing real estate based solely on the amount of money generated, as the traditional methods do, has proven inadequate to measure success in meeting the purpose of investing in real estate. Time of receipt is equal in importance to the amount in determining the worth of an investment.

Financial analysis is to a large extent a process of measuring the effect of time on money. Real estate financial analysis can be applied to measure two different time frames.

1. Actual past performance forward to the present.
2. Projected future performance back to the present.

Both applications involve measuring the effect of cyclical change on funds invested in a specific property. The increase or decrease in wealth is determined by when, as well as by how much, cash flow was received or paid in the past or projected to be received or paid in the future. Purchasing power is a function of both the timing and the amount of the cash flows.

Money received sooner has greater value than money received later. There are a couple of good reasons for this. First, you can put it to use; second, the risk of loss is eliminated sooner. The utility of money gives it time value. The sooner you can get money out of an investment the sooner you can put it to use as you choose. The sooner you can get it, the more liquid it is. Liquidity shortens the time between perception of potential loss and conversion of market value to cash.

One of the drawbacks of real estate is its lack of liquidity during inactive market periods. Because real estate is a credit-dependent industry, its liquidity also often depends on the availability of credit. You can't sell unless there is credit or a cash buyer.

Conversely, expected loss of purchasing power during inflationary cycles is why bonds are discounted in price to offer a higher yield. It is also why the expected appreciation of real estate is more valued than the liquidity of cash. Purchasing power can diminish in some cycles so fast that the need to protect it outweighs the desire for liquidity. Consequently, assets that appreciate in value during inflation cycles are more in demand than liquid investments.

Beginning an investment program at the right time in the cycle may be the single most important factor in long-term investment success. The long wave cycles of inflation followed by deflation and stability and then new inflation are major forces in the appreciation of property values. Entering the market at the top of an inflationary cycle can mean loss of your investment. Entering the market at the beginning of an inflationary boom can mean financial security. The timing of an investment program in real estate can be a significant factor in the growth or loss of funds during the investment period.

The opportunity to put money to use to earn rent or interest carries the cost of lost opportunity. Money that is not earning rent over time is a loss. The concept of opportunity cost follows naturally from the concepts of time value and utility. Money that is not put to use over time loses the opportunity to earn money over that lost time period. It can never be replaced.

This has a very practical application to income property. Rents that are even a few dollars too high, which nudge tenants to competing space, can never be justified when the otherwise rented space remains vacant for even one month—a month that never will return and a rent that can never be replaced as time marches forward.

A similar circumstance can occur when property is placed on the market just as a cycle is peaking and turning down and buyers are starting to exit the marketplace. If property is priced just slightly too high and the trend turns down, the opportunity to sell, to become liquid, to do all the wonderful things with that large profit, may be lost. And in some cases the entire property that one day seemed so valuable suddenly is unsalable, worth less than the debt it secured and ultimately repossessed.

That is what the utility of money, opportunity cost, and the time value of money means in the daily real estate market. Renting for a little less than your competition and selling for an amount slightly under the market can sometimes prevent the problems illustrated above and may be the only practical course of action in a contracting market. The opposite danger exists in an expanding market with rising prices. This is when asking a little more than the market value can be the best approach.

Pricing should be ahead of the trend of the cycle. If activity is expanding and prices are rising steadily, pricing ahead of the market is practical because as time passes the price will move to you. When the market is contracting and prices are falling as buyers exit, pricing below the market in order to catch the trend can prevent a lost sale.

The point to remember is that there is always risk, and the nature of risk can be seen in the real estate cycle and the way the cycle affects rents and sales prices. When the cycle is strong and activity is high, the risk is in renting or selling for less than top dollar. When the cycle is contracting and activity is low, the risk is a vacancy that can never produce income or a lost sale that can never be retrieved. Both are opportunity costs. Both are the loss of utility of the money that could have been in hand to earn more money or used to afford a higher quality of life.

Discount rates reflect the time preference for money based on current marginal utility. Discounting is largely a process of imposing expectations on market values. The lower the expected future purchasing power the higher the discount rate. The higher the expected future purchasing power the lower the discount rate applied to future cash flows. The discount rate is the market mechanism for integrating inflationary expectations and real estate values.

Discounting reduces all cash flows, which are spread over many different points in time to a single time value; that is, the value at the time of initial investment. This point in time is usually the beginning of the project, which is the time of initial investment or acquisition. But in certain applications it may actually have occurred in the past. For example, when measuring the return of a property to determine the acceptability of a sales price you discount the known cash flows, which have already occurred, back to the time of initial investment, which occurred even earlier in the past. Consequently, cash flows are discounted to the present value at the time the investment started, which is not necessarily the time at which the financial analysis is performed.

Putting Risk in Perspective

One of the useful aspects of analyzing real estate investments in the context of cycles is that it forces attention on the levels of risk and opportunity at different stages of the real estate cycle. When cycle risk and the risks of a specific property are combined, it is possible to evaluate the probability of ownership benefits making the transition to cash flows. The combination is important because competitive advantages of specific properties offset unfavorable market conditions and vice versa.

Cycle risk addresses the possibility that the market is entering a time of high or low risk. Property risk addresses the competitive performance of the investment during changes in the cycle. Both contribute to or detract from the likelihood of transferring purchasing power through time. Both are of equal importance.

Therefore, it is important when evaluating the benefits of owning a property to ask:

1. How much cash flow will this investment produce?
2. When will the cash flows occur?
3. How likely are the cash flows to occur?

The financial analysis of real estate is in large part an attempt to accurately answer these three questions. Whether you are investing in land, office buildings, apartments, or rental houses, the questions will always apply. In a way this is fortunate because when you look at different types of real estate from a financial point of view, you are always dealing with three familiar concepts:

1. Quantity—How much?
2. Time—When?
3. Risk—How Likely?

The financial analysis of real estate does not have to be an intricate mathematical process or search for some undiscovered mathematical formula. Overly complex approaches to value analysis tend to obscure the practical, concrete, and essential elements of financial analysis—cash flows and time.

7

Using Net Present Value to Analyze Real Estate

The purpose of a financial model is to see the effect of change on the timing and amounts of cash flow. When you have all the cash flows (negative and positive) in one model you can see how changes in the property and in the market affect financial performance. This is how you can tell if an investment is maintaining purchasing power, increasing wealth, or losing money.

A financial model structures cash flows so they can be analyzed. The analysis process may involve measuring past performance, verifying current performance, and forecasting future performance. It can be the basis for deciding to purchase, sell, remodel, demolish and rebuild, and to lease or buy real estate.

The usefulness of financial analysis depends on the financial analysis technique and accuracy of the data and assumptions which form the foundation of the cash flows in the model. The level of detail depends on the complexity of the properties or project being analyzed. The objective is to be thorough, but not at the expense of clarity.

Establishing Discount Rate Criteria

In its most basic form, financial analysis is a process of determining which investment alternative will produce the largest increase in real wealth as measured in present value dollars. This use of discounted cash flow analysis, and net present value (NPV) in particular, allocates limited investment capital between alternative investments. In this use it is a decision criterion.

Present value analysis can be used to determine and compare the present value of any set of cash flows for a number of financial purposes. Consequently, it can be used to make any variety of cash flow–related decisions from acquisition, during ownership, to disposition.

NPV is a useful financial analysis technique because it compares sets of cash flows from different properties and lease structures on the level playing field of present value dollars. This is one reason NPV is rapidly becoming entrenched in office leasing as a tool for evaluating seemingly incomparable leases. As a logical extension, projecting and discounting lease income for an entire building over its useful life can be used to determine the value of an office building.

Present value analysis adjusts for differences in cash flow amounts and cash flow timing, providing a single dollar amount that accounts for the time value of money. Net present value applies a designated discount rate to reduce cash flows to the present value and nets them; that is, the present value of the positive and the negative cash flows are offset against each other to produce a single dollar value. This dollar value is the net of the present value amounts that, invested in the present, would compound at the chosen interest rate to generate the projected cash flows. The formulas for calculating time value illustrate the inverse relationship between discounting and compounding:

Discounting: $\text{Present value} = \dfrac{\text{Future value}}{(1+i)^n}$

Compounding: $\text{Future value} = \text{Present value} \times (1+i)^n$

The following illustrates calculation of net present value using the 8 percent discount factor. Discount factors are calculated with slight modification in the discounting formula to allow multiplication: $PV = FV \times (1/(1+i)^n)$.

Year	Cash Flows	Discount factor (8%)	Present value
0	($300,000)	1	($300,000)
1	20,000	0.92593	18,519
2	25,000	0.85734	21,434
3	30,000	0.79383	23,815
4	25,000	0.73503	18,376
5	575,000	0.68058	391,334
		Net present value	$173,478

Each cash flow has a nominal and a time value (present value). When a cash flow is received or paid in the present, the nominal and the discounted values are the same. This is how the initial cash flow or down payment is treated. Since no time has past in the life of the investment, the initial cash flow is not discounted. In a sense it occurs in year zero, which is sometimes referred to as the beginning of year one. Since no time has passed, its nominal value is its present value. The other cash flows are treated as being received at the end of the year.

The discount rate is the key element of net present value. It should be chosen with an appreciation for the underlying purpose of investing. The cost of capital (prime rate or commercial paper rate) is a useful source for a discount rate. The cost of capital for top corporations reflects the debt market's perception of the purchasing power lost to inflation plus the profit requirement for invested funds.

Assuming cash flow projections have been reduced by all expenses and taxes, the cost of capital represents a minimum adjustment for inflation and profit. Since this is a minimum, a positive NPV represents an increase in wealth. This application of NPV represents the minimum financial basis on which to proceed with a project and is signaled by a positive NPV when the cost of capital or minimum rate is used for discounting.

If you use the rate of inflation for a discount rate you can determine whether an investment meets the minimum requirement of transferring purchasing power through time. This application illustrates the basic measurement function of net present value as a gauge for transferring purchasing power through time. An IRR that is the inflation rate represents breakeven in time value, which occurs when the negative and positive cash flows are equal, producing an NPV of zero after discounting at the rate of inflation.

Calculating the Transfer of Purchasing Power

Year	Cash Flow	Discount rate (CPI 4%)	Present value
0	($200,000)	1	($200,000)
1	15,000	0.961538	14,423
2	20,000	0.924556	18,491
3	$200,000	0.888996	$177,799
Net	$ 35,000	Net Present Value	$ 10,713

Difference: $24,287

The net nominal value of the cash flows is $35,000. The net present value is $10,713. The nominal increase in value above the $200,000 investment is $35,000. The real increase in value above the $200,000 investment is $10,713 after the loss of purchasing power to inflation of 4 percent.

This investment generated $210,713 in positive cash flows after inflation. When comparing nominal and present values it is apparent that during the first year, $577 was lost to inflation ($15,000 less $14,423). During the second year, $1,509 was lost ($20,000 less $18,491) and $22,201 was lost during the third year ($200,000 less $177,799).

Therefore, using net present value to monitor the loss to inflation we can see the relationship between nominal and present value.

Annual Loss in Purchasing Power (4%)	
Year 1	($ 577)
Year 2	(1,509)
Year 3	(22,201)
Total	($24,287)
Nominal gain	$35,000
Less inflation at 4%	(24,287)
Real gain (NPV)	$10,713

In this illustration the real gain in purchasing power exceeds the loss to inflation by $10,713 when inflation is running 4 percent. This loss is the erosion of inflation and the first barrier to meeting the goals of investing. It is a cost just like operating expenses and taxes and therefore cannot be ignored.

Inflation is built into the future of our monetary system. The only question is how high it will go during the next long wave cycle. But the inflation component is only one part of the usual minimum discount rate used in present value analysis and accounts for the first barrier to meeting the objectives of investment. The other barriers which are contained in the discount rate account for risk, profit, and possibly other designated factors such as indirect overhead expenses. Each can be included in the rate. By adding cost items to the discount rate you can customize it in a way that meets your corporate or individual requirements.

For example, assuming that the cost of capital includes inflationary loss, add an overhead allocation to establish the minimum discount rate. Then discount equity and debt capital as cash flows put in or taken out of the project. If the net present value of the cash flows is positive, the project breaks even and exceeds the minimum rate of return requirement.

Ten Applications of NPV to Real Estate

Use of net present value analysis in the real estate industry has expanded through the years, demonstrating its value and ability to adapt to the needs of the marketplace.

Net present value represents an insight into the significance of the time value of money and can change the way one views financial analysis. There is probably no investment field that has recorded this change more clearly than real estate. In fact, the process is still under way as new applications of NPV continue to surface.

Here are ten applications of net present value to real estate analysis.

1. Net present value as a cutoff criterion for making an investment. The discount rate used to compute NPV serves as the minimum rate of return for proceeding with an investment. A positive NPV is confirmation that the minimum return is likely and serves as a confirmation signal for the transaction. If the NPV is negative the investment is canceled.

2. NPV as a criterion for choosing between alternative investments. Two sets of cash flows that vary in timing and amount of both negative and positive cash flows can be reduced to present value amounts using the same discount rate. NPV allows the investment alternatives to be compared on an equal basis to determine which provides the greatest increase in wealth.

3. NPV as a criterion for accepting a purchase offer. An offer to purchase can be analyzed using past cash flows and the sale proceeds of a proposed sale to determine if a minimum rate of return is achieved by the offered price. If the minimum rate is not met, a counter offer can made at a price that will provide a positive NPV at the desired rate of return.

4. NPV as a technique for establishing a listing price. Another application of NPV for determining real estate pricing occurs when analyzing property to be put on the market for sale. The basic motivation is to sell for the highest price the market will bear. Sellers who have unrealistic expectations of property values do themselves financial harm by pricing property out of the actual market price range as the cycle is moving down, thus missing an opportunity to sell. Determining the NPV realized at a projected sale price can provide a financial context for listing property. The primary pricing mechanism comes from market conditions and the characteristics of the property; but, determining the real gain in wealth and the interest rate that the gain represents can provide a financial perspective for decision purposes, which may counterbalance the unrealistic hopes of the seller.

5. NPV as an analysis tool for investments with no initial investment or down payment. Investments that involve no down payment cannot be measured by conventional rate of return methods. Because there is no initial investment, percentage rates of return do not apply, but the basic investment objective of increasing wealth does. Nevertheless, this real estate scenario is common especially in projects where the developer creates value and cash flow through expertise, entrepreneurial effort, and the use of borrowed funds. NPV provides a technique for evaluating the financial performance of this common real estate practice.

6. NPV as a tool for determining the purchase price of a negative cash flow asset. Property that does not produce income such as underperforming rental property or vacant land can be evaluated with NPV to determine when and for how much the property should be purchased and for how much it must be sold in order to offset negative cash flows. Determining the required future sales price can help establish a low enough purchase price to increase the likelihood that a future sale that will generate the desired return.

7. NPV as a tool for determining the purchase price of a leasehold interest. A leasehold interest in land on which a retail center or office complex is built can be evaluated using NPV to determine the present value of the lease payments at a required discount rate. This procedure establishes the present value of the leasehold based on its future cash flows. In this application NPV, in effect, appraises the leasehold.

8. NPV as a decision criterion for capital improvements. Major remodeling is a preventive as well as remedial measure in the attempt to slow the economic obsolescence common to real estate. NPV can match the negative cash flows of remodeling against the positive cash flows from rent and potential resale value to help determine if remodeling is worth the cost.

9. NPV as a tool for monitoring real estate operations. NPV can be used to monitor the financial effect of changing market conditions on a property during ownership. In this application NPV is used to monitor the trend of vacancy, rental rates, and price.

10. NPV as a buy or lease decision criterion. Any company that uses real estate is faced with the decision of whether to purchase real estate or to lease. The question is whether the cost of leasing is cheaper than the costs of ownership. Typically, the final decision is based on the assumption that a company can make more money in it own business than in the real estate business. Nevertheless, buying at the right point in the cycle can prove less expensive than leasing. NPV analysis can clarify the alternatives.

Seven Guidelines for Interpreting Net Present Value

The preceding list of applications of NPV to real estate does not by any means exhaust the possible applications. Each of these and all of the other applications of net present value involve specifying and discounting the positive and negative cash flows. In some cases the cash flows occur in the past, and in others they are projected into the future. But in all cases NPV determines the worth of a project by discounting the value of the cash flows to determine the extent the investment transfers purchasing power through time and builds real wealth.

There are guidelines that apply to each application of NPV and help interpretation of its meaning for financial performance. It's apparent that NPV can be useful in choosing between properties for allocation of a limited amount of investment capital when there is a clear choice. But the reality of the real estate market is that finding a single good deal is difficult enough, much less two that are so good that it's difficult to choose between them.

More often, a potential investment property is analyzed alone without reference to other possible acquisitions that are equally attractive, financially. Consequently, there must be a meaningful way to interpret financial performance that is within general market guidelines and does not require a choice between two properties. Percentage rate of return measures have generally attempted to meet this requirement.

In fact, the use of a discount rate and the requirement that the NPV be positive at that discount rate, is application of NPV as a single investment criterion. Here, the discount rate is actually the meaning behind the positive NPV. Vary the rate and the NPV changes. When inflation and interest rates increase, the discount rate should increase. When inflation and interest rates decrease, a lower discount rate is probably appropriate.

Net present value can be interpreted in the context of the discount rate to provide a percentage basis for comparison with the general investment market returns. The net present value dollar amount is also an interpretation guideline. Both the present dollar value and the discount rate can be meaningful and can provide insight into the worth of a property. The point to keep in mind is that the NPV figure is a real dollar amount, not some mysterious product of a financial formula. Also, the discount rate used to calculate NPV is only a compound interest rate, applied in a different manner. The following are guidelines for interpreting net present value.

1. A positive net present value means the cash taken out of the property exceeds the cash put in, when discounted at the chosen rate.

2. A negative net present value means the cash put in the property exceeds the cash taken out of the property, when discounted at the chosen rate.

3. A net present value of zero means the value of the cash put in the investment and the value of the cash taken out of the investment are equal.

4. As the net present value approaches zero it approaches the internal rate of return.

5. A positive NPV means the property generates a rate of return greater than the discount rate.

6. A negative NPV means the property generates a rate of return less than the discount rate.

7. A net present value of zero means the discount rate is the internal rate of return.

Net present value provides a dollar amount, and with a slight expansion of application it also reveals a percentage rate of return. Keeping in mind that discounting is the inverse of compounding, the discount rate used to establish NPV is the compounded rate of return represented by the cash flows from the property.

For example, what is the present value of $100,000 received in three years when discounted at 8 percent?

$$\$100,000 \times 0.793832 = \$79,383$$

What is the future value of $79,383 when compounded at 8 percent?

$$\$79,383 \times 1.259712 = \$100,000$$

How do you calculate the compound interest rate factor for 8 percent and discount factor for 8 percent used in these two problems?

Discount Rate Formula

$$\text{Present value} = \text{Future value} \times \frac{1}{(1 + i)^n}$$

$$\frac{1}{1 + (1.08)^3}$$

$$\frac{1}{1 + (1.08 \times 1.08 \times 1.08)} = 1.259712$$

$$\frac{1}{1.259712} = 0.793832$$

Compound Rate Factor Formula

$$\text{Future value} = \text{Present value} \times (1 + i)^n$$
$$1 + (1.08)^3$$
$$1 + (1.08 \times 1.08 \times 1.08) = 1.259712$$

The emphasis here is on interpretation of the net present value of the cash flows of a real estate investment. The purpose of the example in the above table is to demonstrate that each present value amount that, in sum, produces a single net present value has meaning that can be found in the concept of compound interest. Each discounted cash flow is the present value amount that could be invested today at the discount rate-interest rate to compound or grow to the nominal cash flow amount before discounting.

Using Net Present Value as an Investment Criterion

There are three functions of a financial model. The first function examines known and projected cash flows. The second function requires modification of the known or forecasted data under different market scenarios and with different degrees of certainty. The third function of the model measures the financial effect of the possible scenarios in terms of net present value. These three functions can be defined as a process of analyzing cash flows in terms of:

1. Existing conditions.
2. Possible changes in the existing conditions.
3. Variation in financial performance as a result of the possible changes.

Using the framework developed earlier we can structure the analysis process in three steps to arrive at net present value.

Step 1: Specify the cash flows.

Step 2: Discount the cash flows.

Step 3: Modify the cash flows.

Step one involves determining the amount and time of occurrence of the past and/or future cash flows. Specifying past cash flows is a challenge of sorting known data. Specifying future cash flows is a challenge of projecting the terms of leases, estimating sales prices, and determining the parameters of uncertainty.

Step two is mechanical and can be done with present value tables, business calculators, or by computer. Even though the procedure is routine, it does require an understanding of the concepts of discounting and compounding, which form the basis of net present value.

Step three is a process of exploring variations in cash flows that might result from change. This includes modification of the cash flow structure to determine the change in net present value under different scenarios using different discount rates.

Together these three steps comprise a model. The active analysis process occurs in step three when the cash flows in the model are changed to observe the effect on financial performance. This is how real estate analysis becomes an interactive process reflecting the effects of change on financial performance. Cash flows change as market conditions and property characteristics change. A model allows immediate observation of those changes on financial performance as measured by net present value.

A customized model for financial analysis automatically provides checks and balances on investment expectations. It forces measurement of what you expect from an investment and allows you to measure the financial results of the expectation.

For example, after surveying the market you have located a property that appears to have solid potential. It will require remodeling during the first year and replacement of the mechanical system in about 5 years. A sale is anticipated a the end of 10 years. The property is priced at $850,000 and is likely to provide the following after-tax cash flows. Will it meet the 12 percent return requirement?

Net Present Value Analysis—Discount Rate, 12%

Year	Cash flows	PV factor	Present value
0	($150,000)	1	($150,000)
1	(50,000)	0.89286	(44,643)
2	5,000	0.79719	3,986
3	10,000	0.71178	7,118
4	15,000	0.63552	9,533
5	(35,000)	0.56743	(19,860)
6	20,000	0.50663	10,132
7	20,000	0.45235	9,047
8	25,000	0.40388	10,097
9	30,000	0.36061	10,818
10	500,000	0.32197	160,985
Net	$390,000	Net Present Value	$ 7,213

Since the net present value of the cash flows is positive, the rate of return is at least 12 percent, and the project is acceptable by that minimum rate of return criterion.

Verifying that the property is likely to produce and possibly exceed a 12 percent return establishes that the performance is comparable to investing a total of $235,000 in a tax-free savings account that compounds at more than 12 percent over 10 years.

The above calculations indicate the projected cash flows generate a positive net present value when discounted at 12%. A slight change in the amount or the timing of one of the crucial cash flows would have resulted in a negative net present value and rejection of the investment.

The implication of the narrow margin for error is that the assumptions on which the cash flow forecast is based must have a high likelihood of occurring. This use of NPV to provide an accept-or-reject criterion is one of the most frequent applications.

Using NPV to Choose Between Investments

Real estate cash flows are by their nature different in amount and timing. This fact of the marketplace is one reason comparing different properties on equal grounds is virtually impossible without discounting the cash flows. One of the major benefits of net present value analysis is the solid basis it provides for evaluating the relative worth of two seemingly different investment opportunities. This application of NPV allows selection of the investment with the greatest increase in wealth. The greater increase in wealth is determined by the amount of cash flow as well as the timing of the cash flow.

Present Value Analysis—Discount Rate, 8%

Year	Property 1 cash flow	Property 2 cash flow	8% factor	Property 1 PV	Property 2 PV
0	($40,000)	($30,000)	1	($40,000)	($30,000)
1	3,000	(10,000)	0.92593	2,778	(9,259)
2	3,500	3,500	0.85734	3,001	3,001
3	3,500	3,500	0.79383	2,778	2,778
4	(3,500)	3,000	0.73503	(2,573)	2,205
5	50,000	46,500	0.68058	34,029	31,647
Net	$16,500	$16,500	NPV	$ 13	$ 372

Although these two cash flow streams have the same nominal net amounts, the discounted value is different. This illustrates the time value adjustment function of net present value analysis. The cash flows are already equal in amount, but they are not equal in time value. Therefore, property two provides a greater increase in real wealth. It transfers more purchasing power through time than property one. The two investment opportunities project the same total nominal cash flow but different financial performance due to the timing of the cash flows. NPV provides the financial information necessary to allocate investment funds to the property that maximizes wealth.

Using NPV to Evaluate a Purchase Offer

You have received an offer to sell property that has been on the market for two years. Several people have made offers but none was for the amount you want. This time the outcome is going to be different because you have a new use for the money. Consequently, you have decided that the criterion for accepting or rejecting this offer is going to be financial rather than emotional. Since an offer is on the table you do some research and conclude that if the offer represents a 14 percent return on your investment you will sell. The question is how to determine if the after-tax return is actually 14 percent. To start you isolate the annual net after-tax cash flows generated over the entire time you have owned the property. Then you calculate the after-tax net of the sales offer and discount the entire set of cash flows at 14 percent.

Purchase Offer, NPV Analysis at 14%

	Cash Flow	Factor	Present value
Year 0	($120,000)	1	($120,000)
Year 1	7,000	0.87720	6,140
Year 2	5,000	0.76947	3,847
Year 3	9,000	0.67497	6,074
Year 4	10,000	0.59208	5,921
Year 5	12,000	0.51937	6,232
Year 6	240,000	0.45559	109,342
		Net Present Value	$ 17,556

The sales proceeds and the cash flows from rental operations combine to produce a compounded rate of return in excess of the required 14 percent necessary to accept the purchase offer. The actual return was about 16.9 percent.

Net present value is not limited to the time value measurement of projected cash flow from potential investments. It works just as well on past cash flows. The process of discounting to present value does not actually limit application of NPV to cash flows that are forecasted for the future. It only takes a slight shift in view to apply the concept to measure past financial performance. The discounting-compounding concept is equally valid in both cases. The present value tables, calculator, and computer don't know whether the cash flows have occurred in the past or are expected to occur in the future. In both time frames the cash flows are just amounts of money paid or received at points in time, and the formula for solving net present value is the same in each application. In all cases the cash flows are discounted to the beginning of the investment, which may have actually occurred in the past or not yet at all, as is the case with a projection.

Using NPV to Evaluate Projects with No Initial Investment

The custom of making a down payment and a series of equal monthly payments until the debt on a property is paid probably evolved out of the home sales market and the lending practices upon which real estate depends. In reality, deals in the marketplace are not that rigid. The nature of the real estate market dictates the actual financing structure, and there are as many possibilities as there are unusual circumstances.

There are many transactions that do not involve a cash outlay on the part of the buyer that would be properly considered a customary down payment. In fact, under certain conditions, a seller may pay a buyer to take over the debt on a property. In these cases the personal objectives of the seller outweigh the popular notion of a conventional real estate transaction involving an initial down payment.

Furthermore, real estate development is a process of creating value, which may not involve the outlay of equity by the developer. Borrowed funds are typically the source of money for real estate development. Although this practice can carry high risk during certain phases of the real estate cycle, it remains central to the development process.

In each of these cases and in similar situations, net present value can be used as a technique for evaluating the cash flows generated by the projects, even when there is no initial investment in equity or when borrowed funds are used. The application of net present value to investment scenarios of this type fills a gap left by traditional rate of return techniques which require an initial investment for comparison to annual cash flows.

For example, a builder has offered you a deal to take over the debt on a recently completed building. This office complex is partially rented but is not quite covering debt service. The office market is in a slump, and the building is not in a desirable location. The immediate future of the market is questionable. The long-term growth of the city is promising. The building is professionally managed, and the owner is doing everything possible to market the remaining vacancies. There simply are no tenants now. The owner wants to move on to other opportunities.

Although this is a no money down opportunity, the question remains as to whether the debt is more than the current market value. The owner is paying out of pocket to keep the building afloat. What kind of deal makes sense? Should the owner pay you to offset the first few year's operating losses? Should the owner buy down the debt? Or, is there some combination that makes sense? Each alternative has an effect on cash flow.

The problem with the property in the following example began as the result of a combination of debt that was predicated on an ever rising real estate cycle that turned down. The cycle turn combined with initial poor management and leasing efforts to place the building in financial trouble. The end result was an owner who wanted out of the debt liability and was willing to sell with no down payment.

Under the right acquisition structure, the property will generate positive cash flow the first year. With no investment how do you evaluate the worth of the building?

Nothing Down Purchase, Net Present Value Analysis at 8%

Year	Cash Flow	Discount factor	Present value
1	$ 5,000	0.92593	$ 4,630
2	6,000	0.85734	5,144
3	6,500	0.79383	5,160
4	12,000	0.73503	8,820
5	13,000	0.68058	8,848
6	20,000	0.63017	12,603
7	23,000	0.58349	13,420
8	24,000	0.54027	12,966
9	25,000	0.50025	12,506
10	525,000	0.46319	243,175
Totals	$659,500		$327,272

By obtaining longer term financing, the office building generates a positive cash flow. The sellers were happy to just get out of the debt obligation, which reflects the power of expectations during different phases of the cycle. One person's real estate problem is often another's retirement fund.

There are several questions related to the cash flow of this property. Since there are no negative cash flows involved is it really a net present value analysis? There are no negative cash flows against which to net the positive cash flows. Isn't this a present value analysis that can be totaled to determine the present value of the cash flow stream? Does it even matter what you call it? The really important aspect of investment analysis is the conceptual foundation, not the name used to describe the calculation process. To simplify the process and move away from limiting jargon, why not agree that any set of cash flows can be netted, even when they are all positive or negative.

The underlying concept in this case is time value and the discounting process used to calculate it. Accept that the worth of any investment is the present value of its future cash flows discounted at the rate you choose. Then you can determine real value regardless of the cash flow scenario or the terms used to describe the discounting procedure.

Positive cash flow is the reward for taking on the problems characteristic of real estate ownership. Net present value can help determine if the projected cash flows warrant the risk and provide sufficient reward for the buyer to take on the obligations of ownership.

Since there is no equity investment in this property, evaluating it on a rate of return percentage basis is meaningless. Furthermore, there are no negative cash flows, which by definition prohibits use of IRR, since it is the discount rate at which the positive and negative cash flows are equal.

Nevertheless, the cash flows can be discounted and the acquisition can be judged on the present dollar value alone. Investment is acceptance of burdens and responsibilities that go far beyond the textbook definitions of deferring current consumption in order to increase future consumption.

Accepting risk is an investment of time energy and allocation of personal effort, even though it may not be monetary. Measuring the potential cash flows that result from accepting risk has a purpose. In this case the decision must be based on whether the amount of cash involved is sufficient reward for taking on the burdens and responsibilities of ownership and the ever-present risk that the cash flows will not meet expectations.

Using Net Present Value to Analyze Negative Cash Flows

During certain phases of the real estate cycle, negative cash flow from rental income is accepted with little analysis. Usually, this level of risk acceptance indicates expectations of an eventual sales price with a positive cash flow from sales proceeds that is greater than the negative cash flows from rent.

A more popular characterization is that the purchase of negative rental income property depends on a greater fool to sell to in the future. In fact, the requirements of turning around underperforming rental property is much more of a management challenge than expressed by either view. Nevertheless, expectations of increasing rents is a valid basis for expectation of increasing sale prices. Both rely on growing demand from a growing population reflected in a gradual increase in the level of prices in our economy.

Traditional rate of return percentage measures are useless in evaluating acquisition of negative cash flow property. For example, how can you measure the return on investment of an apartment complex purchased with $50,000 down that loses $5000 a year from rental operations? When transactions like this were made during the topping process of the last 18-year cycle, analysts could only look on in disbelief. It didn't appear to be rational investment behavior, and in some cases it wasn't. But in other markets rents did rise, and the end result was profitable. Both results depend on the combination of the property potential and the trend of the cycle.

If the cycle is trending down it may be impossible to raise rents even if the property itself is highly desirable. If the cycle is trending upward it may be possible to raise rents even if the property is not desirable. Both cases can be expressed as cash flows.

In the following example an apartment complex was acquired for a $55,000 down payment. Rental income was insufficient to pay operating expenses and debt service; consequently, the property lost money each year, requiring an ongoing investment. By the fifth year the owner was tired of the strain of management and losses and accepted an offer that netted the following after-tax cash flows.

Year	Cash flow	8% Discount factor	Present value
0	($55,000)	1	($55,000)
1	(4,000)	0.92593	(3,704)
2	(3,000)	0.85734	(2,572)
3	(2,500)	0.79383	(1,985)
4	(2,000)	0.73503	(1,470)
5	3,000	0.68058	2,042
5 sale	60,000	0.68058	40,835
Net	($ 3,500)		($21,854)

Discounting negative cash flows to the net present value illustrates the significance of the time value of money. As these cash flows indicate, the nominal loss was only $3,500; but, the present value loss was six times as large. There are a couple of reasons for this. First, the rental income losses each year, although diminishing in time value amount, do accumulate and add to the overall loss. Second, the time value loss of the down payment, which may be viewed as returned in the $60,000 received from sale proceeds, has diminished to just under $41,000. Consequently, the loss in purchasing power and the loss of opportunity to earn interest increases the real loss of this investment far beyond the nominal $3,500 in unadjusted cash flows.

The time value of money takes on a new perspective when seen in the context of negative after-tax cash flows. Negative cash flows can be partitioned to illustrate the loss in purchasing power to inflation as well as the loss of opportunity to earn a riskless return above the rate of inflation; for example, discounting the after-tax cash flows in the last example by the rate of inflation estimated to be about 4 percent produces the amount of the loss attributed to the inflationary portion of time value.

Year	Cash flow	4% Discount factor	PV
0	($55,000)	1	($55,000)
1	(4,000)	0.96154	(3,846)
2	(3,000)	0.92456	(2,774)
3	(2,500)	0.88810	(2,220)
4	(2,000)	0.85480	(1,710)
5	3,000	0.82193	2,466
5 sale	60,000	0.82193	49,316
Net	($ 3,500)		($13,768)

Looking at inflation alone, the investment generated a real after-tax net loss of $13,768. Adjusting for lost purchasing power does not consider the lost opportunity to earn money above the inflation rate, which was reflected in the prior calculation at an 8 percent discount rate. The message of this set of cash flows is a nominal loss of $3,500, but a real loss in purchasing power of $13,768.

Using Net Present Value to Measure Breakeven

Breakeven analysis has significance that goes beyond the limitations of its usual application to income from operations. It has evolved into a more meaningful use embodied in discounted cash flow analysis.

For example, there are two applications to real estate that are appropriate for breakeven analysis.

1. Breakeven is the balance point between income and expenses on an annual operating basis.

2. Breakeven also reflects whether an investment meets the minimum requirement of transferring purchasing power from the beginning of ownership through to the end of ownership.

In fact, the internal rate of return is the breakeven rate at a given discount rate. It is the exact discount rate at which the positive and negative cash flows are equal. This application of breakeven has meaning when considering the effect of inflation on purchasing power. In this sense, breakeven in actual purchasing power occurs when the positive cash flows equal the negative cash flows when discounted at the inflation rate. Consequently, the positive net present value produced after discounting at the inflation rate represents the real increase in wealth.

Investment capital must be protected from loss before it can increase wealth. By recognizing the effect of time on investment funds it is possible to see that protection of investment capital means more than ending the investment with the nominal amount of money that was invested initially. True breakeven occurs when an investment is liquidated with no loss in purchasing power, which means that the amount of the cash flows taken out must at least equal the amount of cash put into the property when discounted at the rate of inflation.

Breakeven analysis can be used with cash flow modeling to forecast the minimum cash flows needed for a property to break even over the ownership period. Then the required scenarios for the projected cash flows can be examined in terms of market conditions and property characteristics. This approach to forecasting establishes the minimum breakeven point then examines whether the property and the market are likely to achieve the goal.

1. Specify the amount of cash flow necessary to break even in real terms; and then,

2. Determine if that level of performance is a realistic expectation in terms of market conditions and the characteristics of the property.

This slightly different approach starts by forecasting cash flows based on the discount rate rather than likely market and property scenarios. It assumes a minimum cash flow then tests it against the cycle. As a result, a minimum breakeven base is produced against which to evaluate financial performance. The model starts with a financial minimum against which to test assumptions rather than starting with assumptions to create a cash flow forecast.

Net present value as an investment cutoff criterion actually uses this approach. The marginal cost of capital such as the prime rate makes a useful discount rate for minimum breakeven analysis that encompasses purchasing power lost to inflation and minimum profit requirements. But to emphasize the importance of minimum breakeven cash flows, the profit portion of the discount rate is eliminated and the after-tax cash flows are adjusted to determine the minimum financial performance level required to transfer purchasing power.

Rather than make assumptions concerning the market and the property, then project cash flows based on those assumptions, we run the cash flows first at a minimum rate then see if the market is likely to meet the projections. In other words, rather than ask whether a set of cash flows is likely to occur under certain assumptions we specify the minimum cash flows then examine the market and property assumptions required to meet that after-tax cash flow pattern. Note the variation in the following cash flows.

Year	Projection 1	Projection 2
0	($55,000)	($55,000)
1	(4,000)	(3,000)
2	(3,000)	(2,000)
3	(2,500)	(500)
4	(2,000)	1,000
5	3,000	3,500
5 sale	60,000	70,000
Net	($ 3,500)	$14,000
NPV/4%	($13,768)	$ 1,089

By reducing the negative cash flows in the first years of owner-ship and increasing the sales proceeds by $10,000, it is possible to bring this property to a slightly positive net present value of $1,089 when discounted at a minimum 4 percent rate. The second cash flow projection comes close to a minimum breakeven in purchasing power after tax.

Generating a projection for cash flows during ownership of an underperforming property that reflects a slightly positive net present value at a minimum discount rate for loss in purchasing power establishes a basis for evaluating the upside potential of the investment.

The upside potential of a property is a good reason for pursuing ownership. Knowing the minimum cash flows needed to break even after inflation is one benefit of using net present value analysis at the inflation rate. It provides a framework for evaluating the market and the property from a baseline set of cash flows and puts the risk-reward relationship on paper and in a measurable form.

Acquisition of underperforming property has proven to be a consistently successful real estate investment strategy. These real estate bargains are not necessarily the properties with negative rental cash flows. Furthermore, success with this strategy is as much dependent on the trend of the real estate cycle as it is on the specifics of the property itself. Modeling the minimum break-even purchasing power cash flows before you make an acquisition decision can provide a quantified structure for evaluating the work necessary to keep cash flows above the purchasing power baseline.

8

How to Analyze the Financial Performance of Land Investments

Real estate investment starts with land. Putting land to use gives it value and generates income; in fact, quality land development is an active entrepreneurial activity that creates value and generates income by improving the use of land. Land speculation is, on the other hand, a relatively passive investment activity that involves holding land for price appreciation until demand for development and actual use exists.

Demand can originate from use as well as speculation, and both sources can drive up land values with equal force. In speculative markets investor expectations are very important. In user markets the availability of capital and the actual supply-demand relationship for usable land is of greater importance.

Well-timed speculation occurs just ahead of actual use. A speculative purchase during a topping market when actual use and new building turn down misses the market. In both cases price appreciation results from the expectation of use.

Cash flow from land investment in most cases depends on sale proceeds. Except for land that produces income, such as leased land and farms and ranches, land investment is probably the closest to pure price speculation of all forms of real estate. Although commercial and residential land leases are probably more widespread than commonly realized, land remains largely dependent on sale proceeds for cash flow. Land leases are likely to become more widely used as the population grows, putting more pressure on desirable land.

Cash flow from land usually comes only as a lump sum payment when you sell, often accompanied by a stream of income through the following years when a portion of the sale is carried by the seller on a land sales contract.

Typically, investing in land involves ownership for years until population growth permits development or a change in zoning allows income-generating use. Land often passes through several owners before development and use. Speculative demand tends to increase as the time approaches for actual income-generating use. But regardless of the source of the demand (actual use or speculation), it is the increase in price during the ownership period that produces cash flow from resale proceeds.

There are two things that hopefully occur as a result of an investment in land:

1. The acquisition price will at least hold purchasing power. Accomplishing this requires acquisition at the right price (low) and at the right time in the cycle (bottom).

2. The price will increase during ownership more than the rate of inflation. Accomplishing this requires acquisition of land that is likely to increase in price due to employment and population growth.

Although at first glance it may seem that these two points are inherent requirements of all real estate investments, they carry extra weight with land. For instance, it is possible to acquire income property and for the market price to drop yet still make a profit from rental income and equity buildup. Land investment does not usually enjoy the extra margin of error provided by rental income. Land must appreciate to produce cash flow.

Furthermore, unlike income property, when the market for land sales takes a cyclical downturn, there are often no buyers at any price. This is especially true when the market depends on speculative purchases. But this risk source can be reduced by purchasing land that appreciates as a result of natural supply-demand factors and avoiding investments that must be sold to other speculators.

Land that does not produce income depends on cash flow from

sale proceeds to meet the minimum investment objective of transferring purchasing power through time and increasing wealth. Consequently, because of the long-term nature of land investment and the carrying costs involved, a land investment deserves special care when analyzing market cycles and the specific supply-demand characteristics of the property.

Applying Net Present Value to Land Investment

The financial performance of a land investment can be measured using net present value, regardless of the source of the cash flow. Lease income during ownership, proceeds from a sale, and income from owner-financing or any other source can be expressed as cash flow and discounted to a present value. This application of discounting is especially useful when analyzing sales that involve owner financing.

For example, 15 years ago an investor purchased 40 acres for cash at $3,500 per acre for a total investment of $140,000. He sold the parcel for cash to a home builder for $1/ft^2 which was a before-tax price of $1,742,400. Property taxes and other expenses were nominal during the holding period and are ignored for this example. He paid transaction costs and taxes on the sales and received a net cash flow amount as follows.

After-Tax Sale Proceeds

Sales price	$1,742,400
Less sale costs	(150,000)
Before-tax sales proceeds	1,592,400
Less basis	(140,000)
Realized gain	1,452,400
Less approximate tax due	(385,492)
After-tax sales proceeds	$1,066,908

The owner anticipated a 12 percent after-tax return on this land investment. His success in reaching the objective can be determined by calculating the net present value of the investment using the 15-year present value discount factor for 12 percent. A positive net present value at a 12 percent discount rate indicates that the anticipated return was achieved.

Financial Analysis, Land Investment

Size: 40 acres
Purchase price: $3,500/acre: $140,000
Sales price: $43,560/acre: $1,742,400
After-tax sale proceeds: $1,066,908
Discount rate: 12%

Year	Cash flows	Discount factor	Present value
0	($ 140,000)	1	($140,000)
15	$1,066,908	0.18270	$194,924
Net present value			$ 54,924

This analysis indicates that the investment exceeded the anticipated 12 percent compounded rate of return. In fact, paying
$54,924 more for the property would have resulted in precisely a
12 percent return. One of the interesting ways of analyzing net
present value is to think of the amount of NPV as the margin for
forecast error that is built into the purchase price. This is what
buying at the right price means. In the above example the right
price for a 12 percent return is $194,924. The margin of error in
the forecast was built into the acquisition at a lower price allowing
$54,924 to offset risk. In this sense NPV represents an insurance
margin that is negotiated at the time of acquisition, again
illustrating that NPV is much more than some senseless number.

Since the rate of return is greater than 12 percent we can discount the sale proceeds at a higher rate to come closer to the actual return. Using the discount factor for 14 percent produces a
net present value as follows.

Net Present Value at 14%

After-tax sale proceeds	$1,066,908
Discount factor (15 yr, 14%)	× 0.14010
Present value	149,474
Less initial investment	(140,000)
Net present value	$ 9,474

This additional calculation indicates that the rate of return is
greater than 14 percent because the net present value is still positive. This means that paying $149,474 for the property would have
produced exactly a 14 percent return.

To determine the compounded rate of return for this property we can discount the sale proceeds at 15 percent and then interpolate for the internal rate of return.

Net Present Value at 15%

After-tax sale proceeds	$1,066,908
Discount factor (15 yr, 15%)	× 0.12289
Present value	131,112
Less initial investment	(140,000)
Net present value	($ 8,888)

Interpolating for the Internal Rate of Return

$$IRR = 14\% + \frac{9,474}{(9,474 + 8,888)}$$

$$IRR = 14\% + 0.515957$$

$$IRR = 14.52\%$$

Net present value and the internal rate of return can be calculated by business calculators and computers, but there is no substitute for the understanding that results from first going through the analysis process using the discount factor tables. Understanding the meaning of discounting and the basic math formula is all the more important because you will find slight differences in the NPV and IRR answers with different calculators and software due to rounding. These variations are unimportant when you understand the principle involved. As with tax rates, if you want perfection you know how to get it.

Analyzing Land Transactions Involving Owner Financing

Converting a land investment to cash flow often requires the seller to carry a portion of the sales price on a real estate contract or purchase money mortgage. Also, land sales to individual users often involve the necessary incentive of a low down payment and minimum monthly payments on the balance. This financing technique produces a stream of income, which follows the initial down payment.

For example, compare the net present value of the earlier example with the financial result of the owner carrying a portion of the sales price rather than receiving all cash.

In this illustration the owner sells the property for the same price of $1,742,400, with transaction costs of $150,000, a down payment of $350,000, and a real estate contract for $1,392,400 payable at 10 percent interest only for five years at which time the balance is due. This transaction structure results in the following cash flows.

Cash Flow Analysis

Year	Cash flow	PV factor (12%)	Present value
0	($ 140,000)	1	($140,000)
Year 15:			
Down payment	$ 350,000		
Less costs	(150,000)		
Less tax	(60,196)		
Net cash	$ 139,804	0.18270	$ 25,542
Year 16:			
Interest	$ 139,240		
Tax	(45,949)		
Net cash	$ 93,290	0.16312	$ 15,217
Year:			
17	$ 93,290	0.14564	$ 13,587
18	$ 93,290	0.13004	$ 12,131
19	$ 93,290	0.11611	$ 10,832
Year 20:			
Interest	$ 93,290	0.10367	$ 9,671
Principal	$1,392,400		
Less basis	($ 122,447)		
Gain	$1,269,953		
Tax due	($ 419,084)		
Cash received	$1,392,400		
Tax paid	(419,084)		
Net cash	$ 973,316	0.10367	$100,904
		Net present value	$ 47,884

The transaction structured with a land sales contract produces a net present value of $47,884 at the 12 percent discount rate. The alternative of a cash sale when discounted at 12 percent produces a net present value of $54,924.

Cash Sale

Year 15 after-tax cash flow	$1,066,906
12% discount factor	× 0.18270
Present value	194,924
Less investment	(140,000)
Net present value	$ 54,924

Net present value allows the cash sale and the sale with owner-financing to be compared on the equal basis of time value. Not only is the NPV of the cash sale higher, it also eliminates the risk of foreclosure.

Net Present Value Comparison at
12% Discount Rate

NPV of cash sale:	$54,924
NPV with owner financing:	$47,884
Difference	$ 7,040

The cash sale generates an increase in wealth $7,040 greater than the sale with owner-financing under the assumptions used above. This result can change. A higher interest rate could nudge the owner-financed alternative into a higher NPV, illustrating the usefulness of present value analysis during the negotiation stages of a sale.

Cash is the common denominator of all investments. Financial performance must be defined in terms of cash to have consistent meaning. Present value analysis accomplishes this by discounting cash flows to an equal value at the time an investment is made. As a result both debt and equity investments are valued on equal cash terms at the same point in time—the beginning of the investment. For illustration purposes, the above example considers owner-financing as a continuation of the land investment. In actual practice the market values owner-financing as a separate asset and sets its own discount rate.

Secondary markets establish the prices of purchase money mortgages, trust deeds, and real estate contracts based on the present value at the market discount rate. The process of moving from land ownership through paper to cash is a common liquidation sequence. The value of owner-financed paper is determined by discounting the cash flows from these debt instruments to yield the return desired by the purchaser.

Typically, secondary market purchases are made by investors who specialize in debt instrument investments. Consequently, they are able to spread risk over portfolios containing a balance of real property security consisting of homes, commercial property, and land.

In regions such as in many parts of the West, where there is an active market for owner-financed paper, the market value of the paper can be determined and negotiated into the sale terms to match the proceeds of cash sale.

Analyzing Land Use in Terms of Cycles and Time Value

Real estate is typically classified by use. For example, residential real estate includes single-family and multifamily dwelling units. Land for multifamily units typically sells for a higher price per square foot than single-family land because more dwelling units can fit on a multifamily acre than on a single-family acre.

As a result, land zoned for multifamily use produces more income for its size and therefore sells for more. In this case, the use is distinguished only by intensity; that is, both uses are residential, but they differ because more people use a square foot of multifamily land than is used for single-family homes. This increased utility has value. Consequently, the higher density commands a higher land price.

Commercial uses differ from residential uses in kind as well as in intensity. Commercial land use is a broad classification that is conventionally applied to land uses that involve just about everything except residential and farm and ranch uses. The colloquial use of the word *commercial* actually encompasses retail, office, and industrial land uses. In practice, commercial real estate is loosely defined by custom as any type of real estate use other than residential and farm and ranch. Industrial uses have their own classification but are often lumped with commercial property in the sense of real estate involved in commerce. Then, commercial and residential can be further classified as to the intensity of use, which generally refers to the size of the building structure permitted on the land and the number of people expected to make use of the property on a given day.

The density and intensity of use for a specific land site is controlled by the zoning powers of the governing authority of the city or county in which the property is located. Therefore, in addition to the economic factors of supply and demand, land must be evaluated in the context of governmental factors, including the permitted use. Or, it must be viewed with an eye toward accomplishing the risky and sometimes laborious task of obtaining a change in zoning. One successful investment strategy involves locating property that is zoned for a less intensive use, then acquiring and rezoning it to increase its value. This much-used tactic is at the heart of the land development process and the creation of added value through land-use planning.

For the purposes of investment analysis the intensity of use and density of construction on a given land site directly affects financial performance. These two factors limit the cash flow that is possible from a given quantity of land. For example, commercial uses tend to generate more cash flow and therefore command a higher price than residential uses.

Land use illustrates the practical application of the theory of utility, which is fundamental to the time value of money. The more financially productive the use of land, the more cash flow it produces in a specific time period and consequently the higher the price the market will pay.

Clearly, the economic value—the price—of land is determined by its use and the cash flow the use generates. Real estate cycles are fluctuations in activity. When demand drops off for a given use, activity contracts. When demand increases for a given land use, activity expands.

Land use, cash flow, and cycles are interrelated and ultimately show up in land prices. The use relates to the intensity and density that accompanies the different classifications of real estate uses. Land uses produce cash flows that reflect the intensity and density of use. Cycles relate to the expansion and contraction of buying, selling, and leasing activity in response to the need for a given land use.

Superimposed on this economic foundation is the human element that appears in politically motivated tax incentives and disincentives that distort the normal commerce of the real estate market. In addition, the human element appears in the speculative boom-bust patterns that flow from the extremes of investor expectations. The following summary illustrates this interrelationship.

1.   The real estate market is economically based on the intensity of land use and the density of construction permitted, responding to employment and population growth.

Residential: single family; multifamily

Commercial: office; retail; industrial; farm and ranch

2. The financial performance of real estate follows from the use of land and is measured by the amount and timing of cash flows from all sources during the entire ownership period.

Cash Flows: rental income; tax savings; refinance proceeds; sale proceeds

3. Real estate cash flows fluctuate within generally regular time cycles characterized by expansion and contraction of market activity in response to fundamental and governmental factors.

The Long Wave Cycle (about 54 years)

The Business Cycle (about 48 months)

Real Estate Cycles
   Residential (about 7 years)
   Commercial-investment (about 18 years)

Fundamental factors influencing cycles:
   Capital availability (both debt and equity)
   Supply-demand relationship
   Expectations

Governmental factors influencing cycles:
   Tax laws
   Regulations
   Monetary policy

Land use, cash flow, and cycles are at the core of the real estate market. Land is put to use. Use generates cash flow. Market activity fluctuates in cycles. Cycles affect cash flows. Capturing cash flows within cyclical change is the task of real estate investment. Financial analysis measures how well the task is accomplished and provides a mathematical basis for choosing between investments, deciding when to buy and sell, and managing rentals in the attempt to maximize wealth over time.

The Standard Land Speculation Formula

The overriding requirement for land investment is to accurately estimate the time necessary to hold land for the price to increase sufficiently to meet investment objectives. Or, in the alternative, to have plenty of cash reserves to prevent a forced sale at a low point in the cycle.

Risks associated with land investment center on carrying costs and lack of liquidity. Even very experienced land investors and developers occasionally find themselves the proud owners of large plots of dirt at times when they had expected to have cash flow from increasing lot sales.

Although land prices do tend to increase over the very long term, the only certainty is that prices fluctuate. The problems with holding costs for lots surface during the shorter cycles. For example, the housing cycle (7 years peak to peak) and the business cycle tend to dominate price fluctuations in residential land. Larger land parcels and farms and ranches tend to cycle in price with the 18-year investment cycle which is more closely linked with inflation, interest rates, and commodity prices.

There is a time-tested approach to land investment that has evolved through the years. It is based on a strategy that attempts to ensure holding power over the time period necessary for an area to grow sufficiently to warrant development. There are five parts to the standard land speculation formula:

1. Minimum down payment. If possible, structure the down payment as interest for the first year.

2. Pay interest only on the balance. Use a land sales contract with the seller carrying the balance of the purchase price at the lowest interest rate you can possibly negotiate.

3. Delay amortization of the principal balance of the loan as long as possible.

4. Acquire with no personal liability.

5. In the alternative pay all cash for a lower price.

Land investment has special risks because most land acquisitions are not self-supporting. Rarely do they generate sufficient income to support debt service. Consequently, all the help possible from the initial acquisition structure is important. This means putting as little cash in and getting as much cash out as possible in the shortest time possible.

Therefore, a minimum down payment is the first step in maximizing the present value of the future cash flows. This strategy is based on the premise that the less invested, the less pressure for higher future cash flows to meet present value objectives. In other words, the smaller the negative cash flows, the smaller the positive cash flows needed to meet minimum after-tax investment objectives. Or, the lower the price, the lower you can sell and still make a profit.

Since land does not wear out like buildings, it provides one of the more pragmatic real estate vehicles for transferring purchasing power and building wealth through very long time periods. Considering the long-term nature of real estate appreciation, land investment has practical merit for those who do not want to be burdened with the management requirements of improved property ownership.

Analyzing the Financial Performance of a Land Lease

Land leases are likely to gain in popularity with the general growth in population. Leasing land can provide advantages for all parties that are not available through a sale and purchase. For example, the owner is able to generate income for the term of the lease, and the tenant is able to avoid the initial capital outlay required by a purchase. Land that is available for lease only tends to offer benefits of location that allow the owner to require a lease rather than selling.

Financial comparison of a lease and a purchase can be easily made using present value analysis. Although land lease opportunities are often available because the owner doesn't want to sell, the value of comparable land can be determined by reviewing market prices so they can be compared with the present value of the lease payments. This requires that the proposed land lease payments be discounted to a present value for comparison to current market prices.

For example, compare the relative merits of purchasing two acres compared with the alternative of a 30-year lease of two acres. One parcel is available for lease only over a 30-year period at 10 percent of the $5/ft^2$ value. Another parcel is available for purchase at $5/ft^2$. Both parcels are equally suitable locations for the intended use.

The purchase will be made with after-tax dollars; but the lease negotiation occurs based on market rates without consideration of the purchaser's tax situation. Consequently, the tax due on the lease payments should properly be reduced by the amount of the tax that would have been paid on the payment were it not paid toward the lease. This tax benefit is based on the premise that a portion of a deductible lease payment is paid in tax anyway, and therefore should not be considered in the capital cost allocated to the lease.

In effect, funds are being taken from tax payments and combined with investment capital to make the lease payment. Consequently, the alternatives of a purchase or land lease are best analyzed after consideration of the tax consequences.

For analysis purposes the land is forecast to be sold at the end of 30 years at the original purchase price. Since it is sold at basis there are no tax consequences at that time. Property taxes are paid whether the land is purchased or leased and are therefore ignored.

The unknown factor in this analysis is the sale price at the end of 30 years. As with any long-term projection, tax rates are likely to vary with the time and affect the net cost of the lease. These different possibilities can be explored, and the most likely outcome can be chosen.

Size: Two acres (87,120 ft^2)		
Purchase price: $435,600 ($5/ft^2)		
Lease payment	$ 43,560	
Less tax benefit	(14,375)	
Net lease cost	$ 29,185	
Discount rate: 8%		

Year	Purchase PV	Lease PV
0	($435,600)	
30 sale	43,289	
1–30		($328,558)
NPV	($392,311)	($328,558)

Other outcomes of this transaction can be explored with slight changes in the cash flows. One obvious possibility is to assume appreciation of the land to see the effect on net present value of the purchase alternative. Variations in the tax benefit can also be calculated. Each "What if?" produces an effect on NPV.

What if Land Appreciates at 3% Per Year?

Purchase price	$ 435,600
compound factor, 3%, 30 yr	× 2.427262
equals future value	$1,057,315
discount factor, 8%, 30 yr	× 0.099377
Present value	$ 105,073

Effect on the NPV of the Purchase vs. Lease Decision

Year	Purchase PV	Lease PV
0	($435,600)	($328,558)
30	105,073	
NPV	($330,527)	($328,558)

Appreciation of the land brings the NPVs closer together. The question then becomes whether the money for a cash purchase can be put to better use earning a higher rate of return than possible by investing in land. Under the conditions considered above, the lease involves lower cash outlay. But it involves certain liabilities and may be more difficult to liquidate if necessary. There are numerous factors that go beyond financial considerations that may influence the choice to lease or purchase.

The third alternative is to borrow the cash for a purchase and amortize the loan over a 30-year term. This would result in annual payments of $38,693 including interest of 8 percent. This alternative has the advantage of leasing (no large cash outlay) as well as the advantage of ownership at the end of the 30-year loan. The question here is whether a loan is available for land acquisition and if so is it available at an interest rate that is competitive with the terms of a lease. The important point is that each of the alternative acquisition structures can be evaluated and compared on the equal financial basis of present value cash flows.

Investing in Land to Meet Development Demand

The most prudent way to invest in land is to buy within the context of the development process that flows naturally from population growth. Growth pressure pulls dormant land supply into productive use. Without growth there is little economic demand for new usable land. Consequently, unless you intend to sell land to other investors it is important to consider the likely time period it will take for natural growth pressures to draw land into actual use.

Land development is a high risk business. Usually done by well-financed companies, it involves selecting appropriate raw acreage, designing a land-use plan acceptable to the municipal authorities, annexing, and zoning, as well as construction of the streets and water and sewer lines. Land development is essentially a process of packaging land for resale to builders. Because of the high cost involved and extreme risk of dealing with zoning authorities, builders are less willing to be directly involved in developing raw acreage. There is good reason for this.

Land development is largely influenced by a city's political climate and the resulting vision for the future. If a city is against growth or unable to fund the services that municipal expansion depends on, the land development process can come to a standstill. Consequently, a working relationship with the city authorities is essential although not always readily available. Required quality of life improvement costs, paid for by developers and imposed by cities, are passed on to home buyers. These added costs are part of doing business in today's world. And they are one of many reasons why home ownership requires increasingly higher incomes to cover loan payments.

The residential home market is the backbone of the real estate business and to a large extent one of the largest contributors to employment and the economic well-being of the country. New home purchases stimulate durable goods purchases, such as appliances, and provide a true ripple effect in the economy. Consequently, land development for residential housing and the retail and office services that naturally follow form an essential link in the national economy.

Lots for homes are the front line for cost recovery in land development. Developers look to residential lot sales to home builders to return the majority of costs (60 percent to 100 percent) involved in a large land development project. Then, the larger profits are gradually earned by selling commercially zoned tracts as the population of the development grows. Land use is one segment of this interdependent relationship. It reflects the sequence of growth that contributes to solid economically based real estate price appreciation.

- Employment growth leads to . . .
- population growth, which requires . . .
- land development for sale to . . .
- home builders who sell to people with jobs . . .
- who shop and therefore stimulate . . .
- commercial development, producing . . .
- retail centers for goods and . . .
- office development for services.

This relationship involves a time lag that illustrates one of the likely fundamental reasons the housing cycle differs from the real estate investment cycle. Demand for land to build retail centers pushes prices to a profitable sale value two to three years after the surrounding housing is occupied. Land zoned for offices takes somewhat longer, coming on line about five years after the housing is fully occupied. Land zoned for multifamily or apartment development is usually the last to reach its development potential. This is because multifamily land requires an established economic base (services and employment) in the subdivision area before its profitable value is reached.

Zoning regulations illustrate the link between use and value. The old real estate industry cliche that admonished appraisers to value based on the "highest and best use" of land refers to the amount of money that can be generated by an appropriate use of the property. Ultimately, the use of land is subject to the regulatory power of the officials who approve or initiate the zoning use. This governmental factor is an influence on the cash flow generated by a given land parcel and will play a greater role as the trend continues toward increased governmental regulation.

Using Cycles in a Land Investment Strategy

The question is how to cash in on the land development process. One way, if you are wealthy and have the staying power that comes from large cash reserves, is to buy and hold large tracts for 10 to 20 years until growth reaches the site. This long-term holding strategy usually requires large amounts of equity with little dependence on borrowed funds or concern for investment timing. The prerequisite is to purchase in the path of progress, which is the objective of land speculation in general. But there are other land investment strategies that are not as financially demanding.

For example, the seven-year housing cycle can be used in land investment planning. At the beginning of recessions, which follow this cycle with eerie regularity, smaller builders tend to be caught with lots and no buyers for the houses they would like to build. Since tight credit (low availability of capital) is the usual cause of recessions, which end when the Federal Reserve eases, the housing cycle tends to track the business cycle. The housing cycle tends to peak about three years before the trough in the Gross National Product (GNP).

Housing cycle peaks	GNP troughs
1972	1975
1979	1982
1986/87	1991/92

The relationship between new home sales and the health of the economy is tightly bound. High interest costs lead the economy into recession as the Federal Reserve tries to control inflation by raising interest rates. These regular credit crunches catch builders with lot inventory that can often be acquired at distressed prices. For the builder it is a chance to get out of the high interest carrying costs at a time when there are few if any home buyers.

If you have the staying power, buying lots at what amounts to distressed-sale prices and holding them for an eventual economic recovery and profitable resale is one way to step into the development process as an independent investor. This approach to land investment is, of course, a timing strategy. The key is to acquire when there are signs of a recovery from a recession, but before actual housing demand picks up. If you buy too soon, you may get caught with land during a local depression. If you buy too late, the distress may have been reconciled and the price advantage lost.

Because of the carrying costs associated with land it is important to take advantage of buying opportunities when supply drives down prices. Often this means working with banks that have foreclosed on builders. The opportunity to sell occurs during the subsequent recovery when pent-up housing demand and newly available credit drive prices back up.

Another technique to participate in the land development process without a lot of cash is to obtain an option on land that is likely to be developed during the coming recovery. A slump in your economic region is an opportunity to tie up land with an option. Then when the market recovers sell the option to a developer or builder who will carry the project through rezoning and site planning. The risk in such short-term land investments is that the market will not improve sufficiently to create the demand required to sell the option. Consequently, structuring the term of the option with the timing of new demand for land is crucial.

Another technique for taking advantage of the land development process is to buy a small well-located parcel in the general area where large developers are active. This can be especially profitable if you can acquire a tract between larger parcels owned by developers. Land that has the potential for commercial zoning can be overlooked for years even when surrounded by major development activity. All that is necessary is for someone with a different perspective to discover the parcel.

Land investment is among the more risky real estate investments. Engineering and planning costs as well as the costs of building streets and utilities put considerable pressure on the project to start producing cash flow as soon as possible. Generating internal cash flow is the fastest way to offset the interest costs on a development loan and sustain the project while the project is built out.

Occasionally a land developer will go through the land-planning process but be forced to sell certain well-located, commercially zoned parcels to generate the cash flow necessary to finance the balance of the project. Buying at this early stage in the development process takes advantage of the added land value of a growing population that will eventually create demand for retail services and, in turn, demand for commercially zoned land.

There are numerous ways to make money investing in land. Watching the direction of growth and tying up property near the locations of major national chains can put you in a likely location to profit. Inevitably, the larger national chains, whether motels or restaurant, attract feeder businesses and increase the values around their locations.

Land acquisition that is timed with the appropriate real estate and economic cycles places you in an advantageous position to profit from the appreciation that follows employment and population growth. The value of land flows from its use. And with land ownership, as with improved property, financial performance is the combined result of market conditions and the specific characteristics of the property.

Risks to Guard Against in Land Investment

When you plan to hold land for years, the chance is ever-present that adversity will strike at least temporarily during the ownership period. A prolonged nationwide economic contraction can affect even the most recession-proof market areas at least psychologically, triggering a drop in demand for real estate. The regular credit crunches engineered by the Federal Reserve to slow inflation can completely stop housing construction and thus eliminate the need for residential land.

On the supply side of the equation, overbuilding when conditions are favorable can completely saturate the market and overwhelm demand. This is an especially regular phenomenon in office building construction, which cycles with the availability of credit. When an oversupply of building occurs, whether commercial or residential, it takes time for the market to absorb the supply. There is little need for additional land until the absorption process is complete.

The willingness of governing bodies to extend sewer and water to new land development projects is also a risk factor of growing significance during the periods of debt liquidation characteristic of the final stages of the long wave cycle. Cities are as strapped for cash as corporations and individuals. Consequently, cities attempt to shift expenses to developers in the attempt to reduce their own financial drain.

For example, the development approval process through the city or county authority is a prerequisite to land use. In exchange for planning and zoning approval, developers face growing pressure to pay for the extension of services and to donate land for open space.

The trading of zoning approval in the form of development credits toward open space and parks and other quality of life facilities is now an established part of the zoning-development approval process and therefore another cost factor. Although these added land development costs are passed on to the home buyer and the final user of the developed site, they carry an increased risk and debt burden for all involved, including the city.

The burden is for the city to perform on its promise to provide the improved quality of life that attracts an improved employment base. Higher paying jobs are required to qualify for the payments on the more expensive homes that result from the additional services cities and counties attach to land development. The movement within the nation that attempts to impose open space costs on land development carries the implication that people without sufficient incomes to afford the higher priced homes will not be part of the population enjoying the improved quality of life.

Ultimately, attempts to impose land development standards

that leave the choice of appropriate quality standards to city employees who don't have to pay for the cost runs the risk of excluding people from adequate housing because of financial limitations.

Employment opportunity is a prerequisite to population growth. Increased land value follows the increased housing demand of a growing population. Centrally planned quality of life requirements, imposed by municipal authorities, add only one thing with certainty—higher costs and debt burdens for the homeowner. And ultimately, that cost is likely to be as much a detriment to increased jobs as an attraction. Employers must consider the added costs to their employees when relocating facilities to a new city. Cities that promote business and encourage reasonable development without undue expense to the citizens tend to attract jobs more easily.

Techniques for Rural and Mountain Subdivision Analysis

The costs imposed on developers and ultimately homeowners by the city planners result in the final solution of citizens who vote with their feet and live outside the limits of the central planners and the debt burdens they foster. Affordable land outside the city in villages and rural areas offers an opportunity for a simpler approach to land development with its own requirements and risks.

There are certain services that must be provided in a successful rural subdivision. Seven factors work toward financial success— each is taken for granted in a city subdivision, but they must be planned with care in a rural land development.

1. A reliable, affordable water system, whether by individual well or private service.

2. Electric power and phone service.

3. A road system that provides all-weather access.

4. Terrain that offers variety, trees, and if not an actual panoramic view, a feeling of being away from the crowded city.

5. Lots that are generous in size with a maximum of usable land areas.

6. Purchase terms that are flexible enough to get sales activity started.

7. A capital base sufficient to make it through economic downturns and periods of slow or no sales.

There is a formula for pricing residential land that has evolved through the years. The formula produces a ratio useful as a general guideline for acquiring land for subdivisions: acquisition costs of raw land should be limited to between 20 percent and 25 percent of the per acre sales price of finished lots.

For example, land acquisition costs of $1,600 to $2,000 per acre project lot sales at the $8,000 range for the project to be profitable. This represents a factor of four to five times the raw acreage cost.

Per acre acquisition cost	$1,600
	× 5
Finished lot price	$8,000

A similar percentage relationship exists between city lots and the price of the finished house. Builders try to keep their lot costs at 20 percent of the house sale price. Unfortunately, this has become increasingly difficult with generally rising price levels through the years. Consequently, finished subdivision lots where land is in short supply can range from 25 percent to 28 percent and more of the sale price of the finished house.

Acquisition cost	$2,000/acre
Times factor	× 4
Sale price	$8,000/acre

In one small subdivision, 70 acres were acquired for $3,000/acre and placed on the market at $15,000/acre. Actual sales were negotiated at $13,600/acre (4.53 times land cost). Prices of finished lots fluctuated in this subdivision in response to demand.

Consequently, the factor dropped below four or rose above five depending on the strength of demand. Here is the allocation of costs of a subdivision project, which explain why development activity needs to stay within the ratio guidelines.

20 percent to land acquisition costs

20 percent to advertising and promotion

20 percent to lot preparation and development

10 percent to sales commissions and advertising

30 percent to overhead and profit

This distribution is subject to considerable variation. The lot absorption rate dictates the allocation of certain items in the budget. For example, if demand is strong, advertising can be reduced and more can be paid for other budget items. If a land sales project is extremely large, the chance is high that sales activity will endure at least one recession, thus necessitating a large advertising budget. Infrastructure development costs must also contain a considerable margin for variation. Increased road development costs because of rocks in mountain areas illustrate the type of risks that are sometimes hidden in land development projects. Furthermore, the availability of water is a primary concern in certain rural areas and always a prerequisite for housing development.

Certain amenities that are taken for granted as part of city lots are not expected in rural areas. For example, access to natural gas and community sewer are not expected by purchasers of home sites in rural areas. Subdivisions that are able to provide unexpected amenities at minimum expense gain an immediate competitive advantage. Providing more than is expected results in expansion of the market, increasing both the number of potential buyers and the rate of lot sales, assuming prices remain competitive.

Building a Model for the Financial Analysis of Land Sales

Guidelines for subdivision development are intended for use with flexibility to meet the specific configuration of the project. Ultimately, a well-financed land subdivision should be analyzed on the basis of the cash flows it is likely to produce. Cash flows from lot sales define the financial performance of the project, whether in cities to builders or in rural areas to people who want to build their own homes.

As with each segment of the real estate market, land sales are best viewed in terms of cycles. Cash flows anticipated for lot sales should be projected within the context of the regional effects of the long wave cycle and the seven-year residential cycle.

For example, during the contraction phase of the long wave cycle, significant increases in regional unemployment greatly increase risk. Added risks of high unemployment combine with the relatively consistent seven-year residential cycle to form time and risk parameters for bringing new projects on line.

The following analysis assumes a maximum three-year sales period, in an area of homes priced in the $150,000 range. The subdivision consists of 40 acres recently annexed to the city, which will provide water and sewer services. Raw acreage will produce 4.5 lots/acre net after streets and will sell for $30,000 each, finished and ready for building.

Therefore, the project is expected to produce 180 finished lots selling at a minimum of $30,000 each to builders of homes selling in the $150,000 range. It is anticipated that in a strong economy lot prices will be increased. The lots are coming on line during an apparent recovery and upswing in the residential cycle; consequently, the minimum lot price of $30,000 is expected to be exceeded.

A minimum 15 percent internal rate of return is required for the developer to proceed with the project. Consequently, the cash flows in the following projection are discounted at 15 percent to determine if the net present value is positive and if the project should proceed.

Optimistic Scenario

Size: 40 acres; 180 lots
Lot prices/year: $31,000; $33,000; $35,000
Three phases of 60 lots/year

	Year 0	Year 1	Year 2	Year 3
Lot sales	0	1.86	1.98	2.1
Raw land	(1.6)			
Design	(0.2)			
Improvements	(0.4)	(0.42)	(0.45)	
Overhead	(0.1)	(0.1)	(0.1)	(0.1)
Cash flow	(2.3)	1.34	1.43	2.0
Net present value (15%)				$1,261,535
Internal rate of return				43.67%

These projections represent the optimistic scenario, including sufficient demand to raise lot prices, which assumes increasing demand for single-family homes. The following project presents a less optimistic scenario.

Pessimistic Scenario

Size: 40 acres; 180 lots
Lot prices/year: $24,000; $25,000; $25,000
Three phases of 60 lots/year

	Year 0	Year 1	Year 2	Year 3
Lot sales	0	1.44	1.5	1.5
Raw land	(1.6)			
Design	(0.3)			
Improvements	(0.5)	(0.52)	(0.53)	
Overhead	(0.2)	(0.2)	(0.2)	(0.2)
Cash flow	(2.6)	0.72	0.75	1.3
Net present value (15%)				($552,034)
Internal rate of return				2.92%

In the pessimistic scenario, lot sale prices are lower and costs are higher. Lot sales here are based on sales to builders of lower priced homes, which may do better in an economic downturn. Clearly the minimum 15 percent return is not achieved.

The projection is based on the mostly likely middle ground between the optimistic and pessimistic scenarios.

Most Likely Scenario

Size: 40 acres; 180 lots
Lot prices/year: $28,000; $30,000; $32,000
Three phases of 60 lots/year

	Year 0	Year 1	Year 2	Year 3
Lot sales	0	1.68	1.8	1.92
Raw land	(1.6)			
Design	(0.2)			
Improvements	(0.4)	(0.42)	(0.45)	
Overhead	(0.2)	(0.2)	(0.2)	(0.2)
Cash flow	(2.4)	1.06	1.15	1.72
Net present value (15%)				$522,232
Internal rate of return				26.66%

As each of these scenarios illustrates, financial projections do not have to be overly detailed and complex to be useful for decision purposes. It is possible to complete the NPV and IRR analysis using a standard business calculator or spreadsheet software on a personal computer. Furthermore, the model you design can be expanded to the level of detail most useful for you.

The most important point to keep in mind is that the future is unknown and uncertain; to expect exact projections is unrealistic. Projections that express detail of a range of potential scenarios can only provide a starting point for planning and revising strategy as the future unfolds.

A Simple Way to Monitor Land Appreciation

Although uncertainty is the condition of forecasting real estate performance, it can be reduced by using a structure for measuring historical performance. All you need is a few specific dates and prices in the past to establish an appreciation rate. Then the compounding rate can be used to project land values into the future. The procedure uses both discounting and compounding and illustrates the interrelationship between the two.

There is a six-mile-long farming valley outside of a major metropolitan area where farm land is gradually giving way to new home construction. A road runs through the middle of the valley, which is bound on the east by a river and on the west by hills and dry plains. Land between the road and the river is in high demand because of the trees and proximity to the river. It is limited in supply and has experienced steady appreciation through the years. The question is, what has the appreciation rate been between the road and the river along the six-mile valley and what can an owner of the minimum-sized one-acre lots expect in the way of future appreciation?

Price History Based on Actual Sales of One-acre Parcels

Per-acre sales	Rate (%)
1956: $ 1,050	
1971: $ 5,000 / 1956 to 1971 = 15 years	10.96
1975: $ 8,500 / 1971 to 1975 = 4 years	14.19
1981: $28,000 / 1975 to 1981 = 6 years	21.98
1989: $55,000 / 1981 to 1989 = 8 years	8.81
1992: $62,500 / 1989 to 1992 = 3 years	4.35

The rate of land appreciation in this area tracks the progress of the real estate cycle with the highest appreciation rate between the mid-1970s recession and the beginning of the long wave topping process in the early 1980s. As with most markets, prices jump around—they don't move smoothly except in averages. The future of land appreciation in this valley is likely to proceed in similar fashion, responding to surges in demand or a total absence of demand as is typical of cycle activity. Nevertheless, an average appreciation rate can be constructed from this data and used to project future price appreciation.

Since there are four blocks of time with different rates of appreciation in response to the stages of cycle activity, they can be smoothed by using a weighted average appreciation rate which could be applied to the long-term potential. But because the long wave has peaked, it is unlikely that a very high growth rate (21.98%) as occurred from 1975 to 1981 will repeat.

In fact, it is unlikely that the same strong appreciation experienced during the last 30-plus years will be possible, and it is more likely that the most recent rates from 1981 to 1989 of 8.81 percent and 1989 to 1992 of 4.35 percent are more representative of the trend. In fact, the trend of the rate of appreciation reversed after the 1980s peak and is now slowing and might drop more as the upper boundary of the 4:1 ratio of land-to-building costs is hit.

Consequently, a projection of the land values can be made using the appreciation rates with an eye on the housing values implied by the land-to-building ratio. Ultimately, the upper limit of land values will be defined by the ability of buyers to afford higher priced homes implied by the increased land value. The projections represent a conservative projection based on the current phase of the real estate cycle and recent increases in values.

Land Value Projection at 5% Appreciation Rates, 4:1 Ratio

Year	1992	1997	2002	2007
Land value	$ 55,000	$ 70,000	$ 89,300	$114,000
House value	$220,000	$280,000	$357,200	$456,000

This illustration is a rough guideline for monitoring land values in relation to home values in combination with appreciation rates. There are other factors of equal importance to the trend of land prices. For example, per-acre costs tend to decrease with larger tracts. Higher prices tend to encourage new supply to come on the market, holding demand in check and keeping prices within reason. And ultimately, home prices will only rise to the extent that buyers' income levels are high enough to permit affordability. Usually this final consideration hinges on the quality of jobs in the area and the number of highly paid executives who are able to afford higher priced housing, implied by increasing land values.

9

Financial Analysis of Office Buildings and Leases

The financial value of real estate ultimately results from its use. Land is leased, or improved with buildings that are in turn leased or owned by the occupants. The purpose of the tenant, whether renter or owner, is to use the property. Use is the source of financial value.

When property can't be used in the way the market wants, its value diminishes and in some cases is nonexistent. Restrictive zoning and natural preservation ordinances represent conditions which limit or prevent market uses and thus eliminate the property from the market. When property cannot be used it rarely retains any financial value at all for investment purposes.

Market value is really the price of property. It is the natural outcome of market activity. It is the end result of the interaction of the availability of capital attempting to balance the supply-demand relationship, based on expectations of use and increased financial value. Restrictive-use ordinances illustrate the growing influence of governmental factors on real estate values. Tax laws, regulatory requirements, and monetary policy are at the core of the growing body of governmental influences on market value.

205

Distinguishing Between Market Value and Financial Value

Financial value differs from market value primarily because of the influence of time. Financial value goes beyond market value to encompass the time value of money. Investing in real estate is an attempt to increase financial value by taking advantage of changes in market value, or prices, during the time the investment is owned. Financial analysis measures how well a specific property is able to benefit from changes in market value during a given time period. Consequently, financial value reflects the influences of the market activity on prices as well as the influence of time on money.

Market value can be isolated by appraisal and by comparison with rental rates and prices paid for similar properties in the recent past. But financial value must be determined in relation to the amount and the timing of the cash flows generated by a given property or lease.

Financial value can actually stand on its own out of the context of the market, provided the use of the property has a benefit for the tenant or owner that can be specified as cash flow. Therefore, financial value can be measured based solely on time and cash flows. This can be done without market comparables to evaluate the investment performance of a property.

One of the best illustrations of the difference between financial value and market value occurred in a small government research town. There was no growth to speak of and few real estate transactions other than an occasional home sale. The government owned all the office buildings with the exception of one, which it leased.

The particular government agency that leased this older building needed a larger facility. Their plan was to buy the building, remodel, and expand. This location was essential because of the proximity to related research facilities.

There were no comparable sales in town to determine land or building value. Essentially, there was no real estate market in this town. And the office building was of no use except to the government and only to the agency currently using it.

Nevertheless, the building had considerable financial value for the investor who owned it. He had received substantial cash flow over the past 20 years and was looking forward to continuing income for the balance of his life. He was 60 years old when the government approached him to sell the property. He was willing to sell only if he received financial value comparable to the income he currently realized each year. But since there was no real estate market in this town, how could the value of the property be determined? It had no market value, because there was no market. But the property definitely had financial value for the owner and a specific usage value for the government.

At the time he was approached to sell, the owner was receiving about $8.57 per ft² in rent on a triple net lease for the approximately 35,000 ft² building. He had grown accustomed to this level of income and wasn't particularly interested in selling. And he was very clearly aware of the financial value of this building and was unmoved by the government's arguments that it was too old and too small for their needs and had no market value.

For the owner, this office building had a specific financial value, which he calculated based on the income he anticipated receiving over the balance of his planned ownership during the next 25 years. Based on this premise he made the following assumptions.

1. The financial value of the building to him was the $25,000 in rent he received each month.

2. If he sold today he would have to be assured of receiving the same income.

3. The money he received from the sale could be invested in government bonds and notes and other diversified investments to yield a minimum of 7 percent rate of return during the next 25 years.

4. Consequently, he could sell for the equivalent of $25,000 per month paid for 300 months discounted at 7 percent.

5. At the end of 25 years he assumed that the building would have no value (as the government assumed was the case now), but the land would be worth one year's rent of $300,000.

The question of taxes presented a special problem. He had written off the building and received no tax benefit under the current lease. But when he sold, the capital gains tax would diminish the investment capital available necessary to ensure his same level of income, and he would still be faced with tax on the income from the new investments.

Although the government argued that the land had no market value, he countered that the fact that they wanted to buy it to build on the land today disproved that contention. Consequently, he calculated the financial value of the building for his investment purposes as follows:

Before-Tax Financial Value

Present value of $25,000/month discounted at 7%	$3,537,172
Present value of $300,000 received at the end of 25 years discounted at 7%	$ 55,275
Financial value	$3,592,447
Less adjusted basis	26,500
Realized gain	3,565,947
Tax rate	× 28%
Less tax payable	$ 998,465
After-tax proceeds	$2,567,482

The after-tax proceeds of $2,567,482 represented an income of $220,312 for 25 years provided it could earn a minimum of 7 percent per year. Because of the capital gains tax on this sale, the owner was faced with about a $70,000 a year reduction in income. The solution, of course, was to increase the price above the nominal financial value by an amount sufficient to pay the capital gains tax and leave approximately $3,500,000 after tax, which could be invested to provide $300,000 per year for 25 years. This amount was $4,900,000, and the only price at which he would sell.

The value of this property resulted from the use. There was only one possible user. There was no real estate market to establish value using conventional comparison methods. But the financial value was easy to establish using the cash flows. In fact, the owner could care less about market value. His only interest was the financial value of the property which was the discounted value of the future cash flows. The income from the use of the property was the value of the property.

Although this example is somewhat unique it illustrates what happens on a more complex basis with every office building. Simply put, the discounted cash flows generated by the building determine the financial value of the property. Given this premise the task is to choose the appropriate discount rate and project the amount and timing of the cash flows.

The procedure can be done regardless of the number of leases involved or the size of the property. Financial value is the measure of how an investment meets the objective of transferring purchasing power through time while building wealth. It is the only meaningful way to measure the value of an investment. Although financial value changes with the influences of market forces, it can be determined outside of the context of the real estate market, based solely on the time value of the cash flows of the property.

How Competition Influences Rent and Building Value

During periods of oversupply, tenants have the upper hand in lease negotiations. Conversely, as supply is absorbed, building owners are more likely to have an advantage. The give and take during lease negotiations reflects the interrelationship between the office market cycle and the characteristics of individual properties.

Lack of business activity typical of a contraction in economic activity shows in the office market as lack of demand for office space. High activity typical of the expansion phase of the economy shows as increased demand for office space. This expansion-contraction cycle in business activity generates and then eliminates the need for the office support service provided by real estate. As the population and related businesses grow, demand for offices increases. As a result, rental rates rise and new supply is created, usually overshooting the immediate demand.

Rents are the referee in the supply-demand balance contest. When demand increases to the point that supply is greatly reduced, rent increases slow demand until new supply is available. In this way high rents check demand. Then in turn, competition from new supply holds rents in check. As supply increases, rental rates and lease terms soften. Rents react to competing supply whether due to economic contraction and vacancy, or new construction, or both. If the trend toward excessive supply continues while businesses cut back during a contraction, prices drop to attract tenants.

The way to take advantage of this natural supply-demand balancing process from a building owner's perspective is to negotiate leases that expire when demand for space is greatest. And for tenants, the ideal is to have a lease expire when market conditions are soft. Of course, this is easier said than done, but owners who know the cycle use the technique.

Office buildings are like individual businesses. Each is a profit center and each competes with others for tenants by trying to offer better services at better rates. In a local economy that is stagnant, low rents in buildings with high vacancy attract tenants whose leases are expiring and encourage them to move. Given roughly comparable office conditions, the competition of a well-managed building with lower rental rates is often ample incentive for tenants to move. This equalization process during periods of oversupply spreads the existing tenants among the available buildings, allowing more of them to survive until the oversupply is absorbed.

The speed with which a market absorbs new supply best reflects the relationship between business expansion, the demand that results, and the supply on the market. Each year a certain amount of new supply comes on the market and a certain amount of supply is absorbed by the market. For example, a market area may have a total of ten million ft² of office space with an 8 percent vacancy rate, approximating 800,000 ft². The absorption rate may be running about 400,000 ft² a year, and another 600,000 ft² in new construction may be in planning and various stages of construction. Of the existing vacancy, half may be older Class C space; 25 percent may be Class B space, and the balance may be newer Class A space at the higher end of the rental range. The class of a building depends on the location, age, and quality of construction. As buildings age, they change from Class A to Class B, and, depending on the demand for the location, to Class C. This long-term process of change toward economic obsolescence can be slowed through remodeling.

New Class A space tends to attract the larger professional firms that are trying to maintain a prestigious image of being the top professionals in their field. The largest law firms seem to think it important to maintain offices on the top floor of the newest Class A buildings, signing 10- to 15-year leases with 5-year options. Expansion by legal firms often marks the top of the office building cycle in local markets.

Local office market cycles provide a limited time frame for attracting tenants to a building. For example, tenants are only in the market for new space when their existing leases are up for renewal. Expansion needs are usually first filled in the current building, if space is available, or can be made available by moving smaller tenants around.

Strong markets don't feel the financial strain that is apparent in overbuilt areas where new buildings must begin to generate cash flow as quickly as possible. New buildings need cash flow, which puts competitive pressure on existing buildings, including the ones that are full who must fight to retain their tenants. As new buildings begin the rent-up phase, offers of incentives to attract tenants become common. Free rent, generous tenant improvement allowances, free parking, moving cost allowances, lease buyouts, and private restaurant memberships are lures offered in lease incentive packages of well-financed buildings.

In markets where high supply is competing with low demand, the incentive package can be crucial to filling the building with the limited number of available tenants. In slow markets the attractiveness of the lease incentives and the aggressiveness with which a new building is introduced to the market can be essential to the success of the leasing efforts.

For example, owners are understandably reluctant to give away what seems like an overly generous lease incentive package during the early marketing efforts. But buildings that are trying to market space during recessions don't enjoy the luxury of filling up on their own schedule. They can only fill up on the tenants' schedule. And if there is not a general expansion of business activity bringing new jobs to the area, this means taking tenants from other buildings by giving them a better deal.

Unfortunately, lack of aggressive competitiveness is common with the committee-dominated corporate environment. Insulation from the local market areas about which they are making armchair decisions seems to inhibit timely competitive action. Weak competitive posture is a common result of out-of-town corporate management. In some cases it takes time to realize that owning an office building is not a passive investment.

Reluctance to implement competitive rents is understandable when a property has recently been acquired based on rent projections used to justify the purchase price. Lowering rents acknowledges that not only were the rent projections off, the company paid too much for the property. Lower rental rates devalue the building. It's like selling a stock that is trending down. If you don't sell you don't take a loss. In both cases the value is determined by the market, whether the rents are lowered or the stock is sold. The question is, do you lower the rent and fill the building or wait for the market to come back? Do you sell the stock and reinvest the proceeds or hold on and hope it trends up once again?

But there is a competitive alternative that accepts the current market, good or bad, and builds value into the lease as the ownership period progresses. This approach is based on the reasoning that a building with high vacancy today is worth less than a building that is full but has lower rental rates.

This competitive strategy encourages tenants to lease at lower rental rates during the first few years of the lease. As the term of the lease progresses, the rental rate gradually steps up to the objective of the owners, justifying a higher value for the building at the end of the lease term. This strategy involves a one-year intensive marketing effort to fill the building at very competitive rates. The first two years of the lease are at rates too attractive for prospective tenants too ignore. Then during the third, fourth, and fifth years, lease rates are increased to meet the established rental objective and support the building value.

Standard Techniques for Evaluating Office Leases

An office building is as valuable as the income it produces. Consequently, the leases and potential for leases under existing market conditions ultimately determine the worth of the structure. Every lease contributes to value. Often leases are hard-won rewards of a competitive marketing effort. They should never be taken for granted or assumed to be the entitlement of ownership. There are always competitors waiting who may value your tenants more than you do and be willing to offer the leasing incentives to prove it.

Consequently, the methods used to evaluate rental terms become crucial to the decision-making process during lease negotiations. Traditional methods that use average rental rates over the term of the lease to produce an "effective rate" have long been the accepted practice of comparing individual lease proposals.

Recently, the more financially aware building owners have augmented this standard guideline with net present value. Introduction of NPV to office lease evaluation recognizes the significance of the time value of money as a component of the leasing decision process. Nevertheless, as with other ingrained traditional analysis methods, the old structure is still in use and is therefore of importance in certain markets. Unfortunately, decisions based on this approach alone have no financial context. They are at best passive responses to market forces that compare competitors rather than measure the intrinsic financial value of a specific building or lease. That is, without time value the lease rates can only stand in relation to other lease rates in the market. And of what use to financial management is that information alone?

If nothing else the older methods provide a summary of market information and a context for moving from the paper format and averaging tradition to the computer and net present value analysis criteria.

In the following analysis the building owner based acceptance of lease offers on the rental rate at the end of the lease term. The marketing strategy was to fill the building, recently acquired out of foreclosure, as fast as possible. The leasing agent was given great latitude, provided a certain rental rate was in place during the last two years of the lease. Higher rent at the end of the rent-up phase of the lease term was essential because the plan was to price and sell the building based on the higher value reflected in the higher rental rate.

Prior owners had ignored this building and viewed it as a portion of a large portfolio. It was used as a negotiation chip in an attempt to work out of a larger loan problem. Consequently, the building had remained practically empty and without financial or management backing for several years. By the time the current owners entered the picture, this attractive office complex was the epitome of the real estate turnaround opportunity.

Some of the best real estate acquisitions result from management neglect. Often the signs are obvious. In this case the owners lived out of town in one city and the "hands-on" manager lived out of town in a different city. Furthermore, the actual decision maker was insulated by three layers of corporate management.

Every leasing agent in the city was aware of the botched management of the prior out-of-town ownership. They had refused to negotiate competitively or provide the leasing support necessary to fill the building even under the relatively favorable market conditions that had existed for several years.

Although it was a puzzle to many who had not attempted to negotiate leases with the prior owners as to why such a well-designed and efficient building was so long vacant, it was no mystery to the agents who had worked on it. As part of a corporate real estate empire, this relatively small building was insignificant to the larger problems. Or, so it seemed to the management in control. Had such numerous and seemingly insignificant problems been addressed with businesslike professional attention, it is possible that the combined total of "insignificant" problems would not have resulted in gradual foreclosure of this real estate empire, portfolio by portfolio.

In this case, one company's growing disaster again proved to be another's opportunity as the free market made the ultimate management decision. Location, a good design, and reasonable market conditions are not enough to ensure financial success of an office building. Ownership must work with management and leasing agents to make the competitive decisions necessary to thrive and in some cases survive in the cyclical office market.

When the new owners took over, new leases were negotiated at $12/ft^2$ for the first year in contrast to the lease rates of $16/ft^2$ asked but not received by the prior owners. But more importantly, local management was put in place, and the word got out fast to independent leasing agents that deals could be made and relatively high commissions could be earned.

Furthermore, a renovation plan was established, and the remodeling and updating of the lobby was started. Clearly, things had changed. New life was being breathed into a shell, and the dynamics of the local office leasing market focused on this building. Within nine months it was fully occupied. There are two obvious reasons: competitive lease incentives for tenants and responsive market-aware decisions by the owners.

The pension fund that acquired this building used a very simple, well-organized method of analyzing each lease proposal. The financial terms of the lease were summarized on a single page, which correlated with the lease. This management presentation is a traditional analysis format that served the needs of the owners for basic information. It follows, with some minor modification.

Lease Summary

Tenant: Grant, Fritz, and Grow, P.A.
Business: Law Firm
Net leasable area: 16,500 ft^2
Term: 5 years

Rent provisions:
Rent/ft^2/yr: $12; $13; $13; $14; $15
Ave. rent/ft^2: $13.40
Rent/month: Year 1 $16,500; Year 2 $17,875; Year 3 $17,875;
   Year 4 $19,250; Year 5 $20,625
Rent/year: Year 1 $198,000; Year 2 $214,500; Year 3 $214,500;
   Year 4 $231,000; Year 5 $247,500

Lease incentives:
Free rent: None
Tenant improvement allowance: $15.64/ft; $258,000 total
Moving allowance: $2.00/ft^2; $33,000 total
Buyout: None

Escalation provisions:
Expense stop: $6.00/ft^2
Passthroughs: None
CPI escalation: None
Security deposit: $16,500

Cash flow analysis:

Total of lease income	$1,105,500
Other income	0
less free rent	0
less tenant improvements	(258,000)
less moving allowance	(33,000)
less commissions	(70,310)
Net lease income	$ 744,190

Effective lease rate	$9.02 ft^2/yr
less operating expenses	5.85 ft^2/yr
Net operating income	$3.17 ft^2/yr

In this example the effective lease rate is calculated by dividing the net lease income by the square footage of the lease, which is in turn divided by the number of years in the lease term.

$$(1) \quad \frac{\$744,190}{16,500} = 45.10 \qquad (2) \quad \frac{45.10}{5} = \$9.02$$

This standard summary form for lease provisions served the needs of the company for projecting income over the term of the leases and comparing the various leases in the building. This approach to analyzing a lease is very limited financially. For example, the capital improvements are not treated as an investment which produces a return. They are instead subtracted from the lease income. These initial negative cash flows represent an investment and prerequisite for the positive cash flows from rent to follow. They are improvements which will contribute to rental cash flow and ultimately to the potential sale proceeds when the building is sold.

The key point here is that average lease rates do not provide information related to the financial value of the lease. They only provide comparative market data. Consequently, using an average lease rate as a basis for comparing various leases tells you nothing about their relative financial value. This makes it almost impossible to compare complex incentive packages on an equal basis.

Lease Income Averages

Lease income	$1,105,500
Lease incentives	(361,310)
Gross income	744,190
Operating expenses	(482,625)
Net Rental income	$ 261,565
Average/ft^2/yr	3.17

The criteria used by this company was very simple: If a lease proposal averaged $3.00/ft^2 or more per year after incentives and expenses, they would accept it. The obvious gap in this reasoning is that there is no consideration of the return on investment relationship between the funds invested to establish the lease and the income it generates. That is, there is no measure of the time value of the cash flows and therefore no measure of the financial value of the lease.

Relying on market averages provides comparative market-related information, but no financial information. Not only are the owners operating a business in a financial vacuum, but they are also missing a competitive opportunity to attract tenants by offering better financial value.

Office leasing is a very competitive area of real estate with a range of seemingly incomparable incentives designed to attract tenants. Discounting the cash flows of a lease can serve as both a financial decision-making tool for the owner and with a slight variation as marketing information to attract tenants.

It is a question of value:

1. What financial value does the lease have for the building owner?

2. What financial value does the lease have for the building tenant?

3. What competitive advantage in financial value does the lease offer when compared to other leases available in this market area?

These three questions cannot be answered with market averages. These are financial questions that can only be answered in terms of cash flows and time value.

Financial value for a building owner is a function of the money invested in relation to the money generated as a result of the investment. Lease incentives amount to an investment that is required in order to compete with other buildings for a limited number of tenants. Incentives are part of a strategy designed to balance the financial value and service provided to the tenant with the financial value received by the building owner.

Evaluating a Lease Using Net Present Value

The pension fund that owned this building had recently employed a new financial vice president who was in the process of evaluating all of the leases on the buildings in the real estate portfolio. This was one of the first new leases that came across his desk for financial review. As a matter of routine, he plugged the numbers into his personal computer spreadsheet and developed a financial analysis for the cash flows over the entire lease term.

Rather than lumping the annual performance of the lease into an average square foot rate over the entire term, he took all the cash flows when they occurred and entered them in his spreadsheet model month by month. His reasoning was that each lease contains somewhat unique terms based on the dynamics of the market at the time the lease was negotiated. The cost of capital and the inflation rate were in the usual state of flux, adding additional uncertainty to the portfolio value over the balance of some of the older leases.

Furthermore, he had approval authority for all new leases and planned to implement a negotiation system to outbid competing building lease deals by selling space based on a principle of providing more financial value to the tenant. Recognizing that he was in the service business he decided that one of the services he would provide would be better financial value.

Consequently, he implemented a model for purposes of comparing all new leases based on the financial criteria of present value analysis. This allowed him to compare the capital investment required to attract each tenant with the lease income generated. In a sense he could then weigh both sides of the ledger in the context of time value and determine the financial value for the company as well as the tenant.

Since the mix of financial information for this analysis originated in the field, he also decided to train all of the resident leasing agents to use the model when negotiating a lease. This was a competitive management decision on his part to outsell other buildings by showing tenants the higher value the pension fund's buildings could offer.

He established a minimum discount rate as part of an objective financial criterion to eliminate the haggling that slowed down the signing of leases. This had been a problem in the past because there was no objective financial criteria for accepting an offer.

Consequently, the committee that reviewed prospective lease terms would often reject a key element, which was of no financial consequence to the company but of significant importance to the prospective tenant. Since they were operating on market averages instead of financial criteria, they never realized what they were doing. In fact, they had killed deals over lease provisions that made little if any difference in their financial net.

The following lease analysis structure was designed to change the manner in which lease deals were evaluated by the company. Emphasis was placed on the bottom line return generated by the terms negotiated in each lease. Each provision of a lease was evaluated objectively based on the contribution it made to financial performance rather than being arbitrarily rejected or included without acknowledging the financial impact.

The evaluation model presented the financial detail of a lease using the discount rate criterion that met an acceptable rate of return minimum for the company.

Lease Analysis

Building 031
Tenant 03129
Net leasable area: 16,500 ft^2
Rent/ft^2/year: 12/13/13/14/15
Operating expenses/ft^2/year: 5.85/6/6/6/6
Discount rate: 15%

Investment:	
TI's	$258,000
Moving	33,000
Commission	70,310
Total	$361,310

Operating Cash Flows:

	Year 1	Year 2	Year 3	Year 4	Year 5
Monthly lease income:	$16,500	$17,875	$17,875	$19,250	$20,625
Less monthly expenses:	(8,044)	(8,250)	(8,250)	(8,250)	(8,250)
Net monthly cash flow:	$ 8,456	$ 9,625	$ 9,625	$11,000	$12,375
	$ 8,456	$ 9,625	$ 9,625	$11,000	$12,375
	$ 8,456	$ 9,625	$ 9,625	$11,000	$12,375
	$ 8,456	$ 9,625	$ 9,625	$11,000	$12,375
	$ 8,456	$ 9,625	$ 9,625	$11,000	$12,375
	$ 8,456	$ 9,625	$ 9,625	$11,000	$12,375
	$ 8,456	$ 9,625	$ 9,625	$11,000	$12,375
	$ 8,456	$ 9,625	$ 9,625	$11,000	$12,375
	$ 8,456	$ 9,625	$ 9,625	$11,000	$12,375
	$ 8,456	$ 9,625	$ 9,625	$11,000	$12,375
	$ 8,456	$ 9,625	$ 9,625	$11,000	$12,375
	$ 8,456	$ 9,625	$ 9,625	$11,000	$12,375

Total	$612,972
Present value at (15%)	$428,473
Investment	(361,310)
NPV at 15%	$ 67,163

Presenting the actual cash flows of the lease so the total performance per month can be reviewed allowed the building owners to compare several leases with varying rent and time characteristics on an equal basis. The above analysis indicates that the owners could invest an additional $67,163 to meet the needs of the tenant and still meet the 15 percent rate of return criteria. Knowing this type of financial information gave them an advantage over the competition.

By establishing a financially based decision criterion, the company gained an increased flexibility in the negotiation of leases. The reason, of course, was that the focus of decision making moved from often irrelevant market detail to significant financial concerns. The amount each lease contributed to the financial performance of the building became more important than haggling over an increase of 50 cents/ft^2 in the lease rate halfway through the lease term. The decision makers were able to choose lease structures based on measurable financial criteria and avoid the past practice of killing financially meaningful deals over financially insignificant issues.

For example, one of the officers of the fund had argued against accepting lease deals that were less than $12 per ft^2 the first year of the term. He was adamant about this and unconcerned with much of the related factors such as the amount of tenant improvement allowance and other incentives. But his view changed when he saw the insignificant financial effect of varying the rents and understood that it could be an important consideration for some tenants.

The following lease proposal put his concerns in financial perspective. Note that a discount rate applied to monthly cash flows is divided by 12 months to reflect the appropriate rate when calculating NPV on a spreadsheet (i.e, 15%/12 = 1.25%).

Lease Analysis

Building 031			Investment:		
Tenant 03125			TIs		$247,500
Net leasable area: 16,500 ft^2			Moving		33,000
Rent/ft^2/year: 10/11.5/14/14.5/15			Commission		70,000
Discount rate: 15%			Total		$350,500

Operating Cash Flows:					
	Year 1	Year 2	Year 3	Year 4	Year 5
Monthly income	$13,750	$15,813	$19,250	$19,938	$20,625
Less monthly expenses	(8,044)	(8,250)	(8,250)	(8,250)	(8,250)
Net monthly cash flow	$ 5,706	$ 7,563	$11,000	$11,688	$12,375
	$ 5,706	$ 7,563	$11,000	$11,688	$12,375
	$ 5,706	$ 7,563	$11,000	$11,688	$12,375
	$ 5,706	$ 7,563	$11,000	$11,688	$12,375
	$ 5,706	$ 7,563	$11,000	$11,688	$12,375
	$ 5,706	$ 7,563	$11,000	$11,688	$12,375
	$ 5,706	$ 7,563	$11,000	$11,688	$12,375
	$ 5,706	$ 7,563	$11,000	$11,688	$12,375
	$ 5,706	$ 7,563	$11,000	$11,688	$12,375
	$ 5,706	$ 7,563	$11,000	$11,688	$12,375
	$ 5,706	$ 7,563	$11,000	$11,688	$12,375
	$ 5,706	$ 7,563	$11,000	$11,688	$12,375

Total income	$579,984
Present value at 15%	$404,496
Investment	(350,500)
NPV at 15%	$ 53,996

The important financial goal was for each lease to meet the minimum 15 percent rate of return criterion. This financial outcome determines whether a lease is profitable, not the market rate in the first year alone. Financial performance is a function of the relationship between the investment in the lease and the total present value of the income from the lease. This relationship is not reflected in market rates alone. Therefore, market rates can't be used by themselves to make financial decisions, especially when many financially aware tenants are comparing offers by competing office buildings on a present value basis to make their selection.

How a Tenant Can Analyze a Lease Using NPV

Tenants look at a lease proposal with the purpose of comparing alternative offers and choosing the best deal among often complex and seemingly incomparable lease incentives. The challenge here is to compare the financial benefit of two or more lease proposals with varying incentives on an equal basis. Typically, any two leases will have different rents, varying periods of free rent if any, different moving allowances, and other provisions, which must be compared financially in order for a tenant to make a well-informed financial choice.

Building owners have essentially the same challenge, but with a different purpose. They must analyze the lease incentive package they offer to prospective tenants within the context of both the building's financial performance and the competitive advantage they want to have in the marketplace. Of course, this is a balancing process designed to maintain a competitive operation while maximizing rental income. In slow markets this can result in a decision to live with a high vacancy rather than meet the competitive requirements of what is hoped to be a short-lived slump in the market. It can also result in the decision to become highly competitive, fill the building, and look toward raising rents as leases expire. In either case the decision is best based on a comparison of how the building's lease competes with other buildings trying to attract the same tenant.

Consequently, the tenant and the building are faced with several interrelated market factors, all of which are best resolved with financial analysis based on net present value. The building can compare the costs of the competitive lease incentives it must offer to the present value of the lease income. The tenant can also compare the lease rate and related additional costs such as rent escalation, operating cost pass-throughs, building load factors, parking costs, and other building specific costs on a present value basis. In this manner tenants can determine which lease is the best financial value.

For both the tenant and the building, the process is one of comparing the intrinsic financial value of the cash flows. The building determines whether the intrinsic financial value of the lease meets minimum investment criteria established by the chosen discount rate. The tenant determines whether the intrinsic financial value of one lease is greater than the intrinsic financial value of other lease proposals.

For the building owner, determining financial value is a process of discounting projected lease income to the present value and netting that present value amount against the investment made in the form of lease incentives. A higher net present value has greater financial value for the building.

For the tenant, determining financial value is a process of discounting the lease payments and adding other payments related to the lease such as improvement costs and parking. Since there is no income flowing to the tenant that must be "netted," the analysis is technically limited to present value of the rental payments and other costs. An exception to this, of course, is when the tenant subleases a portion of the space. Since tenants deal almost exclusively with negative cash flows, a lower present value has greater financial value for the tenant.

To begin the process of comparing leases, let's look at the relative financial value of the two leases in the prior example. But this time let's look only at the cash flows in terms of the rental rate on a square footage basis before expenses. This is a comparison of money paid by the tenant as rent only, which represents negative cash flows.

Tenant: 03129
16,500 ft^2
Rental rate: 12,13,13,14,15/ft^2/year/12
Monthly discount rate: 15%/12

$16,500	$17,875	$17,875	$19,250	$20,625
$16,500	$17,875	$17,875	$19,250	$20,625
$16,500	$17,875	$17,875	$19,250	$20,625

$16,500	$17,875	$17,875	$19,250	$20,625
$16,500	$17,875	$17,875	$19,250	$20,625
$16,500	$17,875	$17,875	$19,250	$20,625
$16,500	$17,875	$17,875	$19,250	$20,625
$16,500	$17,875	$17,875	$19,250	$20,625
$16,500	$17,875	$17,875	$19,250	$20,625
$16,500	$17,875	$17,875	$19,250	$20,625
$16,500	$17,875	$17,875	$19,250	$20,625
$16,500	$17,875	$17,875	$19,250	$20,625

Present value: $773,483
Present value/ft^2/yr: $9.38
Total lease value: $1,105,500
Lease value/ft^2/yr: $13.40

Tenant: 03125
Size: 16,500 ft^2
Rental Rate: 10,11.5,14,14.5,15

$13,750	$15,813	$19,250	$19,938	$20,625
$13,750	$15,813	$19,250	$19,938	$20,625
$13,750	$15,813	$19,250	$19,938	$20,625
$13,750	$15,813	$19,250	$19,938	$20,625
$13,750	$15,813	$19,250	$19,938	$20,625
$13,750	$15,813	$19,250	$19,938	$20,625
$13,750	$15,813	$19,250	$19,938	$20,625
$13,750	$15,813	$19,250	$19,938	$20,625
$13,750	$15,813	$19,250	$19,938	$20,625
$13,750	$15,813	$19,250	$19,938	$20,625
$13,750	$15,813	$19,250	$19,938	$20,625
$13,750	$15,813	$19,250	$19,938	$20,625

Present value: $749,507
Present value/ft^2/yr: $9.09
Total lease value: $1,072,500
Lease value/ft^2/yr: $13

Comparison summary	03129	03125	Difference
Present value:	$ 773,483	$ 749,507	$23,976
Present value/ft^2/yr:	9.38	9.09	0.29
Total lease value:	$1,105,500	$1,072,500	$33,000
Lease value/ft^2/yr:	$13.40	$13.00	0.40

These two leases are in the same building and compare closely to each other. But competing buildings strive to quote rental rates that are within market ranges while offering incentives that are difficult to compare financially.

For example, in the following case a prospective tenant is presented with two proposals for a three-year lease with a two-year option to renew. Both locations are suitable for the company and offer the same general amenities. The significant differences between them are the expense stops and the tenant improvement allowances.

Summary of Lease Proposals

	$/ft^2	
	Proposal A	Proposal B
Rental rate		
Year 1	$20	$19
Year 2	21	21
Year 3	21	22
Expense stop	5	6
Tenant improvements	15	19

Traditional methods of comparing leases based on the nominal amount of rent per square foot averaged over the term of the lease do not consider the time value of money and consequently do not permit comparison of variations in the timing of rental payments and expenses. Furthermore, simply looking at the amount of the expense stop and the allowance for tenant improvements is not informative unless they are evaluated within the context of the financial effect on the tenant. In this simplified example, a $5 expense stop in a building that has operating expenses of $5.75/ft^2 means an additional $.75/ft^2 in negative cash flow for the tenant. Also, a tenant improvement allowance of $15/ft^2 that is short of actual costs necessary to meet the design specifications of the tenant will result in negative cash flow during the first year or possibly over the term of the lease, if the overage is amortized.

Consequently, in order to be financially meaningful, the two lease proposals must be stated in terms of actual cash flows rather than marketing proposals.

Cash Flow Analysis

Assumptions:
 Projected tenant improvement costs $24/ft^2
 Projected expenses $6/ft^2

	Proposal A	Proposal B
Expense stop	$5	$6
Projected expenses	(6)	(6)
Net expense	($1)	0

If expenses hold at $6/ft^2 Proposal A will cost $1/ft^2 more than Proposal B as a result. This effectively raises the rental rate of Proposal A.

The point here is that rental rate and expenses are both cash flows, and can be analyzed in terms of amount and time. The same is true of each cost and each benefit offered in a lease proposal. Consequently, the two lease proposals can be summarized and compared based on cash flow.

Proposal A

	Year 1	Year 2	Year 3
Rent	($20)	($21)	($22)
Expense stop	5	5	5
Projected expenses	(6)	(6)	(6)
Improvement allowance	15		
Projected improvements	(24)		
Net cash flows	($30)	($22)	($23)

Proposal B

	Year 1	Year 2	Year 3
Rent	($19)	($21)	($22)
Expense stop	6	6	6
Projected expenses	(6)	(6)	(6)
Improvement allowance	19		
Projected improvements	(24)		
Net cash flows	($24)	($21)	($22)

Simply comparing the two sets of cash flows is a fast way to judge the relative cost of the two leases. This is a situation that illustrates the importance of at least specifying the cash flows as the first step in financial analysis. The next step is to determine the financial value of the leases by discounting the cash flows. This is a simplified method of comparing leases using the rental rates. Using the monthly rates would be more accurate and possibly necessary in a detailed comparison, but for illustration of this shortcut method we can separate the initial capital costs of net tenant improvements paid by the tenant at the beginning of the lease from the operating costs of rent and expenses during the term of the lease.

Proposal A

		PV factor (8%)	Present value
Year 0	(9)	1	(9)
Year 1	(21)	0.925926	(19.44)
Year 2	(22)	0.857339	(18.86)
Year 3	(23)	0.793832	(18.26)
		Present value	(65.56)

Proposal B

		PV factor (8%)	Present value
Year 0	(5)	1	(5)
Year 1	(19)	0.925926	(17.59)
Year 2	(21)	0.857339	(18)
Year 3	(22)	0.793832	(17.46)
		Present value	(58.05)

The financial cost of Proposal B is 88.5 percent of Proposal A. Or, Proposal B is 11.5 percent more financially valuable to the tenant. This shortcut method of comparing leases can provide the necessary information for a rough comparison of alternatives. And it can be particularly useful to compare the two on the basis of their percentage relationship. But for the final decision between leases, a complete accounting of the cash flows on a monthly basis is preferable.

Note that this is a comparison of negative cash flows using net present value. Even though the cash flows are negative, each lease alternative has a financial value. And the financial value of each lease can be compared with the financial value of any other lease on an equal time value basis. In one sense an office tenant is making an investment in office space and services each month. The return on that investment comes from productivity and morale of the employees and the image and convenience of the location as perceived by clients.

The intrinsic financial value of any set of cash flows can be computed by discounting. But the investment value of the cash flows can only be determined by the values of the company or individual making the investment. Determining the financial value is a significant step in gathering the data necessary for answering the question of whether an investment in a lease or an office building is worth the commitment. That commitment in time and energy and money goes far beyond financial considerations alone, which is why buyers and office tenants often determine, after it's too late, that they did not give sufficient weight to financial considerations when the initial commitment was made.

The use of incentives in office leasing presents an interesting challenge for tenants who want to compare different lease proposals on an equal basis and for owners who want to demonstrate their competitive advantage to prospective tenants. For example, how is a tenant to evaluate competing office space that varies in rent per square foot, load factor, free rent, moving allowance, parking charges, and tenant improvement allowance? Each incentive varies from building to building, presenting a seemingly unsolvable maze of unrelated choices. But each incentive is related. They are all related as cash flows with time value.

Consequently, each incentive and each rental charge can be expressed as a cash value received or paid at a certain point in time. When incentives are expressed as a positive or negative cash flow per square foot of usable area they can be discounted to a present value and compared to see which lease proposal presents the best value.

Building owners can also use the discounting process to evaluate the financial benefits of a lease. Every lease, regardless of how seemingly different in rental concessions, can be compared on an equal basis of rent per square foot. And the cash flows from the total of the leases during the ownership of the building represents the financial value of the building itself. This is not necessarily the market value, which may be higher or lower, depending on the fundamental and governmental factors at the time the investment period ends.

Applying Cycles to the Office Space Market

Real estate cycles are patterns of investment activity that tend to repeat with a degree of regularity. Often these activity patterns coincide with the business cycle and the longer-term cycles that affect the national economy. For example, the seven-year housing cycle tends to peak slightly before the GNP and bottom and then rise slightly ahead of GNP, leading the economy to recovery. This is a logical relationship when you consider the important economic role of durable goods purchased for new homes. The 18-year real estate investment cycle is more closely related to the broad monetary changes that we see as inflation and fluctuations in interest rates. Three 18-year cycles complete a 54-year long wave of capital expansion and contraction.

At the extremes, cycles move from shortage to overbuilding; from pessimism to optimism; from highly restrictive lending policies to loose credit and deregulation. This movement in the supply-demand relationship, investor expectations, and credit availability affects real estate prices and ultimately plays an important role in determining the financial value of real estate.

The opportunity to invest in concert with cycles is always present. The challenge is to develop a cyclical view of the present when it seems that it will never change. It is difficult to accept that the expansion and prosperity of today could really again disappear as completely as in the past; or that offices could be in such oversupply once more; or that shopping centers could experience such a drop in occupancy and revenues; and that so many farms could be so heavily mortgaged that selling to pay off the debt was not even a viable alternative to foreclosure. Nevertheless, these patterns surface again and again.

The characteristics as well as the investment timing opportunities inherent in the cyclical phases of various segments of the real estate market differ. The office market differs from the activity cycle of the apartment market. But the core elements of the supply-demand relationship, investor expectations, and the availability of capital embody the significant causal factors of cyclical fluctuations in each segment of the real estate market.

The supply of office space tends to roughly follow the expansion and contraction of business and the general economic health of corporate America. Shopping center revenues tend to be more closely tied to population growth and the stability of retail sales, which in turn are more directly dependent on employment levels and the expectations of the buying public for continued job security. The ups and downs of the farm land cycle are sensitive to longer-term inflationary forces that appear in fluctuations of livestock and crop prices.

Understanding the Office Building Cycle

The office space market has a relatively well-defined cyclical activity pattern. When a regional economy begins to recover from a recession, office space demand increases as businesses expand into existing vacancies. As the expansion phase of the normal business cycle creates new demand, rents increase, encouraging development of new offices. The longer the recovery lasts, the more office buildings spring up. Building gains a momentum of its own as actual demand becomes secondary to the process of development.

As long as money is available, offices continue to be built. If lenders lend, builders build because that is what both do. Consequently, lack of demand does not check supply if capital is available and expectations of a continuing economic expansion dominate investment decisions. The longer the recovery the larger the supply of new offices that will eventually hit the market. Extended economic recoveries tend to produce an extreme oversupply of office space.

The relationship between the business cycle and the construction of office space is logical. Businesses need office space. If business is good, more office space is needed. If it is really good, new office space is needed. Commercial lending is a business. If the lending business is good, banks need new offices. The most successful and largest law, accounting, and banking firms must have the newest (expensive) and most image-enhancing office space. Therefore, as the expansion reaches it peak and new and expensive office space comes on the market, you can literally see the largest office-dependent businesses move into the newly developed space, often just shortly before the next contraction begins.

It is probably inevitable that a large portion of the new supply of office space comes on the market as an economic expansion is ending and demand is weakening. Depending on the severity of the subsequent recession, it can take years for the oversupply to be absorbed and for confidence to recover to the level necessary to support another surge of office development.

Projecting office space needs with a high degree of accuracy is no less difficult than projecting the fluctuations of the general economy. It is difficult to let go of optimism until the market turns negative and there is no other alternative than to admit that the expansion is stalling. It is equally difficult for many (especially lenders) to develop confidence until an economic expansion is well established.

Consequently, it is virtually impossible to avoid periods of shortage and periods of oversupply. Both are natural to the office space market and reflect the interaction of the supply-demand relationship, capital availability, and investor expectations. The need for office space as businesses grow out of a contraction combines with newly available capital and renewed optimistic expectations to generate new supply.

These swings from shortage to oversupply produce periods of unwarranted enthusiasm followed by excessive pessimism even among the most experienced developers and investors. The confidence of a business boom fosters excessive building. It is an overreaction that can be especially painful for developers of speculative buildings who do not prelease sufficient space to service the loans that financed the project. This risk is traditionally offset by leasing sufficient space to major local or national tenants before starting construction. But during the topping of an extended recovery, such caution is easily overlooked, even by the experienced, who also have the influence to bring a lender into the project before tenants are lined up.

There are two ironic aspects to the office building cycle that relate to investor expectations. First, the amount of new office space needed is difficult to project until the recovery is well under way and existing office space is fast disappearing. Second, the oversupply of office space that subsequently develops is not seen as a problem until it is clear that the economy is in a recession, ending the demand for new offices.

Furthermore, it seems to be the nature of cycles that extreme fluctuations follow each other. Possibly there is a causal relationship here as equal and opposite reactions attempt to establish balance. The magnitude of enthusiastic overbuilding is an indication in itself of the severity of the slump to follow and the depth and length of the pessimism that eventually surfaces.

Certainly, the larger the oversupply, the longer it takes for the clearing process of the market to work the supply through the system. An extreme oversupply of office space is characteristic of the end of a long wave cycle and a logical outcome of the preceding decades of business expansion, ending with easily available credit, and unrealistic expectations for unending prosperity.

Conversely, reluctance to repeat past overbuilding mistakes inhibits new development, resulting in shortages until the economy is roaring along, thus practically ensuring that much of the new supply will come on line at the end of the expansion and the beginning of a new contraction. Confidence is highest when risk of oversupply is greatest, as the cycle is topping. And equally so, confidence is lowest when risk is low as the cycle is bottoming and new demand is about to hit the market. Taking an investment position against mass expectations has its place in the office market cycle.

Recognizing that existing office space will eventually be absorbed and responding to the approaching wave of demand with new construction is difficult. You can never be sure how much office space will really be needed at any given time in the future. Furthermore, the nature of the office development market is such that more than one developer is trying to meet the new demand at the same time.

Competition among developers in an attempt to profit from growing demand increases the likelihood that more supply will come on the market than is needed. It takes convincing evidence that the demand for new office space is in fact satisfied before the development frenzy comes to an end, just as it takes convincing evidence that the previous oversupply has been absorbed before new construction begins.

The challenge is to avoid getting caught on the wrong side of the extremes, yet to use them to your advantage. The clue is in the time component of the cycle and its relation to the magnitude of the overbuilding.

The greater the oversupply during the trough of the previous cycle, the greater the resolve of developers (and lenders) not to repeat the same mistake. Consequently, as the signs of a strengthening market become increasingly apparent, there is a natural tendency to hold back further development until the old supply is absorbed. The desire to be cautious at this stage of the cycle combines with the inherent time delay of large building construction to create a shortage. Then by the time new construction begins, the shortage has created overly optimistic expectations which encourage further construction, contributing more to the eventual oversupply.

The momentum of the factors that comprise this cyclical pattern tend to carry the supply-demand balancing process to extremes, which can require years to correct. The opportunity in this recurring process lies in timing the acquisition of office buildings as the economy shows early signs of recovery, but before the pessimism of oversupply changes to the optimism of shortage.

A large oversupply combined with a severe recession lays the psychological groundwork necessary for a shortage when the economy eventually does recover. The longer it takes to work off the previous oversupply, the more serious the subsequent shortage is likely to be. The longer it takes to satisfy a shortage, the more extreme the subsequent overbuilding is likely to be.

From a practical standpoint don't expect even time periods between the peaks and troughs of each cycle. Rather, look for the general pattern of optimism and growing oversupply characteristic of an approaching top. If you can maintain a skeptical outlook that is contrary to the extreme views characteristic of popular opinion, chances are good that you can avoid much of the risk.

A contrary view combined with patience can also be the source of overcoming the pessimistic atmosphere characteristic of bottoms in the cycle. This is when the opportunity for profitable investment is highest. It is the time when you can negotiate the most favorable pricing and acquisition terms and build in the safeguards that will allow you to hold on during future economic slumps.

The prerequisite to this cyclical investment opportunity is choosing a region of the country with growth prospects that go beyond those normally expected during a recovery. You don't want to put your investment dollars in regions that depend on sectors of the economy that are shrinking or that are in a topping process. It is much less risky to enter a market that has been washed out and has adapted economically. For example, the Southwest was devastated by the drop in oil prices during the first half of the 1980s. As we progress into the 1990s, the Southwest has started to come back, giving strong indications of leading the rest of the country into the next expansion.

Our economy is becoming increasingly regionalized. During any given time period one area may be in a virtual depression with 10 to 20 percent unemployment, while other areas hardly notice any discomfort at all. National statistics become meaningless under these conditions. Investment must be based on the specific conditions of the region under consideration.

It is apparent now that the debt liquidation and capital restructuring process of the long wave cycle is moving from region to region of the country. Throughout the 1990s it will be increasingly important to look for investment opportunities that reflect completion of the adjustments characteristic of the long wave cycle. This basing period is the foundation for the next long-term expansion as the new technological advances attract new capital and provide new jobs region by region.

10
Using Cycles and Cash Flows to Analyze Rental Houses

A rental house is the usual start for the beginning real estate investor. Houses are familiar assets and relatively easy to manage. Also, there are many to choose from. The supply base is large and demand tends to be steady as the population continues to grow.

Risk of loss from investing in rental houses is reduced somewhat by the nature of the underlying demand for homes and the active residential market. For example, a rental house that is not meeting investment objectives can be sold to someone who wants to own and live in it rather than rent it.

Houses serve two purposes in our society—they are both an investment and a high-priced consumer item. Homes provide shelter and for many the only source for accumulating savings. The backup consumer market increases the depth of the market, lowers the risk, and increases the possibility of appreciation and a favorable resale.

Because of the size of the housing market it is easier to diversify with a relatively small amount of investment capital. Also, the large market increases the chance of selling when you choose. Even during adverse market conditions buyers can usually be found and the property can be liquidated through concessions in price and terms. An exception to this is the ghost town syndrome characteristic of mining towns in the West and one-industry towns in other regions. In these cases, when the source of employment goes, the people go and the houses remain—vacant.

The nature of the housing market provides a built-in hedge against inflation, while providing a floor under the market, which can help soften the landing when sales activity decreases. This cushion against price declines depends on a growing home-buying population, which in turn depends on employment and income growth in the market area.

But the entire balance can be thrown off with speculative bubbles and the expectations of riches that occasionally grip the residential market. When housing speculation gets out of control demand can disappear suddenly, creating a gap of total inactivity. When this happens sometimes the only thing to do is wait out the cycle.

Single-family homes offer unique investment potential because they are the one segment of real estate that is the embodiment of the American Dream as well as a basic human need. Broadly based demand for homes tends to establish a floor under the market while giving depth to the resale market. Even with these underpinnings the residential market is not immune to loss of jobs, reduced income levels, and population loss. The same market requirements exist for timing and investment area selection as for other real estate segments. Risks exist in rental home investment just as in other areas, especially in highly speculative markets that have enjoyed apparent security for years.

The important element in single-family demand is employment growth and the income level of the investment market. Average national statistics are of questionable use and little significance in our increasingly regionalized economy. The reality of our time is that at any given time a depression can be well established in New England while a recovery from an earlier regional depression can be underway in Texas. The specific economic and market conditions where you invest dictate the strategy for acquisition and sales.

Applying the Housing Cycle to Rental Houses

Housing responds to general economic recovery more directly than other segments of the real estate industry. New home construction is a major factor in pulling the country out of the contraction phases of the business cycle. This somewhat predictable phenomenon in combination with the seven-year housing cycle is a helpful timing tool for rental investments.

We are fortunate to have a clearly defined housing cycle that has recently exhibited a high degree of predictability. The regular peaks hitting about seven years apart seem almost too regular and useful to last. In fact, the housing cycle seems to be a better indicator of our national economic health than the barrage of detailed statistics that dominate business news.

For example, recessions have followed the peaks in new home sales in 1972, 1979, and 1986–1987. This relationship allows the housing cycle to be used as a quasi-leading indicator of the next statistical recession. It seems fairly predictable that once housing sales begin trending down, a national recession eventually hits.

However, local conditions are more important than national statistics. The regional depressions of the 1980s didn't command the media attention of a national recession, but based on local statistical measures, regional depressions are much more significant. These localized contractions are the guidelines to use for timing rental acquisitions.

National recessions differ from regional depressions in important ways:

1. Entire industry segments restructure by permanently eliminating large numbers of jobs and closing plants in an attempt to remain globally competitive.
2. Banks fail, including savings and loans (S&Ls).
3. Banks, or the regulators, restrict credit.
4. Bankruptcies then increase to record levels.
5. Lower interest rates have a limited ability to stimulate the economy out of a depression.

A national recession is a minimum of two consecutive quarters of negative GNP, usually caused by high interest rates, that ends when interest rates are lowered by the Federal Reserve. When you look at the specifics it is obvious that certain states (even cities) and regions can experience depressions while the rest of the country remains relatively active. Examples are the rust belt of the early 1980s; the oil patch of the mid-1980s; the New England financial bust of the late 1980s; and the California real estate bust of the early 1990s. And even worse, during national recessions certain regions can be severely depressed in ways that aren't reflected in the diluted national statistics.

Even with the recent tendency for regional depressions, the housing cycle remains a solid tracking tool for the statistically defined national recessions. The key is that the housing market not only must recover nationally it must recover in your market area. Nevertheless, the housing market with its relatively complete statistics can provide a useful timing guide and gauge of market conditions.

Note the timing relationship over the last two decades between the housing cycle and recessions.

Housing Cycle Peaks

      1972   1979   1986   1993 projected

National Recessions

  1974–1975   1980–1982   1990–1992   1996–1997?

The proximity between the peaks in the housing cycle and the occurrence of recessions a few years later does not imply that a drop in housing activity causes a recession. The unemployment and slump in business that follows a peak in housing activity certainly figures in the drop in GNP that defines a recession. The housing market is about 25 percent of the GNP, but there is more to the specifics of each recession than can be attributed to the housing industry alone.

Conversely, the increase in employment that follows a pickup in housing construction and sales is a major factor in pulling regional economies out of recession. Increased construction is only one factor of many. But it may be more significant in restarting economic activity after a recession than in causing a recession after every seven-year peak. The ripple effect of new housing construction spreads through the economy stimulating housing-related employment.

Peaks in the housing cycle are approximate and based on peaks in new home sales. Housing starts obviously peak slightly before sales. The statistics on housing starts reflect the approaching new supply of homes. Actual sales indicate market activity because they are completed real estate transactions, not just construction activity.

Housing starts, on the other hand, provide an early warning of a peak in the cycle, indicating reduced construction employment and reduced sales of related durable goods, such as appliances and carpet for houses. Housing starts also reflect the beginning of a recovery in the economy, acting as an early signal of the real estate activity to follow.

Residential vacancies, including apartments and rental homes, tend to be low at the bottom of the housing cycle. Low rental vacancies are usually most apparent during the last stages of a recession, corresponding to the bottom of the housing cycle. Lack of construction during the housing cycle contraction provides time for existing supply to be absorbed. After this bottoming process is complete, rents can be raised because demand outweighs the supply of rental homes and apartments. At the peak, more supply comes on the market and consequently the vacancy rate tends to be higher.

A countercyclical relationship applies to residential land also. Demand for land is highest when housing starts and sales are active, but peaking. No doubt this is one reason builders often get stuck with land inventory at the housing cycle peak. Residential land prices are at a high point as the cycle peaks. Interest rates are also at the high point during this stage of the cycle.

Strategically, a countercyclical land acquisition program makes sense. Residential land acquired at the low point of the housing cycle when pessimism is greatest and demand for housing is low allows for more favorable price negotiations.

This is also the point in the cycle when low sales activity in the housing market provides a chance to buy rental property at a favorable price. Cycle bottoms are a low-risk time for rental home acquisition. The lack of new supply during a recession contributes to the low rental vacancy rate.

The fact that low sales activity and low vacancy tend to occur at the bottom of the housing cycle, and often during a recession, makes for a favorable convergence of trends for rental home acquisition. Recessionary market conditions and pessimistic expectations work to make the low point in the cycle a buyers' market.

Financially, buying a home when activity is low means a greater likelihood of selling at a higher price when market activity increases. Furthermore, it means a greater likelihood of renting at top dollar immediately after acquisition. Then, as the sales activity and demand for homes increase during the following years the chance of selling at a profit increases. You make your money when you buy. And it is done by building appreciation potential into the acquisition price.

Expectations of large cash flows from rental homes must be based on anticipated sale proceeds, whether due to cyclical appreciation or as a result of building equity through years of reducing the loan balance. In certain markets and unique neighborhoods, rental cash flows are high enough to contribute to financial performance, but in most cases sale proceeds are usually the major source of cash flow.

Refinance proceeds are also a cash flow source that has the added benefit of being tax free. Although the sales price when you sell will encompass the loan balance, provided the market value holds steady, the absence of tax at the time you receive loan funds significantly increases the present value of a rental home investment. Care, of course, must be taken to ensure that rental income is likely to remain high enough to cover the new debt service.

Timing the acquisition and subsequent sale of rental home investments to profit from supply-demand shifts within the movement of the housing cycle and the recovery-recession dynamics of the business cycle is one way to maximize the increase in wealth. Not paying proper attention to timing can place you in the market when your chances for price appreciation and rental income are slim at best. Cyclically, the way to minimize risk is to act contrary to popular expectations by selling during active markets and buying during inactive markets. But that is not always easy to do.

The period when the real estate cycle is topping is a popular time to invest. Too popular. In the first half of the 1980s the general public was drawn to real estate that had low cash flow but high debt exposure. Even though the rate of inflation was trending down, it was still viewed as the security blanket that would make any real estate investment work out. Conversations at parties seemed to turn to real estate as the necessary protection against inflation with little recognition of the market specifics such as rental rates, operating expenses, and debt service.

Expectations of never-ending inflation prevailed even though interest rates were so high that few people could afford to finance a new home. Consequently, market activity was dropping rapidly. And more importantly, real interest rates were extremely high as the Federal Reserve increased short-term rates to control inflation. Clearly, a top in the cycle was coming whether the public knew it or not. Inflation was not going to be allowed to scuttle the

American economy. This is a fact to keep in mind in any seemingly hopeless inflationary spiral. The government or the market itself will eventually get it in hand, ending the price increase.

Ultimately, a rental home or any other form of real estate investment must be viewed within the cash flow reality of the market and outside the abstraction of daily inflationary expectations reported in the popular media. For example, as this cycle top gradually worked through the economy from 1980 to 1986, many first-time buyers bought rental homes and small apartment complexes based on expectations of inflation rather than actual cash flow projections. The two are far from the same thing. These new real estate investors followed the crowd because real estate was so popular and they thought they could remain safe from inflation.

The mistakes were made in timing and relying on general expectations rather than the specifics of a particular property. There is always money to be made in real estate, but it is very difficult without a sense of market cycles. Unfortunately, many feel safest when real estate is the most popular. But this is often when demand is topping as an increased supply of houses hits the market toward the end of the expansion phase of the housing cycle.

The interaction of supply-demand dynamics and expectations works on emotions at the top of cycles as well. Greed instead of fear goes to work at this stage. Here the asking price hovers just above the price that will close a sale. If the demand frenzy is over, a sale may never occur as buyers leave the market and prices slide faster than owners can adjust their greed to the new market reality.

Obviously, the tendency is greatest for the public to buy at the top or fail to sell during the topping process when the popularity of real estate is widespread. Trends in price appreciation of houses can continue for years, and when activity ends it is often difficult to see the effect on prices. Instead, buying and selling activity simply stops.

There are stages during which you can invest while prices are rising and have sufficient appreciation potential remaining to profit from a subsequent sale prior to the top of the cycle. But there is also the option of holding out for the long term. Timing a purchase within normal cycle fluctuations can make that option more profitable.

But if you are on a tight budget, timing the sale and purchase of a rental home can be crucial because of the cash flow demands of debt service when there is a vacancy. Consequently, it is important to view a rental home investment in the context of the actual cash flow demands during the anticipated holding period. Short-term dips in market activity are not necessarily indications of a long-term problem, but they can disrupt rental cash flow and restrict the possibility of a sale. The major source of cash flow from a rental house is sale proceeds. Therefore, cycle activity becomes very important because price appreciation during the favorable portion of the cycle can, in part, determine that cash flow.

Realizing cash flow from appreciation is more likely when market activity (the number and frequency of sales) is high. A sense of market activity is essential to understanding the crucial role of timing rental home investments. You need an active market to easily liquidate your investment. High sales activity depends on demand. Demand depends on affordable financing and growing employment opportunities in the region.

Selling into a strong market is the way to realize the maximum price for your rental house, and buying during a very inactive market as it just begins to recover is the timing point to acquire rental property for maximum price appreciation during an approaching economic recovery and housing cycle peak.

For example, applying timing to maximum advantage is a process of watching the market activity of the housing industry in the context of the business cycle. Sell when the housing cycle peaks but before the business cycle peaks. Buy when the housing cycle starts its recovery but before the business cycle begins to recover as the recession ends.

New home construction is the important indicator to watch. Market tops are characterized by a growing supply of unsold homes. At the extreme, you can tell a bottom is in place when the builders of excess supply go out of business under the weight of high interest rates, excess land inventory, and low sales activity. Watching the cyclical pattern of the housing market can help you avoid the trap of buying at the top and selling at the bottom of the cycle.

Five Important Factors for Rental Home Appreciation

Timing is an important consideration in all types of real estate investments, but it is only one of many factors that are useful. Each of these factors work together to increase the likelihood of success, or, when ignored, to increase the chance of a costly mistake. These five factors are:

1. *Timing:* Are you buying at the cycle top or bottom?
2. *Financing:* Is debt service higher than rent?
3. *Management:* Is the potential worth the effort?
4. *Location:* Is the property improving or deteriorating?
5. *Market appeal:* Is the property in demand as a residence?

When you have all five factors in your favor you have a definite advantage. There is not much more to be done to increase the chances for maximizing the cash rental house. The task then becomes to monitor appreciation.

Price appreciation with rental homes is among the easiest of cash flow sources to follow because of the relatively frequent sales, which provide price quotes. One investor in rental homes specializes in acquiring property on his block and in the surrounding neighborhood. He acquires a house or two per block through the years as good buys come on the market. Then he gleefully provides price quotes to his friends. "That house just sold for $102,000 and I have a rental right next door. I bought that rental seven years ago and it's done nothing but appreciate."

His strategy incorporated the five essential factors. He only bought during cycle bottoms when the market was inactive and buyers were hard to find and good price and terms could be negotiated. He structured financing as favorably as possible and in a manner that made it likely that the rental would break even. Management demands were kept to a minimum by regular maintenance and the proximity to his own home. Location was confirmed by his own residence in the area and the regular contact he maintained with prices. Market appeal was ensured by the selection of houses and the regular upkeep he provided.

The combination of these factors maximized the potential for appreciation and minimized the management demands on his time. This investor viewed rental houses as individual savings accounts with deposits made by the renters and appreciation provided by the growth of the area.

Adapting Financing to the Business Cycle

Financing is a key factor in the housing market because it is a credit-dependent industry. Credit is also one of the major factors in the business cycle. Tight credit chokes demand for high-priced items that are usually financed, such as houses and cars. Easing of credit restrictions tends to stimulate demand for homes. Similarly, easing of credit stimulates business expansion and jobs in general. This relationship to the availability of credit links the housing cycle and the business cycle.

When interest rates on home loans increase to the point where willing buyers can't afford the monthly payments, sales slow rapidly and market activity drops. When families can't buy homes, rental house investments are not salable as easily or at the best possible price. Consequently, rental vacancies fill, because the alternative of purchasing is less available. Conversely, vacancies tend to be highest at the top of the housing cycle after a period of time when new supply has been introduced to the market. As the peaking process continues, financing becomes more costly as interest rates increase.

In the absence of traditional financing there are solutions based on seller financing and lease options. These adaptation methods usually involve price concessions that are contained in the terms themselves. Actually, increased popularity of seller financing is one strong indication of a drop in housing sales.

Seller financing grows out of the necessity of the marketplace to find a substitute for institutional financing that is priced beyond the means of home buyers. Seller financing can be negotiated to your benefit when acquiring rental property during recessions. A motivated seller, who is willing to finance part of the equity, increases the flexibility of the negotiations and gives you the opportunity to reduce risk and build in a higher return at the time of purchase.

Financing availability ties directly to the business cycle, and consequently is a timing indicator at the extremes of the business cycle. High rates tend to appear at the top of an expansion and serve to choke off demand while low rates tend to appear at cycle troughs when people are reluctant to buy.

Realistic financing is crucial for successfully investing in rental homes. The cost of financing has a direct impact on cash flow. Interest paid on mortgages is an expense item that reduces any cash flow you might receive from rents. A high interest rate has an effect when you sell. The higher the interest rate, the higher the monthly debt service payments and the greater the risk that you will not be able to find a buyer with sufficient income to qualify for financing.

High interest rates can also reduce the price you receive when selling. If you are forced to sell in a slow market, it may be necessary to lower the asking price to offset the impact of a higher interest rate. The same market influences work to sustain a higher sales price when a low interest mortgage is part of the transaction. The level of market activity depends largely on the attractiveness of financing.

The structure of financing can be a major benefit of real estate or a potential hazard. The hazard is not limited to the high interest rates characteristic of a peak in the cycle. Another way financing can burden rental homes is in the form of balloon payments. The danger here is that when a loan comes due it will not be possible to refinance the property to make the relatively large payment.

If you acquire a rental house with a loan that is payable in full within three to seven years after purchase, the risk is increased because of the uncertainty of being able to obtain future financing. This risk reduces the desirability of the property to a potential buyer who may wish to assume the existing financing. The success of the sale may then depend on the amount due on the loan as well as the expectation of future interest rate levels and the availability of credit to refinance the house. Long-term low interest loans that are assumable have real market value and help cash flow. In contrast, short-term high interest loans limit profit potential and increase risk.

Another potential financing problem can be found in adjustable rate mortgages. During a contraction as rates fall toward the bottom and the Fed begins to loosen credit it may appear that rates will never be at the high levels of prior years. The history of cycles provides contrary evidence. The debt overhanging the country will have to be adjusted eventually. This presents a possibility of volatile interest rate markets in the future. Massive national debt carries a potential economic jolt to the country in the form of unexpected and high interest rates. Adjustable rate mortgages that seem safe and popular when interest rates are low contain serious dangers.

The time for an adjustable rate mortgage is when there is downside potential for interest rates, not when they are low and the only way to go is up. What good is an adjustable rate loan for the borrower when the rate is at 7 percent and the chance of the rate being reduced to even 6 percent is remote? Adjustable rate mortgages are for the benefit of the lender and only make sense when rates are high and trending lower. They are as dangerous as balloon payments.

Managing for Maximum Cash Flow

Unwillingness to accept the routine requirements of managing property keeps many people from investing in rental homes. Also, management demands are often the motivating factor that brings small real estate investments to the market. The owners get tired of managing and decide to sell. This often occurs after realizing that real estate is more a long-term investment than a get-rich-quick ticket.

Managing rental housing is a good training ground for apartment ownership and other larger real estate properties. Although managing several houses spread around the city may seem difficult, it is one of the necessary obligations of owning rentals and turning a profit.

Monthly income from rent is rarely adequate to support professional management and still make a positive cash flow. Consequently, as an owner it will most likely be up to you to deal with the daily management requirements. When analyzing the rental house you are planning to acquire, a careful assessment of the management requirements should be a major element of the decision-making process. There are actually two aspects to this consideration.

1. Consideration of the management demands as they fit into the way you live and spend your time before acquiring the rental house.

2. Consideration of the changes in your life and the demands on your time that will result from managing the house.

Managing rental homes is a time-consuming but necessary part of making your investments pay off. It is a factor that can be as important as the location you choose for your real estate investment activity. Maximizing rental cash flow takes energy and time, but the long-term benefits can be structured so that it is worth the effort.

Location Considerations for Rental House Investments

The popular advice for selecting real estate investments is to find a good location. Although location is only part of the formula, it is a very important part. The location of a rental house has as much influence on the resale potential as the timing of the acquisition and the price.

In fact, the standard emphasis on location when buying is an expression of many influences. Location as an analysis criterion for real estate investment choice actually embodies timing considerations as well as the relationship between supply and demand. Location is commonly used as a catchall generalization for many important elements of a rental. It really points to the demand side of the equation and singles out the fact that rental homes are more valuable where people prefer to live.

But for more detailed analysis purposes it is necessary to separate location from the other decision components that are almost unconsciously associated with it. Then we can see the decision-making function of the supply-demand dynamic that directly determines both the price at acquisition and the price at sale.

For example, when you buy a rental house, the location usually separates the speculative inflationary hedge benefits from solid supply-demand related appreciation based on usage and buyer preferences. In most locations rental houses generate the majority of investment return through price appreciation. And, as with any investment market, houses are subject to increases in price that exceed reasonable supply-demand bounds. That is, prices can be driven up by speculators selling to speculators rather than builders or resident-owners selling to people who live in the house.

This type of speculative increase in price provides both an opportunity and a danger. It is an opportunity if you can enter and exit the trend before supply-demand reality catches up with bubble price increases. When the location of rapidly appreciating property is favorable it can provide a floor under the price if the speculative pressure eases.

Preferred demand shows in location. It is often a specific location that is in high demand when a new cycle starts and buyers enter the market in force. When a cycle turns down, the preferred locations are hurt the least. Location attracts or repels demand. A poor location is simply a way of saying it is not in demand. A good location is another way of saying it is in high demand. A preferred location is cash flow insurance when you decide to convert appreciation to sales proceeds.

Analyzing Rental Houses for Market Appeal

The appeal of a rental house is reflected in the price at acquisition and the price when you sell. The appearance, size, floor plan, age, and quality of construction directly influence the practical use and the popularity of the house. The degree of appeal, in part, controls the demand for a house when you sell. Higher prices come from people who actually live in the house. Consequently, the acquisition of a rental should consider its appeal when you sell, or at least the improvements that will be necessary to make the house more attractive to the ultimate buyer who is more than likely going to live in the house.

For example, the possibility of buying low and selling high is increased through timing. The same objective is possible by using market appeal to your advantage. Higher returns are often the result of acquiring property which appears to have little market appeal, thus allowing you to negotiate a lower price and easier terms. You can enhance market appeal by improving the landscaping, repainting and recarpeting, and implementing other physical improvements that build market appeal. The improvement process can be done gradually while relying on rental income to cover much of the remodeling costs. Improvement plans can also be implemented gradually to build increased value through the years of home ownership.

Analyzing for market appeal is part of the process of building profit into the transaction when you purchase. It is also part of the risk protection process, which involves analyzing the market for houses available for sale based on their appeal to potential buyers when you eventually sell.

The potential for resale should be as clearly in mind as possible when you buy. That potential exists when you buy and is the basis for the protection of your investment funds during ownership of the property. For example, there are houses that have limited price appreciation potential. These houses, because of age, location, and construction, appeal mainly to investors who buy them as rentals. Ultimately, they sell to the next wave of investors rather than to someone who buys the house to live in. Acquiring this type of rental house makes it very likely that you will have to sell to another investor. This limits the appreciation potential. If you sell to another investor more emphasis will be placed on rental cash flow and the remaining upside appreciation potential. But someone who lives in the house is more likely to buy based on emotional reasons rather than to meet financial objectives. This increases the chance of a higher price when you sell.

The middle price range house in a growing area is generally in greater demand and consequently has higher appreciation potential than extremely low or high priced homes. The highest returns on resale are houses that appeal to the largest number of buyers. These are often the houses that new families buy when moving up from their first home. This traditional source of demand is a foundation for appreciation and eventual resale at a higher price.

Combining the Five Factors for Rental House Analysis

Timing, financing, location, management, and market appeal are interrelated factors that directly affect the performance of rental houses. They are analysis criteria and a set of guidelines for choosing a rental house investment based on market dynamics rather than emotion.

For example, the thoroughness with which you analyze the potential of a rental house and the demands it will place on your time can make the difference between profit and loss. The most obvious example of this is the effect of management requirements on the property and on the owner. Fortunes have been made by people who turn around poorly managed property. The problems the former owner experienced with the property become the source of opportunity for the new owner. Sellers are often motivated to sell because of the way they view their property based on a history of difficulty and a series of ongoing problems. This stress-filled relationship between owners and their properties can form the basis for negotiating a favorable acquisition.

Market appeal is closely related to management. For example, market appeal can often be increased by relatively minor improvements undertaken over a period of years. But the market appeal of houses as an analysis criterion involves viewing other factors that are not easily changed. The floor plan and number of rooms will influence the demand for the house on resale. A small rental house will have limited resale potential when compared with midsized houses. For acquisition purposes it can help to define the home buyers a rental will appeal to when you are ready to sell. Who is the most likely buyer? Another investor? A new family? A family moving from an apartment to a first house? Or possibly empty-nesters moving from a large house to a smaller one.

Population growth is the underlying source of demand for all types of real estate. Increasing employment opportunity, high incomes, and expanding population constitute growth which in turn creates demand and makes a market profitable for rental estate investment. But the neighborhood location within the market controls the demand for houses. Together these elements of demand that relate to location directly affect cash flow from sale proceeds.

Location within a market as an analysis factor is really a way of emphasizing the importance of investing in the path of growth rather than an area in decline. And, as with the timing of a purchase or sale, it is helpful to build in a margin for error.

Location and timing are strongly tied together by the ability to make a marginal property a success. Location tells you where to invest and timing tells you when. Consequently, both are of equal importance.

Timing investment activity within the fluctuations of the housing and business cycles is an attempt to take advantage of price fluctuations resulting from changes in capital availability, the supply-demand dynamics, and expectations. In the final analysis it is change in price, whether rental prices or sales prices, that determines the success or failure of an investment in real estate. Therefore, the analysis of cycles and the fundamental factors they reflect can help you invest with favorable price trends and avoid the unfavorable trends. In the housing market this process ties directly to the relationship between the business cycle and the housing cycle.

For example, housing activity depends on the availability of financing. Consequently, when loan funds are restricted, market activity contracts, usually resulting in a withdrawal of demand, a slowdown in market activity, and a trend toward more favorable prices and terms for buyers.

Much of this change is due to change in the expectations of

market participants who fear the cycle will not recover. This is the opposite of the case at the top of the cycle when market participants rest comfortably with the false security that buyers will always be ready to purchase, and the rate of price increase will never slow. Without the cycle there would never be a favorable time to buy, and without a favorable time to buy there would not be a favorable time to sell.

Timing, financing, location, market appeal, and a realistic assessment of management demands comprise the essential analysis factors for rental home acquisition. Each factor makes a contribution to the financial success of the rental when ultimately measured as cash flow.

How to Analyze the Financial Performance of Rental Houses

The financial analysis of a rental home is simple to do but seldom accomplished, as with other types of rental property cash flow rules. Not only rental cash flow, but cash flows from all sources. It is the net that counts. As described earlier there are four primary sources of cash flow.

1. Net rental income after expenses and debt service.
2. Tax savings from depreciation of improvements.
3. Loan proceeds from refinancing.
4. Sales proceeds from disposition of the property.

The money made on a rental home is a function of the amount of cash flow and the time it is received. It is determined by the basic process of comparing all the money received with all the money paid. If you want to project the potential of a property, run an estimate of the money you anticipate receiving and compare it with the money you anticipate paying. In other words, compare the positive cash flows and the negative cash flows.

Investing in rental homes is basically a process of making decisions, and financial analysis is the major tool for measuring the outcome. One way of looking at the analysis process is in the context of time and decisions faced during each stage of the investment process. When viewed in this manner there are actually three uses for financial analysis:

1. Prior to acquiring property to determine whether the projected range of likely cash flows will accomplish your investment objectives.
2. While you own the property to determine if it is performing at potential and what you can do to assure that it does.
3. When you consider selling, to determine whether the benefits of selling outweigh the benefits of continued ownership.

In each of these primary applications, financial analysis is used to help in acquiring property, monitoring performance, or selling. For example, let's say you have determined that rental house ownership is an appropriate investment area for you during the next several years. Also, you have determined through careful consideration of the housing and business cycles that there is potential for economic growth and an increase in housing values over the next few years.

After surveying the market you locate a house priced at $92,000 that appears to have appreciation potential. It has been on the market for quite some time, and the price has been lowered a couple of times. The owner is highly motivated now. The question is how much cash flow this house is likely to produce from rental income, tax savings, and sale proceeds.

Although housing sales have been slow over the past year, rental rates have increased lately as vacancies have decreased. After looking into the maintenance and other expenses you generate the following estimate of operating cash flow.

Cash Flow Analysis, Operating Income and Expenses

	Year 1	Year 2	Year 3
Potential income	$10,200	$10,800	$11,400
Less vacancy	(850)	(900)	(950)
Estimated income	9,350	9,900	10,450
Less insurance	(375)	(375)	(375)
Less maintenance	(600)	(600)	(600)
Less property taxes	(900)	(900)	(900)
Net operating income	7,475	8,025	8,575
Less debt service	(6,481)	(6,481)	(6,481)
Rental cash flow	$ 994	$ 1,544	$ 2,094

Breaking even is sometimes a reasonable expectation from a rental house while you wait for natural growth pressures to increase the value. Cash flow from rent is just the first step in this series of calculations. The real value in a house is the home it provides the owner. Consequently, the profit from a rental house is most likely to come from the sale proceeds when someone who wants to live there buys it. Rental income is often just part of a holding pattern that is considered doing well if no major expense arises to wipe out a breakeven operation until a profitable sale can be made.

The next calculation involves determining if there will be cash flow from tax savings that can be attributed to this rental. The first step here is to determine the amount of annual depreciation. Here we must deal with our constantly changing tax laws. As a result, the principle underlying the calculation is more important than the tax rate and allowable depreciation, both of which may very well be changed during the next session of Congress and then changed again in the session which follows two or three years later. But the principle necessary to make the calculation will remain, and all that is necessary is to use the percentages that apply under the new law.

In this case 85 percent of the property value, or $78,200, can be attributed to improvements, which can be depreciated at $2,844 per year. This shelter benefit must be figured into the cash flow calculations because it will reduce taxable income and possibly provide additional cash flow as a result of taxes saved.

Income taxes are a cost of investing and must be accounted for in the calculation of the financial performance of an investment. The specialized treatment of real estate can provide an advantage rather than a cost. Therefore the cash flow analysis can be expanded to include the tax effects as in the following table.

Cash Flow Analysis, Tax Savings

	Year 1	Year 2	Year 3
Rental cash flow	$ 994	$1,544	$2,094
Plus loan principal	593	640	692
Less depreciation	(2,844)	(2,844)	(2,844)
Equals deduction	(1,257)	(660)	(58)
Times tax bracket	31%	31%	31%
Tax savings cash flow	$ 390	$ 205	$ 18

Historically, the tax shelter benefit has been one of the more important incentives for real estate investment. The reasoning behind the benefit is that improvements wear out and must be replaced. Consequently, normal building depreciation should not be taxed since it represents worn out capital. It makes sense to keep capital in the investment market so it can be put to productive work in the economy rather than lost in the tax abyss of government spending. The tax shelter benefit of real estate acts as an incentive to replace structures as they wear out so there will always be sufficient structures to provide support services in the economy.

This same reasoning applies to residential buildings, office buildings, and retail buildings as well as our industrial plant and equipment. Unfortunately, our tax policy has become such a political football that the constant change has caused financial accidents and destabilized the real estate market. But this can be a source of opportunity.

Regardless of the tax law changes in process as you read this, the applicable law has an effect on cash flow. In most financial areas, taxation is an expense that reduces cash flow and financial value. As already illustrated, it can work to increase the cash flow of a real estate investment. To be measured financially, the tax benefit must be stated as a cash flow, whether negative or positive.

Therefore, we can summarize the cash flow from operations after consideration of the tax consequences. This generates an after-tax cash flow analysis.

Cash Flow Analysis, After-Tax Summary

	Year 1	Year 2	Year 3
Rental income	$ 994	$1,544	$2,094
Plus tax savings	390	205	18
Cash flow after tax	$1,384	$1,749	$2,112

Of course, it is possible to have a negative cash flow after tax with income real estate. This could result from any number of circumstances, including a high land-to-building ratio, high rental income, a fully depreciated building, or restriction on deduction of passive losses. When taxes are due on rental income the payment is treated as a negative cash flow which is netted against positive cash flows for the year. Income tax is, in this case, just another expense of doing business that reduces net income just like insurance and maintenance; thus, under these circumstances tax savings disappear as a line item and become taxes paid.

The next calculation in this rental house example is to estimate the cash flow as a result of sales proceeds. This is the cash flow area of greatest potential for significant financial performance. Buying for the right price shows in the sales price when the property sells. Determining the cash flow from sale proceeds requires netting of another set of expense items.

Cash Flow Analysis, Sale Proceeds

Sales price	$125,000
Less loan balance	(71,675)
Less costs of sale	(8,750)
Net sale proceeds	$ 44,575

The amount of $44,575 represents the before-tax sale proceeds. To arrive at the actual cash flow amount, the tax must be calculated and subtracted from this figure. The first step in calculating the tax is to determine the adjusted basis after three years of ownership. This is done by subtracting the depreciation taken during the investment holding period from the original cost and adding back the costs of sales and capitalized costs incurred in preparation for the sale, if any.

Calculating Adjusted Basis

Original cost	$92,000
Less cumulative depreciation	(8,532)
Plus costs of sale	8,750
Adjusted basis	$92,218

The next step is to calculate realized gain by subtracting the adjusted basis from the sale price. Realized gain is the gross profit from a tax accounting standpoint. It is not a cash flow. Rather, it is the capital gain on the investment and is subject to tax at capital gain rates. Consequently, the next step is to determine the amount of gain realized on the sale by subtracting the adjusted basis from the sales price as follows.

Calculating Realized Gain

Sales price	$125,000
Less adjusted basis	92,218
Realized gain	$ 32,782

The amount of $32,782 represents capital gain on the sale that is subject to tax. Obviously, this is a different concept from cash flow, which is actual money in hand after all expenses and taxes are paid. Profit and gain and similar words like *value* and *worth* have different meanings in different contexts and thus lose their ability to help clearly describe investment reality. Cash flow cuts through this problem and zeros in on the bottom line of what you walk away from an investment with. But to determine cash flow, several preliminary calculations are necessary. The next one involves determining the amount of tax due as a result of the transaction.

In this calculation realized gain is multiplied by the tax rate applicable to capital gain. Since the rate changes frequently, the rate used in this example may be different from the rate in effect at the time you calculate the results of an actual transaction. Consequently, the tax rates in effect currently should always be verified before computing actual capital gains treatment.

Calculating Tax on Capital Gain

Realized gain	$32,782
Times tax rate	× 28%
Tax payable	$ 9,179

From an investment view, tax payable on gain is an expense item. As an expense it must be subtracted from the net sale proceeds to determine the after-tax cash flow from the sale. This is the next calculation.

After-Tax Sale Proceeds

Net sale proceeds	$44,575
Less tax paid	(9,179)
After-tax sale proceeds	$35,396

All the calculations related to the sale of this property were made in order to generate the after-tax amount. This is the cash flow net of all expenses, including taxes, that can be used to determine the financial performance of the rental house. This is the financial measure of success of the investment in transferring purchasing power through time while building real wealth. To complete the analysis procedure we summarize all the negative and positive cash flows generated by the rental.

Cash Flow Analysis, Summary of All Sources

	Year 0	Year 1	Year 2	Year3
Down payment	($18,400)			
Rental income		$ 994	$1,544	$ 2,094
Tax savings		390	205	18
Sale proceeds				35,396
Total Cash Flow	($18,400)	$1,384	$1,749	$37,508

NPV at 25% discount: 3,031
IRR: 31.90%

The final calculation determines the net present value of the cash flows. If you establish that a positive NPV at a 25 percent discount rate is the objective of your real estate strategy, the remaining question is whether this meets that minimum. In this case the minimum objective is achieved because the NPV is positive. In fact, the actual discounted rate of return or internal rate of return is 31.93 percent This calculation is easily made on a handheld business calculator. Keep in mind that the internal rate of return refers to the cash flow generated internally from this property only and to be accurate it must include all after-tax cash flows.

As this example illustrates, the key to comparing the performance of different investments as well as determining whether you are making (or losing) money is to:

1. Isolate all cash flows.

2. Discount them to a net present value.

The major question in any rental house investment is whether it will actually make money for you. Basically, this question can be answered with simple addition and subtraction. That is, just add the income and subtract the outgo. This is actually all that is being done when we net cash flows. The challenge is to cover all the cash flows and not leave any out.

This is probably more than most do when they venture into a rental. But then, they may complete the rental ownership cycle never knowing that they lost purchasing power, while thinking they are ahead of the game. Or worse, they may think they have lost money when they actually had not. In either case the way to determine the financial outcome is to isolate the cash flows and discount them to the present value.

Doing basic cash flow analysis is a good first step to determining whether an investment makes or loses money. The preservation of purchasing power and the building of real wealth can only be calculated when cash flows are clearly specified.

Guidelines for Rental House Acquisition

As a general rule when acquiring a rental commit as little cash as possible and when selling get as much cash as possible. This doesn't necessarily mean that you should try to be highly leveraged at all times. Sometimes a better price can be negotiated with a larger amount of cash during a contraction, which can later be recovered through refinancing when a recovery begins.

This strategy will naturally direct acquisition activity to periods of economic contraction when prices and terms tend to be more flexible. These are the buyers' markets that are driven by supply, which are the best times to buy real estate. In contrast, sales activity should be during the expansion phases. These are sellers' markets driven by demand and characterized by high activity and rising prices.

Selling into a strong housing market is especially important when trying to obtain the highest price. Price resistance is not a significant factor in a strong expansion when the public is optimistic about the economy. But when there is a high degree of pessimism about the economy it shows in price concessions and flexible terms.

The expectations of the market participants influence price and terms. Expectations can drive a market and turn it on a dime. And our expectations change with the cycles of the economy and the housing market. The end results show in financial performance.

Expectations take over where actual supply-demand dynamics end. For example, expectations for continued price movement (up or down) in the direction of the trend tend to remain long after the fundamental supply-demand causes end. Consequently, when prices start moving in the opposite direction it can be quite a surprise. Acquisition of rental houses requires consideration of the effect of change on cash flows.

Consideration of change is a process of asking What if? and measuring the financial effect. With rental home investments, asking What if? forces recognition of the range of possible changes in the housing market and in the economy. But to be useful the potential for change must also be considered within the context of the cash flows of the house and the financial value of the investment.

Change in the market and the ability to sell is of no consequence unless it changes the financial outcome of the investment. Financial value is the bottom line of rental home investment just as it is in any real estate investment. Consequently, the time value of the cash flows must be considered in order to measure the financial value of a rental home. This is the purpose of financial analysis as applied through discounted cash flow analysis.

Applying the Housing Affordability Index

The relationship between population growth, income levels, and the cost of financing have an effect on real estate values. These factors work in combination in a direct manner to affect the appreciation of single-family houses.

Population growth and the formation of new families creates the need for housing. Income provides the means to satisfy the need. The cost of financing and the price of housing then combine to determine whether the income level is high enough to qualify for a purchase. The relationship between interest rates, income level, and prices determines whether a potential buyer can afford a home.

The National Association of Realtors developed an index in the early 1970s to monitor the relationship between median income levels and median home prices. It is useful in gauging fluctuations in the home market based on the ability of purchasers to afford houses.

The Housing Affordability Index measures the ability of a married couple with two children to qualify for a loan necessary to purchase a home with a 20 percent down payment, based on the median price. The index is produced by the relationship between median income levels in relation to median home prices in relation to interest rates.

At the beginning of 1992 the national affordability index was 124.7 which means that the median income home buyer had 24.7 percent more income than necessary to qualify for the purchase of a median-price home. The index climbed from 111.2 in August of 1991 to 116.1 in November 1991, reaching levels not seen since the mid-1970s.

The most volatile component of the index is interest rates. Although the index is designed to change as home prices and income levels change, neither is as dynamic as interest rate fluctuations. Consequently, it is no surprise that the index is reaching new cycle highs as interest rates fall into the 1990s.

For example, if median income levels and median home prices hold steady while interest rates drop, the affordability index will increase. In fact, the index trends in the opposite direction of interest rates. As interest rates increase, the index drops, and when interest rates drop the index rises. When the index is at 100 it means that half of the population can qualify for a loan on a median-price house and half cannot at prevailing interest rates.

The Housing Affordability Index is used nationally and in local markets. As the index rises with decreasing interest rates, home demand tends to increase. Consequently, it serves as a measure of the relationship between the availability of capital and demand. And it can be calculated for your market area when you know the median income, median home price, and local interest rates.

The requirement is that home buyers' principal and interest payments not exceed 25 percent of their annual income. With this information you can determine the income level necessary to purchase a house at the interest rate and asking price. It is also possible to establish whether a home price is affordable for the majority of the home buying public in your market.

Assuming the down payment is in hand, income is the prerequisite for buying a house. Therefore, if the median national income is $36,000 and the median home price is $100,000 what is the affordability index if interest rates are at 10.5 percent.

1. The loan amount is 80 percent of the price—$80,000—and the payments on the loan at 10.5 percent over 30 years are $8,782 per year.

2. The annual payments represent 25 percent of the income necessary to purchase a $100,000 house. Therefore: $4 \times \$8,782 = \$35,128$

3. Median income $36,000
   Required income   35,128
   Difference $ 872 ÷ 35,128 = 0.025 + 1 = 1.025

Consequently, a family that earns the national median income has 102.5 percent of the income necessary to buy a home at the median price. Or, half the population earns at least enough to qualify for a loan necessary to buy a home at the median price at that interest rate.

The Index If Interest Rates Drop to 8.5 Percent

Payments on $80,000 at 8.5%, 30 years	= $1,382
$4 \times \$7,382$	= 29,528
$\$36,000 - \$29,528 = \dfrac{6,474}{29,528}$	= 0.22 + 1 = 1.22

This means half the population has 122 percent of the income necessary to qualify for a median priced home, provided they have the 20 percent down payment.

The important point here is that size of the home buying market increases as interest rates drop. That is, families with incomes below the previous median level can qualify for financing on median-price homes. Consequently, demand for homes increases because more first-time home buyers can qualify for a loan needed to purchase middle level quality housing.

In a rational housing market people buy out of need, not because interest rates are suddenly a better deal. They buy because they have the money to buy a needed item—a home. Thus, as rates drop, new families can more easily move from rentals to their own house.

The Index If Home Price and Income Level Are Lower in Your Market Area

Interest rates: 8.5%
Median home price: $85,000 (loan $68,000; payments = $6,274/yr)
Required income: $25,096 (4 × $6,274)
Median income level: $32,000 − $25,096 = $6,903 ÷ $25,097 = 0.275
Affordability index: 127.5
Meaning: The median income level population has 127.5% of the
   income needed to qualify for a home priced at the median level.

The affordability index describes market conditions. In doing so it illustrates the importance of the fundamental and governmental factors in market activity and how these factors work, in part, to create real estate cycles. This index consists of a demand component (required income); a supply component (home price level); a capital availability component (interest rates); and a governmental factor consisting of the manipulation of interest rates to control inflation (monetary policy). All of these basic factors work together to make the real estate market.

But as with most general indexes they are best used to illustrate trends of the components that comprise them. Home prices, income levels, and interest rates are elements of the real estate market that determine cycle activity. Consequently, the affordability index reflects regional market differences and can provide insight to local housing markets.

11

Building a Financial Model to Analyze Apartments

Apartment ownership is the natural and logical progression from an investment in rental houses. The residential rental market has the greatest depth and largest number of participants. Moving from single-family rentals to multifamily complexes is the usual direction of individual investors. This process is a gradual expansion of comfort level and directly related to the management requirements of acquiring property of increasing size.

Realistic assessment of apartment management demands can make the difference between failure and success. In fact, analysis of the management requirements can be as important as selecting the right location and negotiating favorable financing. Tired owners are among the most cooperative, willing sellers of apartments. Find an owner who doesn't enjoy management and you've made the first step in locating an acquisition that will be relatively easy to negotiate.

Management neglect is often visible in the operation of apartments, even with some professionally managed complexes. It shows in the physical appearance and financial performance. Routine maintenance is ignored. Rents are not raised when the opportunity is there. And the possibility of capital improvements to increase financial performance is never considered. Reduced cash flow as a result of poor management rather than market factors is a source of investment opportunity. Improved management is the most efficient way to turn financial performance around. It is also a strategy that blends well with the cyclical nature of real estate.

For example, the high rate of foreclosures during the bottoming of the real estate cycle brings a new type of owner into the real estate investment market. Lenders who must repossess property used as security for underperforming loans prefer not to be burdened with ownership, much less management. Their objective is to convert the real asset to paper—to convert equity to debt. They have already taken the loss, and the concept of entrepreneurial effort and the resulting profit that drives effective management is a distant thought.

Nevertheless, effective management is among the most immediately available methods of bringing an apartment complex to a satisfactory cash flow level. The fortunate aspect of the process is that effective management doesn't cost any more than ineffective management. In fact, poor management is expensive.

It is not only the month-to-month operation that suffers from the problems of poor apartment management. Typically, the difficulties accumulate and eventually show in a discounted sales price as a result of deferred maintenance and low rental income. In contrast, well-managed apartments reflect the attention they receive in higher rents and eventually in a higher sales price.

Buying property that is "operating below potential, bringing it up to potential, then selling" is a way of expressing the objective of a management-based acquisition strategy. Someone's management headache is another's opportunity. Furthermore, an acquisition strategy that ties improved management with the timing guidelines of the housing and business cycles is a natural extension of the housing cycle to multifamily dwellings.

The flow of investment funds into real estate during the 20-year period from 1970 to 1990 marked the maturing of the long wave cycle and the coming of age of the post-World War II baby boomers. As the 1960s ended, this bulge in the demographic profile of the American population hit the real estate market. Not only did this population surge need housing, it also discovered real estate as an investment.

The result was twofold: (1) residential prices increased, and (2) the number of properties operating below potential almost evaporated between 1975 and 1980. Demand pressures from this population component of the long wave cycle suddenly made it very difficult to find property that was operating below potential. The commonly acknowledged problem of experienced real estate operators was finding "good deals." The sleepers of the 1960s real estate market had been discovered, acquired, brought up to potential, and in many cases sold.

This change in the real estate investment inventory also increased the risk of investing. By the 1990s, much of the pre-1980s real estate inventory had been refinanced based on inflationary blow-off values of the 1980 to 1986 real estate peak. This additional debt on the apartment inventory of the country left little potential to be realized. Apartment investment settled back to operations instead of speculation. And once again, management became the primary consideration as the years of foreclosure and debt liquidation began.

Market Factors Influencing Apartments

Excessive construction of the early 1980s combined with the end of tax incentives in the Tax Reform Act of 1986 to put a halt to apartment construction in the latter half of the 1980s. A chart of the apartment vacancy rate shows a downward trend well into the 1990s. The decline in apartment vacancy indicates a growing shortage of multifamily dwellings. This market condition is the inevitable outcome of several converging factors: a change in the tax laws affecting real estate and the peak in the housing cycle, both of which occurred in 1986 at the end of a boom in construction with funds from recently deregulated savings and loans. The question remains whether the shell-shocked lenders of the 1980s will respond to the growing shortage of apartments, developing from region to region during the 1990s.

The recent drop in apartment vacancies is one of the clearest examples of the interaction of governmental and fundamental factors underlying real estate cycles. But this time the impact may be more lasting and less responsive to the normal housing cycle and business cycle recovery. There are reasons for this that go beyond the risk-aversive market orientation of developers.

For one, the population of people renting is growing while the availability of rental units is dropping. This long wave related combination of events reflects the drop in income level and the shortage of low income housing. In addition, apartment construction at the beginning of the 1990s dropped to the lowest level since the mid-1950s. This pace of construction cannot keep up with new family formations and the rate of divorce, which may be the single most direct cause of apartment demand.

Consequently, demographic changes point toward increasing demand for apartments, but the construction industry is showing a very slow response to the need, inhibited by restrictive lending policies. This gap in new apartment development is not surprising in light of the number of lenders who have left the market. The failure of the savings and loan (S&L) industry has created a void in the residential lending market that will eventually affect the ability of the market to adapt to the changing supply-demand dynamics of the 1990s. Local markets will feel this as the lenders continue the credit-restrictive lending policies that extend the period of shortage.

The reluctance to lend on real estate is the natural outcome of a change in expectations resulting from the real estate depression that has moved from region to region in the late 1980s and 1990s. The uncritical acceptance of real estate typical of lenders at the cycle top in the 1980-1986 period has turned to aversion at the cycle bottom. Again, as the cycle begins to turn into the 1990s, the pattern of decision making reflects the popular thinking of the moment, ignoring the cycle and approaching recovery.

Analysis Guidelines Used by Lending Institutions

Real estate investment depends on financing. Easy credit tends to lead to oversupply. Restrictive credit tends to contribute to shortage. When a lender is presented with the opportunity to make a loan on a real estate project there are certain financial performance requirements that the property must meet. These requirements are prerequisites to financing and are directly tied to the income generated by the property. Knowing the lender's guideline in advance allows you to determine the amount for which property can be financed based on the current income.

There are two concepts that work together to facilitate calculation of the amount of a loan that can be placed on a property based on the income available to service the debt at prevailing interest rates.

1. Debt coverage ratio
2. Annual constant

Debt coverage ratio is the relationship between net operating income (NOI, income after expenses, but before debt service) and the maximum debt service payment. Annual constant is the factor that reflects the relationship between debt service and the original loan amount. Together the two can be used to determine the loan that is possible at prevailing interest rates when you know the net operating income of the property. Knowing the debt coverage ratio allows you to determine the feasibility of paying a certain price if you must finance the acquisition. It also allows you to calculate the amount of down payment necessary to keep debt service payments within lending guidelines.

For example, a debt coverage ratio of 1.25 means the net operating income of the property must be 1.25 times more than the debt service. Therefore, the net operating income divided by the debt coverage ratio (DCR) will tell you the potential debt service. Conversely, 1.25 times the debt service produces the net operating income. It seems that lenders who held to these guidelines would never have an underperforming loan. It also seems that with time and professional management, lenders and the RTC could create profit from foreclosed property. But that's not the way the real estate cycle unfolds.

Debt coverage ratios vary with changes in market conditions and lending policy of the financial institution. Consequently, the current ratios should be used in the calculation.

Using Debt Coverage Ratio to Calculate
Maximum Debt Service

$$\frac{NOI}{DCR} = \text{debt service payment}$$

$$\frac{\$150,000}{1.25} = \$120,000$$

The amount of $120,000 is the maximum debt service payment possible on the property under this guideline. The next step is to determine the loan amount that can be serviced by $120,000. This is where the annual constant can be used.

The annual constant is calculated based on the interest rate and term of the loan available under current market conditions. It is the factor which results from dividing the annual debt service payment by the amount of the loan. For example, a 25-year loan with monthly payments, including interest of 10 percent has an annual constant amortizing percentage of 10.91 percent. In other words, each year the debt service will be about 10.91 percent of the original loan balance. Therefore, under these financing conditions we can determine the loan possible on a property with a net operating income of $120,000 using the following calculation.

$$\frac{\text{Debt service } \$120{,}000}{0.1091 \text{ annual constant}} = \$1{,}099{,}908 \text{ loan}$$

The annual constant is normally used to determine the debt service on a property. The loan amount is multiplied by the constant for monthly or annual payments to determine debt service. But the application above uses it to back into the financing possible on a property when you know the NOI. Therefore, if you know the constant you can also determine the debt service payment. Since loans are usually paid monthly, the annual constant is a monthly factor that is converted to an annual figure when used with annual net operating income amounts. Consequently, the monthly payments are calculated first.

Calculating Debt Service Using the
Monthly Constant

Loan amount	$1,000,000
Monthly constant	0.00909
Debt service	$ 9,090

The annual constant for monthly payments is calculated by multiplying the monthly factor by 12.

Converting Monthly Constant to Annual Constant

0.00909 × 12 = 0.10908 or 10.91 percent annual constant

The term annual constant is short for annual constant amortizing percentage. Although there are tables of annual constants it is almost easier to use a business calculator to determine the annual debt service based on monthly payments and then calculate the annual constant. For example, you can compute the annual constant for any term and any interest rate by calculating the annual sum of the monthly payments and dividing that figure by the original amount of the loan. The size of the loan is irrelevant to calculation of the constant, which is the percentage relation between the original loan amount and payments and, of course, is constant.

The annual constant can be calculated using amortization

tables or a business calculator to determine the annual total of monthly payments. That amount is then divided by the original loan amount to determine the annual constant.

Finding the Annual Constant on a 30-year Loan at 9 Percent Interest

Loan amount	$100,000
Monthly payments ($804.62 × 12)	$ 9,655
$9,655 ÷ $100,000 = 0.96555 annual constant	

The mathematical relationship between net operating income, the debt coverage ratio, and the annual constant has a useful application when you want to determine the financial structure of an acquisition. It relates to the price of the property, the equity investment necessary at that price, and the net operating income of the property.

For example, if you are presented with an apartment investment opportunity with a net operating income of $100,000, what is the maximum price you can pay if you have $150,000 cash available for the down payment? Loans are available at 10 percent interest amortized over 25 years. Lenders currently require a 1.25 debt coverage ratio.

The objective of the next example is to illustrate how you can look at an investment opportunity through the eyes of the lender before you apply for financing. In actual practice it is almost a prerequisite for negotiation of a transaction to know the amount of the financing the property will carry. There is no reason to agree on a price only to find out later that the equity you plan to invest is an insufficient amount when compared to the debt coverage ratio requirements of the lender.

Using Debt Coverage Ratio to Determine Price Based on NOI

$$\frac{\text{NOI } \$100,000}{1.25 \text{ DCR}} = \$80,000 \text{ potential debt service}$$

$$\frac{\$80,000}{0.1091 \text{ annual constant}} = \$733,272 \text{ available loan amount}$$

Therefore:

Down payment	$150,000
Available loan	733,272
Price	$883,272

The relationship between the net operating income of a property, the debt coverage ratio requirements of lenders, and the annual constant, which is determined by the interest rates and lending policies prevailing in the market provide the raw data necessary to determine whether a property is priced within a feasible range.

The ratio of debt to the purchase price is also important. If the purchase price is $900,000 and the loan is $600,000, the debt ratio is 67 percent. In addition to minimum debt coverage ratios, lenders require certain ratios between the value or purchase price and the loan. For example, a lender may require a minimum debt coverage ratio of 1.25 and a maximum loan to value ratio of 70 percent. Lending guidelines vary depending on the state of market conditions and the risk tolerance of real estate lenders.

There are several variables at work here which reflect lenders' expectations for the future of real estate, capital requirements imposed on the lender, current interest rate trends, and the rents available in the apartment market. Debt coverage ratios can range as low as 1.10 and as high as 1.30 and above, depending on market conditions and the availability of capital. The usefulness of the ratio is in the connection it makes between income, price, and the total debt the property will support under lending guidelines. The debt coverage ratio and the loan to value ratio are indicators of whether credit is restrictive. Both ratios fluctuate in response to changes in credit market conditions and lenders' expectations as the real estate cycle continues.

Applying the Real Estate Analysis Model to Apartments

Adapting investment strategy to the extensive range of factors affecting investment in the real estate market has become increasingly important in today's volatile market. Here the objective has focused on developing a model of the real estate analysis process that provides a framework to structure a perspective from which market changes can be evaluated.

The basic model has three categories intended to organize information about property in a manner that will help accomplish the purpose of real estate investment, which is transferring purchasing power through time while building real wealth. Cycles are patterns of market activity that reflect change in the fundamental and governmental factors, generally referred to as *market condi-*

tions. They are timing guidelines, for meeting the purpose of investing, that reflect change in fundamental and governmental factors over time. Changes in the level of market activity characteristic of different phases of the cycle can be anticipated and planned for by monitoring the components of market conditions that influence activity.

Property characteristics reflect the specifics of the property, including the effectiveness of management, which rivals location in importance of its contribution to cash flows. The third component, financial performance, is a function of cash flows generated during the entire ownership period.

Property characteristics and financial performance work together during ownership as the reality of economic obsolescence and physical deterioration require periodic capital investment to

The Real Estate Analysis Model

1. *Market conditions:* The expansion and contraction of market activity over time (cycles) in response to changes in the fundamental factors of:
   Capital availability (debt and equity)
   Supply-demand (absorption/employment-income)
   Expectations (optimistic and pessimistic) and governmental factors of:
   Tax laws (incentive-disincentive)
   Regulations
   Monetary policy (inflation-deflation)

2. *Property characteristics:* Including but not limited to
   Physical condition (age, deferred maintenance)
   Location (stable, growing, declining)
   Site characteristics (access, parking, security)
   Management (professional)
   Competitive posture (design, tenant appeal)

3. *Financial performance:* In the form of cash flow from
   Rental income
   Tax savings
   Refinance proceeds
   Sale proceeds

Financial performance, resulting from the interaction of market conditions and property characteristics, produces cash flow. The timing and the amounts of the cash flows determine the financial value of a property, which is measured using discounted cash flow analysis (IRR and NPV).

maintain cash flows. As apartments age, roofs, carpeting, appliances, and in some cases furniture, must be replaced. Ongoing capital investment is part of owning income property. Typically, it is left up to new owners to provide the renovation necessary to maintain cash flows. Consequently, budgeting for capital replacement is not a component of operations for many investors. Nevertheless, the necessity of maintaining rents at maximum levels requires attention to capital improvements, illustrating that the initial down payment is rarely the only capital investment if property is held for an extended period.

The interaction of the components of the real estate model determine how a specific property succeeds as an investment.

Financial value is the bottom line of the model. It measures how well an investment transfers purchasing power through time while building real wealth. It is based on the premise that the worth of an investment in real estate is the discounted value of the cash flows produced over the entire holding period. This type of financial measurement is very much part of everyday corporate business. It is used to allocate capital for investment and measures the cash flow that results. The process of determining financial value of real estate is no different in principle.

For example, the following apartment complex, located in the Southwest and has a financial value based on the actual cash flows it will produce. Since most of these cash flows are in the future, no one knows what the actual cash flows are; therefore, no one knows the actual financial value. Nevertheless it does exist and can be estimated within a reasonable range of probability.

Property Information

Name:	Bay Shore Apartments	
Location:	East Shore, 5752 Central Bay Drive	
Builder:	Beck and Hall Commercial Construction, Inc.	
Completion date:	September, 1986	
Number of units:	100	
Occupancy:	81%	
Size:	Gross	77,100 ft^2
	Net	76,300 ft^2
	Ave./unit	763 ft^2
Parking:	190 spaces (1.90/unit)	
Amenities:	Swimming pool, heated spa, sprinkler system, washer-dryer connections in most units, clubroom, cable television.	

The rental income of the complex averages $0.50/ft²/month. Expenses run about $0.21/ft². Therefore, to keep the operating statement manageable, we can summarize the financial information as follows.

Summary Operating Statement

Potential rent	$457,800
Less vacancy	86,982
Effective rent	370,818
Less expenses	192,276
Net operating income	$178,542

What loan amount will this complex support, given a 1.2 debt coverage requirement and an 80 percent loan-to-value ratio when interest rates are at 9.5 percent for loans amortized over 25 years? This question is answered by dividing the net operating income by the required debt coverage ratio to determine the loan payment the property will support.

$$\frac{\text{NOI } \$178,542}{1.2 \text{ DCR}} = \$148,785 \text{ loan payment/year}$$

The annual constant for monthly payments on a 25-year loan at 9.5 percent interest is about 10.48 percent. Therefore, the amount of the loan this property can support is calculated as follows:

$$\frac{\text{Loan payment of }\$148,785}{0.104832} = \$1,419,271$$

This calculation indicates a potential loan of $1,419,271, which when divided by 80 percent will produce the potential price with a 20 percent down payment.

$$\frac{\$1,419,271}{0.80} = \$1,774,089 \text{ potential price}$$

The potential price represents a cost of about $17,700 per apartment unit, which is within the range apartments were selling for out of foreclosure in parts of the Southwest at the beginning of the 1990s. The buyers stepping in the market during the bottoming of the cycle at these depressed prices knew all they had to do was wait for the market to come back. Buying apartments for half the cost of new construction when capital is unavailable for new competing apartments provides a competitive advantage. Rents are likely to increase several times before new supply comes on the market.

Apartments built in the first half of the 1980s were routinely appraised for $40,000/unit. Ultimately, income determines the value of income property. The fact that apartments cost $35/ft^2 to build and cannot be replaced for $17,700/unit is irrelevant to an investor negotiating the purchase price with the Resolution Trust Corporation (RTC). Clearly, the income is not there to support debt service at a higher price or the property would not have been repossessed. The fact that comparable apartments sold for the $40,000 a unit appraised value six years earlier, before they were repossessed, is also irrelevant. Financial value is the only meaningful measure of income property, and that is a function of cash flows.

When the amount of the loan at the debt coverage ratio is established, the apartment complex can be evaluated based on the debt service requirement at current market rates. The acquisition structure is first determined by the availability of financing. Then the amount of the loan dictates the cash equity the buyer must put into the deal. The down payment is established by the loan amount that the income will support at current interest rates. Backing into the property value based on lending ratios allows financial performance to determine value based on credit market conditions.

Consequently, we can summarize the acquisition structure that results from applying the debt coverage ratio to the net operating income based on the interest rates available in the credit markets (1.2 DCR; 25-year term; 9.5 percent interest).

Acquisition Structure

Price	$1,774,000
Loan	1,419,200
Equity	$ 354,800

This application of the debt coverage ratio allows the credit markets to establish value based on the debt service the net operating income will support. The purchase price then follows based on an 80 percent loan to value ratio. The equity value or down payment is the difference. This is the natural progression from analyzing value based on minimum lending requirements.

Summary Operating Statement

Potential rent	$457,800
Less vacancy	86,982
Effective rent	370,818
Less expenses	192,276
NOI	178,542
Debt service	148,794
Cash flow	$ 29,748

Interest rate markets have placed financial value on the debt portion of this property, which is reflected in the interest rate and loan amount. The lender has also imposed certain restrictions in relation to current income by using the debt coverage ratio in order to minimize risk of loss. But what is the financial value of the equity portion? Is it just what's left?

The financial value to the lender is the cash flow of $12,400/month ($148,794/year) over 25 years bearing 9.5 percent interest. The present value of these cash flows is $1,419,200 which is the present value of the loan payments discounted at 9.5 percent and the amount of the loan. What if we applied the same financial criteria to the current rental cash flows after debt service to establish the financial value of the equity investment made by the owner. In other words, if the rental cash flows hold at $29,748 ($2,479/month) what is their present value when discounted at the same interest rate required by the lender?

Computing the Present Value of the Rental Cash Flows

$2,479 monthly, discounted at 9.5% over 25 years = $283,737

Rental cash flows don't meet current present value requirements of the equity investment or down payment of $355,000. The additional financial value must, therefore, come from other sources, such as the sale proceeds and possibly tax shelter. In addition, there may be upside potential for rental income if the vacancy rate decreases as the cycle moves out of the bottoming process. Also, the added income and potential for rent increases as the market improves could produce additional financial value from sales proceeds.

In this example the property is acquired on terms that make it a good deal, not because it has some fantastic cash flow, but because it has potential to do much better. For now let's assume that the property is able to hold the same average operating performance over a 25-year period. Let's also assume that the rental cash flow is sheltered from tax, but does not contribute to cash flow. Furthermore, let's assume that at the end of 25 years the property sells for the same nominal amount that it was acquired for after paying capital gains tax. And finally let's assume that a 10 percent after-tax rate of return is considered acceptable by the purchaser for the long holding period. What is the present value of the projected cash flows under these assumptions?

Assumptions

1. Operating income holds steady at $29,748/year ($2,479/ month)

2. Property sold at end of year 25 for after-tax price equal to purchase price of $1,774,000.

3. A 10 percent rate is acceptable.

Calculating the Net Present Value
of the Cash Flows

Cash flows:	
Initial investment	($355,000)
Rental cash flow PV, 10%	272,807
Sale proceeds (PV, 25 year, 10%) (1,774,000 × 0.092296)	163,733
Net present value	$ 81,540

This analysis means that the investor could pay $81,540 more for the property at the time of the initial investment and still receive a 10 percent return. It also means that there is an $81,540 present value margin for error in the event that the assumptions of the analysis are too optimistic.

Buying property at the right price is the best way to assure upside potential. What is the upside potential of this property? What if the vacancy rate decreases? What if the rents can be raised? What if the owner is able to sell in 10 years at an appreciated value? Let's make some new assumptions along these lines and see the effect on the financial value of the property.

Assumptions for years 6 through 10:

1. Vacancy decreases to 8 percent.
2. Rents increase to 53 cents/ft²/month.
3. Expenses increase to 22 cents/ft²/month.
4. Sale at end of year 10 for $24,000/unit.

	New	Old
Potential rent	$485,268	$457,800
Less vacancy	38,821	86,982
Effective rent	446,447	370,818
Less expenses	201,432	192,276
Net operating income	245,015	178,542
Less debt service	148,794	148,794
Rental cash flow	$ 96,221	$ 29,748

This new set of more optimistic assumptions represents what upside potential is all about. It is the benefit of buying when the market is depressed and illustrates the significant effect seemingly small increases in rent can have on nominal value amounts.

In addition to the increased rental cash flow we are assuming a sale at the end of 10 years based on a value of $24,000 per apartment unit, which produces the sale proceeds.

Transaction	
Price	$2,400,000
Loan	1,187,436
Equity	$1,212,564
Tax Due	
Price	$2,400,000
Basis	(959,573)
Gain	1,440,427
Rate	28%
Tax	$ 403,320
Sale proceeds	
Equity	$1,212,564
Tax	(403,320)
Costs	(125,000)
Proceeds	$ 684,244

The increased cash flows beginning in year 6 and ending in year 10 with the sale of the property have an effect on the financial value of the investment. Although the improved conditions in this more optimistic scenario are clearly beneficial, to find the net present value we must specify and discount the cash flows.

Year	Cash flow	Discount factor (10%)	Present value
0	($355,000)	1	($355,000)
1	$ 29,748	0.909091	$ 27,044
2	$ 29,748	0.826446	$ 24,585
3	$ 29,748	0.751315	$ 22,350
4	$ 29,748	0.683013	$ 20,318
5	$ 29,748	0.620921	$ 18,471
6	$ 96,221	0.564474	$ 54,314
7	$ 96,221	0.513158	$ 49,377
8	$ 96,221	0.466507	$ 44,888
9	$ 96,221	0.424098	$ 40,807
10	$780,465	0.385543	$300,903
		Net Present Value	$248,057

The net present value of 248,057 indicates that the down payment could be increased by the net present value amount and still produce a 10 percent rate of return. The internal rate of return of these cash flows is 18.01 percent. It represents the rate of return earned on the equity investment in the apartment complex. The rate of return earned on the debt investment is 9.5 percent—the interest rate on the loan. The cash flows generated by the down payment must earn a financial return just as the debt investment must.

Financial value of both debt and equity cash flows is measured the same way. Both debt and equity cash flows have conceptually the same financial value definition. The financial value of the debt investment—the loan amount—is the present value of the cash flows it generates (the loan payments.) The financial value of the equity investment—the down payment—is the present value of the cash flows it generates.

The lender who makes a real estate loan invests in the property. The loan payments are the cash flows produced by the act of investing. The purchaser of real estate also invests in the property. The net rent, tax savings, refinance proceeds, and sale proceeds are the cash flows produced by that act of investing.

In the case of the loan or debt investment, the cash flows are fixed, known, and secured. In the case of the down payment or equity investment, the cash flows are not fixed, unknown, and unsecured. These differences in debt and equity investments reflect different risk-reward expectations but do not change the underlying principles of financial measurement by which each are valued as investments. There is simply more uncertainty placed on specifying the equity-related cash flows. Otherwise, both have investment worth and financial value, which consists of the present value of their respective cash flows. Both are investments with the inherent purpose of transferring purchasing power through time while building real wealth.

Analyzing the Financial Effect of Capital Improvements

The down payment at the time of acquisition is not the only investment made by owners of apartments. Physical deterioration of improvements over the ownership life of a complex requires ongoing capital improvement to maintain rental rates and competitive advantage. Apartments take abuse. They wear out. Carpets need replacement. Roofs don't last forever. Appliances and furniture must periodically be replaced. The cost of these normal but major replacements can only be avoided by selling or letting the property run down and suffering the decrease in rent that follows. Apartments tend to change ownership long before the full amortization of a loan or depreciation of the improvements for tax purposes is complete.

Coincidentally, the sale of apartment complexes often occurs just as the need for capital improvement can no longer be avoided. Depending on the condition of the market, the cost of bringing property up to standard may result in a discount of the sale price or reduction in the down payment. In all cases the age and condition of the property and the cost of bringing it to full potential is of primary concern to a purchaser. Avoiding the capital outlay is of equal concern to the seller.

Capital improvements during ownership of apartments are best planned for and implemented when called for to maintain the operation at maximum cash flow. Gradual replacement of carpet and appliances out of rental cash flow is the preferred and least financially painful way to maintain a quality operation. But occasionally the big requirements hit. Replacing 77,100 ft² of flat roof at $1.15/ft² during a one-year period is the type of major capital improvement that can significantly reduce financial performance. Although it must be done, it won't show or make the units more attractive to renters or facilitate an increase in rent. There are other improvements that can justify higher rents. Usually these are renovations that are more apparent than replacing a roof and improve the apartment for the tenant who in turn is more likely to pay a higher rental rate.

This process of bringing existing property up to new standards during a strong cycle in the rental market is the basis for much of the wealth made during the 1970s by advocates of real estate who appeared in the early 1980s. They had made money during the 1970s in real estate and then made money in the early 1980s convincing others to do the same. This, of course, is another reason good deals became increasingly difficult to find as the decade progressed. Real estate became too popular.

Whether the capital improvements generate more rent or simply allow the apartments to hold the status quo, they have an effect on cash flow, which in turn affects the financial value of the investment. In strong markets the ability to increase rents offsets the risk of not recovering capital investment made to improve the property. In declining areas, improving the property may be wasted money.

Furthermore, making improvements that are of no benefit to the tenants is also a risky use of funds. For example, faced with the choice of allocating a limited amount of improvement capital to new carpet or air conditioners in a climate where air conditioners are neither expected or needed may seem an obvious choice. It is, if the owner can view apartment life as the tenant does. But coming to a new market requires knowledge of the expectations of the renters in that market. Understanding their needs and allocating investment capital in a manner that will meet the needs of tenants is the prerequisite for maximizing rental cash flows.

The entrepreneurial profit that exists in apartment ownership flows from creating value. The requirement is that a market of renters exists that needs the value. This demand side of the equation fluctuates with the change in real estate cycles. Recognizing and acquiring property that has potential for improved value at a time when the cycle is turning positive is the basis of an investment that has the potential to create real wealth.

Acquisition strategies involving underperforming property often have both professional management and a capital improvement program as part of the plan. If timing is fortunate, as was the case for many purchases during the basing period of the 1970s and likely to be in certain regions in the 1990s, improvements can be financed gradually with increased rental cash flows. But more often than not the improvements are planned and financed at the initial acquisition.

During cycle contractions and foreclosure, lenders who thought they had a secure debt investment find that they not only are forced to become equity owners, but they must also bring neglected property up to cash flow standards with unexpected capital improvements. The problems with the physical condition of property repossessed by the RTC are fast becoming legendary as the 1990s progress. The easy money of the 1980s lending spree and the subsequent collapse of lenders left projects unfinished and produced extensive construction quality problems. Consequently, as these properties pass through the RTC to new owners, they require additional investment to generate cash flow to meet financial performance objectives.

There are many circumstances under which property ownership requires capital investment in addition to the down payment. Some have advocated in the past that a separate operating account be established as a reserve for replacements to be paid out of rental cash flows. Under traditional analysis techniques, this anticipated infusion reduced current cash flows. Consequently, the practice was rarely implemented, although it was strongly advocated in theory. When the time came to renovate or remodel beyond the amount the rental cash flow could support, the funds were borrowed and amortized out of operations, or additional equity was invested by the owner.

In practice capital improvements represent negative cash flows during the ownership period. In some cases when the rents are high enough and improvements can be done gradually, the net effect on rents is not negative for the year. In extensive projects the capital infusion offsets the positive cash flow from rent resulting in a negative amount for the year. This common ownership requirement is difficult to evaluate using the older limited investment methods that are tied to the return on the down payment. But they are easily accounted for financially by using discounted cash flow analysis.

There are really two questions related to capital improvements and the financial consequences:

1. Will the improvements add value for the tenants?
2. Will the improvements only maintain the status quo?

Provided the potential exists in the market, it is possible that a positive answer to question one will result in the ability to raise rents almost immediately. Question two relates to maintaining a quality operation that may in the future allow rents to be increased as the market allows. In either case the effect on cash flow can be built into the projections, and the financial outcome can be measured. All that is required is a new set of assumptions.

Using the earlier example, we can modify the operating statement and the cash flow projections to measure the financial value of negative cash flows occurring midway through ownership.

This process of asking What if? and determining the effect on investment performance is the core of financial measurement.

The first step is to modify the assumptions that form the basis of the cash flow projections in order to accommodate the cost of the capital improvements and the additional rental income that is likely to result.

Assumptions

1. Replace carpet in year 3 ($70,000).
2. Vacancy decreases to 10 percent in year 4.
3. Rent increases to $0.52/ft^2/month in year 4.
4. Expenses increase to $0.22/ft^2/month in year 4.
5. Vacancy decreases to 3 percent in year 5.
6. Rents increase to $0.54/ft^2/month in year 5.
7. Expenses increase to $0.23/ft^2/month in year 5.
8. Sale at end of year 5 for $28,000/unit.

	Years 1–3	Year 4	Year 5
Potential rent	$457,800	$476,112	$494,424
Less vacancy	86,982	47,611	14,833
Effective rent	370,818	428,501	479,591
Less expenses	192,276	201,432	210,588
Net operating income	178,542	227,069	269,003
Less debt service	148,794	148,794	148,794
Rental cash flow	$ 29,748	$ 78,275	$120,209

The projected sale at the end of five years for $28,000/unit requires calculation of the net sale proceeds so they can be worked into the cash flows.

Transaction	
Price	$2,800,000
Loan	1,330,044
Equity	$1,469,956
Tax due	
Price	$2,800,000
Basis	(1,406,182)
Gain	1,393,818
Rate	× 28%
Tax	$ 390,269
Sale proceeds	
Equity	$1,469,956
Tax	(390,269)
Costs	(180,000)
Proceeds	$ 899,687

The change in operating performance in this capital improvement scenario increases both the rental cash flows and the sale proceeds. In addition, a sale at an earlier date is possible due to the improved cash flows. The new cash flows can be projected and discounted to determine the financial effect on the investment.

Specifying and Discounting Cash Flows to Net Present Value

Year	Cash flow	Discount factor (10%)	Present value
0	($355,000)	1	($355,000)
1	$ 29,748	0.909091	$ 27,044
2	$ 29,748	0.826446	$ 24,585
3	$ 29,748	0.751315	$ 22,350
3 carpet	($ 70,000)	0.751315	($ 52,592)
4	$ 78,275	0.683013	$ 53,463
5	$ 78,275	0.620921	$ 48,603
5 sale	$899,687	0.620921	$558,635
		Net present value	$327,088

This capital improvement scenario illustrates how cash flows both from rental income and sale proceeds can improve financial performance. In this example the cash flows represent a 26.48 percent internal rate of return.

There are always alternatives available that might increase cash flow. The challenge is in taking the appropriate investment action at the appropriate point in the real estate cycle. Capital improvements at a time when the market cannot support a rent increase may, in fact, reduce the financial value of the investment. Neglect of capital improvement at a time when the apartments require it to remain competitive and support a rental increase is a lost financial opportunity that may only occur during the next cycle.

The Impact of the Housing Cycle on Apartments

Clearly, the housing cycle is linked to the cycle timing of the apartment market. But it is also subject to the influences of the flow of investment capital and interest rates characteristic of the 18-year real estate and interest rate cycles. Historically, apartment vacancies have been the lowest at the bottom of the housing cycle, before new construction brings additional supply on the market.

Low vacancies occurred in 1969 and 1970, and after the 1975 recession before the 1979 housing cycle peak. Then again vacancies were relatively low coming out of the 1980 to 1981 recession increasing into the housing cycle peak of 1986. Since then apartment vacancy has dropped gradually into the beginning of the 1990s.

This apartment vacancy cycle is not random or without cause. It is the result of the interaction of fundamental and governmental factors, which increase and decrease the intensity of the cycle.

The relationship between the vacancy rate and the housing cycle is summarized as follows.

Low apartment vacancy	Housing cycle peaks
1969–1970	1972
1975–1978	1979
1984	1986
1992	1993?

The peak in vacancy rates closely tracks the peak in new home sales of the housing cycle. That is, apartment vacancy rate is highest just before the peak in the housing cycle.

The unanswered question is whether the battered real estate market and the gun-shy lenders who are still in business will respond to the growing shortage of apartments during the 1990s with new construction sufficient to meet the need in the markets that do come back. Indications are pointing to continued shortage of units until rents increase enough to attract investment capital from new lending sources. Also, it is likely that some time will have to pass before optimistic expectations for real estate subside enough to stimulate activity.

It appears that new apartment construction will be less able to respond with the strength characteristic of past cycles. Lenders that are burdened with nonperforming real estate loans in retail and office buildings tend to generalize the difficulties to all real estate. This translates into a general reluctance to lend money for real estate development. Safety is more in government securities than housing for the local community. This, of course is what cycles are made of. Fear is greatest at the bottom when risk in lowest. Caution is forgotten at the cycle peaks and risk is greatest. This is true for debt investors (lenders) and equity investors alike.

Taking the principle of an equal and opposite reaction into consideration, the recovery from the damage to expectations after the S&L debacle is likely to be long in coming. This bodes well for owners of rental apartments who are likely to see a growing shortage of supply as the 1990s progress. The economic and housing recoveries that do occur are likely to be weak and may take on the rolling progression characteristic of the preceding regional real estate depressions.

The lenders who do venture back into the real estate market are likely to be cautious with help in that regard from the regulators. This implies a lack of capital combined with a growing need for low cost rental apartments in the midst of increasing rents, creating a fertile ground for new government incentives and programs in the mid-1990s.

Each phase of the real estate cycle constitutes a trend. The trend consists of buying and selling activity. Low activity is generally considered a poor real estate market. High activity reflects strong demand and favorable market conditions. These characteristics of the real estate cycle apply to every type of property, whether offices, apartments, land, or retail centers. Furthermore, the patterns of market activity for each type of real estate vary in timing. Market activity patterns also vary from region to region of the country.

Consequently, office buildings may be in oversupply in one region at the same time there is a shortage of apartments in the same area. In addition there are time periods when the fluctuations from shortage to oversupply are extreme. These periods of overbuilding, usually in response to a previous shortage, often generate a high number of foreclosures. During the subsequent recovery phase of the cycle, the degree of activity is just as likely to be subdued, even though it still fluctuates between relatively high and low levels with less volatile swings. Therefore, the excesses of the 1980s imply subdued activity in the 1990s.

Regardless of the level of activity, cycles constitute the underlying flow of market transactions through time. Cycles provide insight to market timing, which is important to achieving the purpose of investing in real estate. Cycles have been part of the real estate market as long as there has been a free market, and they are likely to remain the primary timing indicator for real estate investment strategy for years to come.

Sometimes it is difficult to believe that there is a pattern to real estate market activity that has any timing consistency at all. Variations in the strength of job creation, income level, and real estate demand from region to region at different times, and for different types of property, makes finding a pattern seem impossible. But there is a pattern and it does recur. The activity patterns that characterize the real estate market consist of specific factors that can be traced as they unfold.

Because of the large number of variables involved in the real estate market, it is especially important to focus on the underlying factors that constitute cycle activity. Doing so helps simplify the factors classified as market conditions in a manner that permits them to be used for investment planning.

It is equally important to keep in mind the purpose behind investing in real estate: the transfer of purchasing power through time while building real wealth. In fact, the entire process of real estate analysis is designed to define the purpose, provide guidelines to achieve the purpose, and to measure the degree to which the purpose is achieved. Planning investments with an awareness of the importance of timing in accordance with cyclical patterns of activity increases the likelihood of achieving the objectives of real estate investment.

12
Measuring the Financial Performance of Retail Centers

Retail centers are directly linked to the residential housing market. Shopping goes where the people are. When new housing subdivisions are developed, retail services follow. New centers depend on new people. The one requirement for a successful retail center is sufficient population to support the businesses that rent space.

Retail centers perform an essential distribution function in the economy [5]. As a result, the retail space segment of the real estate industry is also linked to the business cycle, employment base, and income levels of the market area. When unemployment is high, retail sales suffer. When real income levels drop, high-end retailers lose customers to the discounters.

Shopping habits reflect the times. Through the years the way retail distribution is accomplished has evolved and changed with the growth and decline of income and leisure time. In the past, stores were outlets for clothing and other necessities and were located in the center of town. National department stores were in the downtown area, as were the local furniture stores, hardware stores, and other merchants. For essentials there were neighborhood grocery stores in the outlying residential enclaves surrounding the downtown area.

Changing Market Conditions and Retail Real Estate

After World War II, as the population began expanding in earnest, supermarkets began appearing in the suburbs for the convenience of the new home owners. The neighborhood grocer faced competition from the new supermarkets, which by the standards then appeared huge and stocked with good buys in food. Some smart retailers located near the new supermarkets and picked up sales from the grocery traffic.

As suburbs radiated from the downtown areas during the 1950s, clusters of retail stores followed, often as branches of the downtown locations operated by local businesses. These clusters centered naturally near the population center of the metropolitan area and shifted gradually as the population grew. Retail clusters were often on the main streets leading to and from the center of town. Much of the expansion of the retail outlets of downtown businesses followed the population center of the city as it shifted away from downtown, as the dependence on the railroad gave way to the car.

Downtown areas were typically at intersections on the roads leading to the city. The main street was usually crossed by a railroad with a depot within walking distance of the business district. The best location for a real estate office just after World War II was on the street that paralleled the railroad tracks across from the train station. That's where the new arrivals first set foot in town, and the real estate agents within line of sight of the train station had the best chance of selling a new home to the new residents as they stepped off the train.

The railroad brought people downtown. Consequently, that's where the retail services were to be found. As automobile use expanded, it allowed the population to move farther from the geographic center of town without being farther away in time. By the mid-1950s, roads leading in an out of growing cities were lined with stores serving the needs of the surrounding housing developments. Use of the car was so much a part of life that residents became less dependent on the downtown area. Although the geographic center of the city was traditionally downtown, the growing suburbs carried the population center outward. As downtown became the primary location for retailing, it was unable to cope with the demands of the automobile for parking and ease of ingress and egress. The needs of the expanding population centered on the automobile, and it had to be accommodated if the public was to be attracted to any area.

As the 1950s progressed, many cities experienced a sprawling growth of housing with stores lining the most heavily traveled streets. It was an efficient if not attractive way to distribute goods and services to the growing population now in lockstep with the car. Neon signs were the attention-getters of the car driver in the 1950s. Every retail outlet in the downtown center saw a glowing neon sign as the way to drum up business of passing motorists. Visibility was the key to retail distribution then, and it is today as well. If they are driving, "they must see it to buy it," was the slogan of the new automobile-based society. Drive-in movies, drive-in restaurants, motels—all were adaptations of retail real estate to the automobile.

As the 1950s ended and the interstate highway system began crossing many cities, the use of automobiles to get retail distribution points reached a new stage. The clusters of shopping outlets away from downtown that were linked by strips of storefronts serving as informal retail centers were faced with new competition. Shopping centers of varying size, serving different population areas, appeared at the interchanges of the new freeways.

These neighborhood centers were designed primarily to accommodate the car. Rather than lining the streets with store fronts, the new centers wrapped around large parking lots. But the lots could not be so large that the store couldn't be readily seen from the street. Visibility was still a requirement to attract the driving shopper, although the use of neon decreased.

The evolution of retail real estate naturally accommodated the car for the convenience it provided the shopper. These new centers used the dominance of the automobile to their advantage by locating on corners where they could be accessed with easy right-hand turns by people on their way home as they exited the new interstate freeway system. Tenants in the centers included the usual lineup along the streets of the early 1950s. Primary anchors were the new supermarkets, a drug store, dry cleaners, bakery, hardware store, variety store, and other retail outlets. Now they moved off the street and back to provide just enough room for parking and easy traffic flow.

The neighborhood shopping center took care of the traffic problem with parking lots. New subdivisions were easily serviced as the population grew farther away from downtown. And with the help of the freeway system, larger regional centers took the example of the neighborhood center and multiplied it tenfold. At first many of the department stores remained downtown. But as the 1960s progressed, lack of parking and the reluctance of shoppers to be inconvenienced with driving all the way downtown caused most merchants to move to the regional centers.

Regional shopping centers began springing up at major freeway interchanges during the 1960s. Furthermore, they had parking lots with free parking unlike the downtown areas. Now the automobile driver didn't have to worry about where to park or about trying to parallel park downtown, and the new centers were closer to home.

With the coming of the shopping centers the adventure was no longer to go downtown. Shopping became a leisure activity and method of entertainment in its own right. Strolling through the local regional shopping center replaced going downtown for citizens with time on their hands. Even local merchants eventually joined the national chains in leaving downtown for the regional shopping centers. Besides, downtown wasn't safe anymore at night and in some cases during the day.

The ability to draw people was so successful that by the 1970s many of the original regional shopping centers were going through major renovation to become enclosed malls. As the population continued to grow, shopping centers grew in size and comfort and evolved into shopping malls. These were the new downtowns where people could shop, enjoying the new entertainment pastime of prosperity.

Neighborhood centers were never threatened by regional centers. They provided different services. Some early regional shopping centers did have supermarkets as tenants, but by the end of the 1970s they had left for more economical and larger quarters, heading toward their own superstore evolution. Shopping centers evolved through various size categories as the population and market area warranted.

But functionally the shopping mall, anchored by several national department stores, dominated the discretionary and leisure activity shopping scene. In contrast, the neighborhood center served as the distribution point for necessities near home. And between the regional and neighborhood centers the strip center of small businesses continued the tradition of providing high visibility and easy access to the driving shopper without a supermarket or major anchor of any sort. In some heavily traveled areas, it almost seemed that there was a drive to build a shopping center on every corner and then fill the space between them with strip centers.

Enclosed malls and major shopping centers are designed for and encourage pedestrian traffic. The major anchors locate at the ends, and the smaller shops line the walkway to draw on the traffic between them. As with the old downtowns of the early 1950s, strolling between stores and window shopping is a way of getting out to see people and pass time—like walking down the main street of the past. At least it has been for those with time and money to spend. There is probably no area of real estate that more directly reflects change in national prosperity than retail centers. The only question is the direction of the next change in this dynamic segment of the real estate market.

The evolution from downtown to regional shopping centers, often surrounded by office buildings, is the natural progression of subdivision development. Functionally, the suburban shopping centers serve as the new central business districts of growing metropolitan areas with the added accommodation of the automobile. As with the evolution of the downtown, as retail outlet storefronts radiated from the city, small strip centers line the main streets leading to the malls. But unlike the storefronts of the past, the new strip centers are set back from the road just enough for parking, acknowledging the importance of the car to the success of the tenants. The loss of leisure time, reduction in real income levels, and the necessity of two-income households provides a hint of the direction of retail real estate in the future.

As more women enter the work force, shopping has become a time drain. With the increased work demands that accompany two-worker families, shopping is becoming more a necessity than a sport, to be done economically and efficiently rather than for fun. Looking for reasonable value is becoming more important than walking the new main street of an enclosed mall. The one social phenomena that is an exception to this trend is the convergence of youth on malls, illustrating the social nature of this replacement for downtown.

The small strip centers of 10 to 20 stores that take advantage of the heavy traffic flows around major shopping areas work well with the requirements of a car-based society. Visibility from the car and easy access and exit by car are the prerequisites to success for these centers. In addition, attractive updated design attracts the convenience shopper. These basic requirements apply equally to the larger neighborhood centers anchored by groceries.

Unlike the malls, ease of access by car is the essential component of a small retail center. People don't stroll the neighborhood center. They shop with what to buy in mind, and after they buy, they leave. It is an inconvenience to go there in the first place, and if the design, location, and traffic pattern in the center makes it even more inconvenient, they are just as likely to find a different, more accessible center.

Small retail centers are not intended for comfort and entertainment like the regional malls. The smaller centers are designed with automobile convenience in mind. That is their service to the customer, and those without automobile convenience and automobile visibility are vulnerable to competition because they don't properly accommodate the technology that created them.

Cyclical Influences on Retail Centers

Retail centers exist because they fulfill an economic need for the distribution of goods and services. This need is the source of real estate value and is based on the use of the property and the function it provides customers. Offices are part of the link in the processing of information; retail centers are part of the link in distributing goods and services [5]. It is the need for this basic support and distribution function in the economy that puts real estate to use. Use generates cash flow, which in turn generates financial value.

Retail real estate is directly affected by the fluctuation of the economy and the changes in income and employment levels. Until the effects of the long wave hit, recessions were to a large degree responsive to the reduction of inventories. In fact, the inventory to sales ratio provided a good indicator of the approach of a recession. And as inventory levels were reduced, a recovery often followed as manufacturing geared up to replenish them. As people starting buying again, the economy recovered and manufacturing began to build inventories back to high levels. As sales slowed, inventories accumulated and manufacturing slowed, layoffs began, and a recession followed until inventories were reduced and the cycle began again. The effects of computerized inventory management has changed this cyclical element and reduced its importance. Nevertheless there is a strong link between retail real estate and the business cycle.

This relationship is especially crucial at the local level where strong job growth or loss of jobs can provide a strong base or decimate retail real estate. When the layoffs of a recession hit a community, retail sales are affected first. When the jobs return, it again shows in retail sales. But the impact of the normal business cycle is not the only cycle felt in retail real estate. Retail centers are designed for the needs of the shopper. The downtowns of the 1950s became obsolete for retail sales as the shopping centers of the 1960s opened in the suburbs. The regional shopping centers of the 1960s have been able to maintain their strength thus far by frequent remodeling, enclosing for climate control, and generally providing comfort for shoppers.

The long wave expansion of the post-World War II period culminating in the overbuilding of the 1980s affected the smaller retail centers as it did other types of real estate. But the reduction in real income levels and the increase in unemployment during the 1990s as the long wave trough works through the economy, is changing the shopping habits of the country. This change may point to the future of retail real estate as large competitively priced warehouse discounters compete for the shopping dollar.

The real estate overbuilding at the end of the long wave cycle during the 1980s hit retail real estate especially hard.

The large regional malls are a highly specialized segment of the real estate business. The smaller neighborhood and strip centers provide the majority of the available investment opportunities and reflect the financial effect of cycles on retail real estate. Often they are built by local developers with equity from local investors and financing by local institutions.

Consequently, these centers are the small business equivalent of the retail distribution segment of real estate. They are subject to the local cycles and because of their size very vulnerable to oversupply.

You can see the impact of the extremes in economic cycles and the impact of job loss and population exodus from cities. The downtown storefronts show the cycle extremes with boarded storefronts. Vacancies in newer centers appear as "For Lease" signs in the windows, large enough to be visible from passing cars. Because of the high visibility of retail real estate it is a clear indicator of the strength of the local economic trends.

Retail real estate was among the first segment to show effects of unemployment during cycle lows during the regional depressions of the 1980s when towns lost whole industries. Since there were no jobs there was no need to distribute goods and less need for retail space.

Nevertheless, the availability of construction capital from the savings and loan (S&L) industry encouraged a surge in building of small centers. These included neighborhood centers anchored by grocery stores ranging to 200,000 ft². There was also a surge in smaller strip centers that were less than 100,000 ft² in size, many speculative, without sufficient lease commitments to cover debt service or an anchor tenant. Many retail centers that were repossessed and eventually ended up in the care of the Resolution Trust Corporation (RTC) fell into this size range. These centers were often newly constructed and reasonably well located, but as with foreclosed property in general, they showed neglect and needed refurbishing to be sold. These centers had been built based on appraisals at the peak of the cycle, and with the oversupply that followed, many of the centers remained vacant. Furthermore, the mortgages based on those appraisals could not be serviced by the cash flows the steadily decreasing rents were likely to generate. The combined effect of the overbuilding from the easy money of the 1980s combined with the rolling real estate depression to increase the supply of small centers while reducing the need for those centers.

In a normal lending environment, the capital available for construction would be restricted by the willingness of anchor tenants to rent space. Anchor tenants' market analysis can work to prevent overbuilding. Their lease commitments become necessary for approval of financing. Unfortunately, many of the speculative centers built at the top of the market were too small to interest anchors or simply went ahead without concern for tenants at all.

Prior to the easy money of the extended real estate cycle top, this traditional prerequisite of an anchor prior to construction of neighborhood shopping centers had served to prevent the type of overbuilding and boom-bust extremes of the office market cycle. But with the peaking of the cycle and easy money during the early 1980s construction money flowed into retail centers without the lease commitments necessary to cover debt service.

Concurrently, oversupply hurt solid developers who lost tenants and had to reduce rents as the glut worked through the system. Speculative overbuilding undercut the traditional procedure for building a new shopping center. The discipline of market analysis forced on real estate developers indirectly through the willingness of major tenants to commit to leasing prior to construction was overwhelmed by easy money. An anchor tenant's estimate of success in a specific market area normally plays a major role in whether a center is actually built. And when financing can be obtained without an anchor tenant, there is usually trouble ahead.

Measuring Financial Performance of Retail Centers

The appraisals at $100/\text{ft}^2$ typical of the supporting documentation for financing purposes that created the glut in retail centers were part of the problem. Lenders thought the appraisal was a statement of value that would hold. Appraisers thought the lenders realized that the value was for one day only. Neither view allowed consideration of the dynamic market that both views helped to create. Appraisals actually contributed to the eventual devaluation of the centers, as more lenders rushed into high real estate values and willingly provided financing for the oversupply that eventually undercut their own loan performance.

Rent projections in the $14 to $16/\text{ft}^2$ range for new centers in the mid-1980s were common, based on rents before the oversupply hit the market. Appraisals in the $85 to $100/\text{ft}^2$ range were also common as a result of the rents in the market. The rush to loan on real estate projects based on peak-cycle rents produced the very supply that drove down the rents that were the security for the loans. Creating oversupply is a circular process. The easy money was self-defeating for the lenders. Relying on appraisals, assumed to be statements of absolute value rather than a price quote for a day, is part of what makes the cycles and trends of the real estate market.

The following description of a strip center illustrates the trend from the peak in 1986 into the bottoming action of the 1990s. This property was appraised at $95/\text{ft}^2$ in 1986 when it came on the market. Rents were projected at $14/\text{ft}^2$. Unfortunately, the center never met projections.

As the financial analysis of the property indicates, rents were at the top of the range and had little room for increases. In fact, the likelihood at the time the center opened was that asking rental rates would have to be reduced to attract tenants. One of the main problems with this project is that there was no major anchor tenant and less than 30 percent of the space had been preleased when it opened. Consequently, the owners were in a position of having to cover debt service. Although they had budgeted leasing expenses and several months of debt service in their plan, they did not anticipate the difficulties would continue for long.

Property Information

Name: Lost Trail Center
Location: 86 Big Bend Road
Completion: December 1986
Number of retail spaces: 15 projected, depending on tenant needs
Size: 45,000 ft^2
Parking: 230 spaces

The initial operating projection for this strip center was based on rents of $14/ft^2. As is customary practice, the tenants were expected to absorb their own utility and janitorial costs. Each retail space was designed for separate utility billings. In addition, tenants were to pay the common area and maintenance (CAM) charges on a prorated square footage basis as well as prorated property taxes and insurance costs. Retail centers are leased on a triple net basis. The tenant pays virtually all expenses related to the leased space. CAM charges cover the lighting and cleaning of the parking lot, landscape maintenance, management, water, sewer, as well as trash removal expense. CAM charges in this area ranged from $1.00 to $1.30/ft^2 depending on the design of the center. Lost Trail Center projected CAM charges at $1.30/ft^2.

CAM charges present a special challenge for retail center owners. They are of little concern when a center is well occupied, but they still must be paid when the center is vacant, along with property taxes and insurance. Management and maintenance is still necessary in vacant centers. Consequently, operating expenses increase for the owner in a vacant center because the tenants are not there to absorb costs. It can get very expensive very fast. Then, of course, there is debt service on the mortgage, which is constant regardless of the occupancy.

The owner-developer of this center was able to obtain financing based on the appraisal of $95/ft^2 and rent projections of $14/ft^2.

One of the great questions of the post-1986 period is whether any of the small centers ever met their initial projections.

The appraised value of $95/ft² for the Lost Trail Center results in a value of $4,275,000.

Appraised Value at $95/ft²

45,000 ft²
× $95
$4,275,000

But land values and building costs can't cover debt service. That is up to rental income. Based on rent projections of $14/ft² and low vacancy with minimum expenses, the center shows the following cash flow potential.

Projected Income at $14/ft²

Scheduled rental income	$630,000
Less vacancy (10%)	(63,000)
Operating income	567,000
Less expenses	(40,850)
Net operating income	$526,150

Net operating income resulting from rental income of $14/ft² and the relatively low expenses involved in operating a center when the occupancy is high indicates the income potential to meet debt service and provide rental cash flow. Since the majority of expenses are passed through to tenants, or paid by tenants, a full center costs less to manage and maintain than a vacant center.

This optimistic pro forma typical of the mid-1980s real estate cycle top does not consider the downside of not meeting the rent projections. This projection reflects the stabilized operation of a center that has completed the rentup phase. The startup budget reflected line items for leasing costs and tenant incentives, operating expenses, and debt service during the nine months estimated to be required to lease the center. One center actually allocated funds to purchase new inventory for retailers who were willing to lease space and open a store in their center. This is the type of incentive that reflects the difficulty of leasing space in a competitive market when there is an oversupply of retail space. These incentives are built into the startup costs and are not reflected in the stabilized income projections after rentup is complete.

The potential loan can be estimated based on the NOI in the income projection for this center.

Calculating Potential Loan Value

$$\frac{\text{NOI } \$526{,}150}{1.3 \text{ debt coverage ratio}} = \$404{,}730 \text{ debt service}$$

The net operating income of $526,150 and a debt coverage ratio of 1.3 indicates a debt service of $404,730 annually or $33,728 monthly.

The annual constant for 25-year loans bearing 11 percent interest is 11.176 percent. This indicates the following potential loan:

Calculating Loan Potential

$$\frac{\text{Debt service } \$404{,}730}{0.117612 \text{ annual constant}} = \$3{,}441{,}230$$

The projected income indicates the center will be able to service a loan of approximately $3,441,230. The annual debt service of approximately $404,730 subtracted from the NOI of $526,150 indicates a rental cash flow of $121,420.

Operating Statement

Scheduled rental income	$630,000
Less vacancy	(63,000)
Operating income	567,000
Less expenses	(40,850)
Net operating income	526,150
Less debt service	(404,730)
Rental cash flow	$121,420

Using the cash flow from rents and a discount rate 4 percent above the lending rate of 11 percent we can calculate the present value of the rental cash flow and add it to the loan balance to estimate the discounted value of the debt and equity. The use of a 15 percent discount rate was common during the mid 1980s by real estate companies. Its construction was based on the internal workings of the companies, but many seemed to be talking to each other. The present value of this cash flow over 25 years when discounted at 15 percent is $784,877. Consequently, the debt value of $3,441,230 and the equity value of $784,877 combine to project a total value of $4,226,000. This is about $94/ft^2 for the center. Tax considerations are ignored in this example because the collapse in value from oversupply makes them incidental.

Calculating Present Value of Debt and Equity

Present value of debt at 11%	$3,441,230
Present value of equity at 15%	784,870
Total present value	$4,226,100

This projection of value is based solely on the income of the center. Both the debt and the equity are derived from the initial $14/ft^2 rental rate. In the real world of price change, when the rental rate changes so does the value. But more importantly, as the rental rates change, so does the ability of the center to cover debt service.

The dynamic nature of the cyclical real estate market would seem to require that any projection be qualified by a statement of likelihood that represents the stage of the cycle and the market conditions on which the projections are based. But projects that come on the market during expansions are usually limited to assumptions that the current conditions and the cash flow reflected by these conditions will continue without change. Furthermore, the implicit assumption is that if change does occur it will be positive. This results frequently from the use of appraisals to establish value that for some reason has taken on meaning that transcends the fluctuations common to all markets.

In this example the rental rates went the way of many centers as time passed and tenants didn't step forward. First the asking rent was compromised by negotiation but not advertised as being lower. Then as time marched on the rates were dropped in marketing efforts to the $12/ft^2 range. Then as the banks foreclosed and tried to rent space without understanding the real estate business, negotiations on potential lease deals seemed impossible. Tight-fisted bankers couldn't seem to make a real estate deal. Then as the banks were taken over by the RTC, management changed again. Of course, the first step was to get an appraisal.

Nothing stops the cost of managing property. The RTC managers seemed as unable to make a deal in the real estate market as the bankers. All the while the smart money was waiting in the background watching prices drop as rents got lower and lower. The more time that passed, the better the prices, and as the 1990s got under way, the prices were getting close enough to make dealing with the RTC worth the effort.

Real estate liquidity is a function of price. The lower the price, the more liquid the property—the more easily it sells. With the repossessed property of the 1980s, the only necessity was for the price to drop to the point that cash flow could be generated. For some retail centers, that price was a far cry from $14/ft^2.

The drop in retail rental rates during the last half of the 1980s illustrates the relationship between true market value and cash flow—the measure of financial performance.

The rental rate on the Lost Trail Center dropped from the original projection in increments of $3/ft^2. Each rental reduction seemed too late to catch the market. The owner was following the trend of rental rates as they dropped. Rather than lower the rental rate below the market, he was chasing the drop in prices and following the trend but never catching the rapidly changing market.

Eventually, the debt service drained his reserves, and the lender foreclosed. The lender failed and the RTC took over. Both had bigger problems to worry about than this center, and the neglect showed. The value continued downward as the few tenants departed for more competitive and better managed space. Each reduction in income translated into lower income, and consequently a lower value based on income.

The change in the net operating income with each drop in rent shows in the summary of operating statements as the rental rates of the center were lowered. The debt service remained the same until it ended with foreclosure.

The developer and the bank lost their investment. The liquidation of debt and equity allowed the center to be competitively priced because no one was fighting for income to pay debt service. Eventually, the center was purchased in a package of property acquired from the RTC. The new owner put money into repairs and remodeling to offset the neglect during foreclosure. He also leased the center below market and paid above-market commissions. Leases were relatively short term in anticipation of raising rents in two to three years.

Summary Pro Forma at Reduced Rental Rates

	Projected $14/ft^2	Actual $11/ft^2	Actual $8/ft^2	Actual $5/ft^2
Income	$630,000	$495,000	$360,000	$225,000
Less vacancy	(63,000)	(346,500)	(280,000)	(45,000)
Less expenses	(40,850)	(67,500)	(67,500)	(67,500)
NOI	526,150	81,000	12,500	112,500
Less debt service	(404,730)	(404,730)	0	0
Cash flow	$121,420	($323,730)	$ 12,500	$112,500

Actual financial performance of the center does not reflect the multimillion dollar potential envisioned when it was first built. The location is the same, the construction is the same. The comparable rents and retail centers on which the value was based were all valid in the mid-1980s when the center was appraised and approved for financing by the lender.

Change, of course is the culprit. It is the downfall of one group and the opportunity for a new group of real estate entrepreneurs. In this case the market moved from relative balance to oversupply, in part because of easily available capital combined with excessively optimistic expectations. The natural weight of the oversupply forced the pricing mechanism to adjust rents to compete in an attempt to generate cash flow.

Measuring Financial Value with a Change of Investors

As the cycle progressed through time, additional funds were invested in an attempt to keep the center open in the hope that tenants could be attracted with incentives and lower rent. The additional infusion of funds by the original developer to cover initial expenses and debt service added a burden that had to be offset by the future rental income if financial value was to be maintained. These negative cash flows changed the financial value of the investment for that investor.

Financial value is the relationship between the investor, the property, and the cashflow generated by the property. It takes an investor to make an investment in real estate. From an investment viewpoint a property does not have financial value without an investor. Then the investor must cause the property to be put to productive use.

Consequently, property becomes an investment when it is owned by an investor who takes on the rights and obligations of equity or debt ownership. When rental income doesn't generate sufficient cash flow to support the obligations of the equity owner, the debt owner repossesses and takes the ownership position. This action ends the investment life for the equity owner.

Each change in ownership begins a new investment life. Each new investment life has new potential as well as actual financial value based on the funds invested and received by the new owner. Therefore, in this sense, real estate has different investment value for each owner, based on the timing and the amount of money invested and received from the property by that owner. Because of this relationship, an investment exists only in the context of the financial circumstances of a specific owner as defined by time and money during the ownership period.

Consequently, as the center changed ownership, the financial potential for the former investor ended and a new potential began for the new owner. An old investment life ended and a new investment life began. By the time the debt had been completely written off, the bottom of the cycle was approaching. The reduced price negotiated with the RTC of $25/ft^2 or $1,1125,000 provided room for price appreciation when rent increases once again became possible as the cycle turned upward.

The cycle of development, repossession, and purchase at bottom dollar price illustrates the movement of ownership through the real estate cycle. The disruption of financial value experienced by the developer and the lender on Lost Trail Center are examples of the effect market adjustments have on ownership.

The period of ownership by the lender represents a gap in the entrepreneurial potential. The developer who created the center put effort into the operation and tried to make it work in spite of the limits imposed by the market cycle. He took an active interest in the success of the center. The lender who repossessed the center would have preferred not to have gone through the process. Repossession is forced ownership, usually as a last resort after most other alternatives have been tried. Therefore, it is understandable that the entrepreneurial effort by lenders in the early stages of a real estate depression might fall short of what is needed.

Lenders without prior experience don't realize the extent of the management obligation associated with real estate. Their role as debt investors is understandably passive, and the same passive attitude tends to carry over after repossession. As a result, the property suffers from the lack of active management interest. For them it is a problem, not an opportunity.

The investor who acquired the center out of foreclosure has the opportunity because of the price reduction and new cycle potential. His role is one of active entrepreneurial effort that creates value, and the chances of success are greater because of it. In this case, the period of ownership by lenders represents a gap in the cycle, during which a caretaker role is assumed until the market changes or the price adjusts sufficiently to interest a new entrepreneur in the financial potential. Starting from a base of $5 rents and a price of $1,125,000 greatly increases the upside potential of the center as the cycle improves.

Risk of foreclosure is eliminated for the investor by acquiring the property for cash at this reduced price. The new financial projections starting from a base at the new rent reflect the new upward trend in the cycle as the 1990s progress.

The investor who acquired Lost Trail Center reduced rents to $4.50/ft^2 and chose his tenants carefully to ensure a good tenant mix. His objective was to fill the center and eliminate the expense of operation. Leases were limited to three year terms. His reasoning was that a full center on triple net leases that covered his holding costs would increase the bottom line. Then as the market improved he could increase rents. This plan resulted in the following financial scenario, which he planned to have in place during the second year of operation:

Operating Statement

Scheduled rental income	$202,500
Less vacancy	0
Operating income	202,500
Less expenses	10,000
Net operating income	192,500
Less debt service	0
Rental cash flow	$192,500

This initial year's operating statement translates into a new projection of financial value over the next several years that involves new financing and an increase in rents. The new investor acquired the center at a price that had little room for downside movement and a lot of room for an increase in rents, loan value, and sale price. This example illustrates the impact of the real estate cycle on the financial value of the property. The financial value was different for each investor, both debt and equity investors, depending on the phase of the cycle during which they participated in the property.

Financial projections for the new investor illustrate the impact of an improving cycle on the performance of the center and the competitive advantage of lower rents. He anticipated increasing rents to $6/ft^2 in the fifth year and $8/ft^2 in the eighth year of operation while maintaining full occupancy.

	Year 2	Year 5	Year 8
Rental income	$202,500	$270,000	$360,000
Less vacancy	0	0	0
Income	202,500	270,000	360,000
Less expenses	10,000	10,000	10,000
NOI	$192,000	$260,000	$350,000

By the end of the eighth year, the value of the center for loan purposes would exceed the bargain purchase price. The calculation was based on the following estimate of loans at that time:

$$\frac{\text{NOI } \$350,000}{1.3 \text{ debt coverage ratio}} = \$269,230 \text{ debt service}$$

This debt coverage ratio would permit a loan of $2,469,000 at 10 percent interest for 25 years. Furthermore, the loan proceeds would be tax free.

The upturn in the cycle as real estate recovers from the overbuilding of the 1980s represents the change in market conditions that makes real estate cycle crucial to planning and timing of debt an equity investments.

Percentage Rents: The Unique Retail Center Cash Flow

Larger retail centers build upside potential into the operation through percentage rents. This rental structure also protects the tenant's operation by ensuring that the rent paid does not exceed performance guidelines for the tenant's industry.

For example, grocery stores anticipate that 1 percent to 1½

percent of their gross sales will be paid in rent. Restaurants antic-ipate that they must keep their rent below 9 percent of gross to remain profitable. Generally, the higher the markup on the retail item the higher the percentage rent paid. Jewelers pay as high as 10 to 12 percent in percentage rent.

Percentage rents can be structured in several ways as a result of lease negotiations. Basically, percentage rents work as a bonus to the center, which is viewed as the result of a good location and well-maintained operation. Although smaller centers do not use percentage rent, they are considered crucial by many developers and are common practice in centers above 100,000 ft².

The structure of the lease provisions for percentage rents can be tailored to the needs of the tenant. For example, during the first year of the lease the tenant may require that the lease be on a percentage basis only so the center shares the risk of slow sales until the location is established.

For example, the center may lease space at a base rent of $12 per ft², which represents $120,000 in rent for a 10,000 ft² tenant. If the tenant has a 5 percent budget for rent, the first year's sale will have to hit $2,400,000 to meet the $12 base rent of the center.

Calculating the Relationship Between Base Rent and Sales

$$10,000 \text{ ft}^2 \text{ at } \$12 = \frac{\$120,000}{0.05} = \$2,400,000$$

Anticipating slow sales during the first year, the tenant may negotiate a percentage rent only with no base rent so that the rent does not exceed the 5 percent guideline. Consequently, if the first year's sales are $1,200,000, the tenant will pay $60,000 in rent.

Calculating Percentage Rent During the First Year

Sales $1,200,000 × 0.05 = $60,000

Then in the second year the percentage rent would start above the $2,400,000 sales level and the base rent of $12/ft² would be payable even if sales do not reach that level. Therefore, the tenant pays the base rent plus 5 percent of gross sales above $2,400,000. For example, if sales were $2,900,000, the second year the rent would be calculated as follows.

Calculating Percentage Rent above Base Rent

Sales above $2,400,000	$500,000
	× 0.05
Additional rent	$ 25,000
Base rent	$120,000
Total rent	$145,000

Center developers look to percentage rents for profit. Base rents often just barely cover the expenses and debt service. Therefore, the developer must look to the performance of the center as a result of design, accessibility, and visibility to attract buyers who will provide enough sales to generate percentage rents.

Percentage rents illustrate the close tie between retailers and shopping centers as a link in the distribution of retail goods and services. Percentage rents within the operating margin guidelines of the tenant combined with the base rent needed for the center to stay in existence benefit both. As sales increase, the cash flow of the retailer and the center increase.

13
Computer Techniques for Analyzing Leases

Leases represent legally defined cash flows. When a tenant and landlord sign a lease, the result is definition of the timing and amounts of cash flow. Prior to the signing there are usually extensive negotiations.

The tenant is likely to be considering space in competing buildings, each of which is offering a different combination of inducements. The objective of the tenant is to minimize the financial cost of the space needed.

The landlord is usually aware of the competition of other buildings and the need to outshine the competition by providing the services desired by the tenant. Concurrently, the landlord is trying to maximize the cash flow of the building without losing the prospective tenant to the competition.

The give and take of lease negotiations can become confusing. It is often difficult for tenants and landlords alike to evaluate the financial value of the seemingly incomparable terms of different lease structures.

Deals are lost by landlords who turn away tenants who have specific needs that make little or no difference in the bottom line performance of a building; yet, the landlord may never have known it or understood how to determine the actual financial effect. So, by turning away a perfectly good tenant, a building's cash flow may continue to suffer for no reason other than the ignorance of the landlord.

Tenants are faced with an even more difficult selection when looking for space. With several equally suitable locations to choose from, the combination of terms and incentives can seem impossible to reconcile and compare on an equal basis.

The techniques that follow are intended to provide information that will help you analyze different types of leases and lease terms. Some of the methods relate to landlords, some to tenants, and some to both. Most common spreadsheet programs can be adapted for use in this type of analysis. Spreadsheet commands and their syntax vary slightly from program to program, but the mathematics of net present value remain constant. Application is all that's needed.

Calculating Constant Dollar Value

Constant dollar value is the present value of a series of cash flows after adjustment for inflation. This calculation determines the purchasing power represented by the lease payments. For example, what is the constant dollar value of a five-year office space lease at $20/ft^2 with no escalations when inflation is 4 percent?

Lease payments are monthly in advance. Consequently, the dollar amounts are best calculated on a 12-period basis, representing monthly payments. To accomplish monthly discounting, simply divide the annual discount rate by 12. Therefore, the command may look somewhat like this, depending on the design of the spreadsheet you are using:

$$NPV (A1:E12,4\%/12)$$

This command tells the computer to calculate the net present value for the amounts in column A row 1 through column E row 12 at a discount rate equal to one-twelfth of 4 percent. Since the rental rate is $20/ft^2 per year it must also be converted to a monthly amount. This is best done separately and entered in the cell as an amount rather than as a separate formula. Therefore, the spreadsheet will discount the monthly rent based on a 4 percent annual rate as follows:

1.67	1.67	1.67	1.67	1.67
1.67	1.67	1.67	1.67	1.67
1.67	1.67	1.67	1.67	1.67
1.67	1.67	1.67	1.67	1.67
1.67	1.67	1.67	1.67	1.67
1.67	1.67	1.67	1.67	1.67
1.67	1.67	1.67	1.67	1.67
1.67	1.67	1.67	1.67	1.67
1.67	1.67	1.67	1.67	1.67
1.67	1.67	1.67	1.67	1.67
1.67	1.67	1.67	1.67	1.67
1.67	1.67	1.67	1.67	1.67

Total 100   NPV 90.68

Discounting indicates that the constant dollar value of the lease payments is $90.68. Or another way of looking at the constant dollar value is on the basis of $/ft^2/year:

Loss to Inflation

$$\text{Total present value of lease} = \frac{90.68}{5 \text{ years}} = 18.14 \text{ CDV}$$

Nominal amount	$20/ft^2
Less constant dollar value	18.14
Loss to inflation	1.86

The application of constant dollar discounting is in comparing the nominal value of the lease payments with their purchasing power value. In phases of the cycle when inflation is high, constant dollar calculation can be useful in setting terms to protect the landlord. For example, a lease with no escalation automatically gives the tenant a discount as each month passes.

Adjusting for Beginning and End of Period Discounting

The net present value formula used by spreadsheets assumes that cash flows occur at the end of the discount period. Lease payments usually occur at the first of the month because they are paid in advance. The fact that they occur at the beginning of the period instead of the end can be adjusted by the way you sum the discounted cash flows in the spreadsheet.

The first month's cash flow is not discounted. It is the beginning cash flow and therefore has a present value equal to its nominal value. This is similar to the treatment of a down payment on a purchase analysis, which occurs at the beginning of ownership before any time has passed. Since no time has passed it is not necessary to discount the first cash flow.

This type of time grouping is one reason it is useful to clearly specify the amount and the timing of the cash flows in a manner that will provide a sufficiently accurate calculation of net present value for decision purposes.

Making the adjustment for lease analysis purposes requires a slight shift in thinking. For example, the NPV function on your spreadsheet will discount and sum the cells you tell it to. Although you may have a 12-month lease, you need to discount 11 months of rent, since the nominal and present value of the first month are equal. Then the first month rent is added to the net present value solution provided by the spreadsheet.

This procedure is no different than is done with a down payment. In most cases the first month's rent and damage deposit function as down payments and therefore are not discounted. The second month's rent is paid on the first day of the second month, which occurs after the last day of the first month. This places the second month's payment at the end of the first discounting time period.

Consequently, in a one-year lease it is necessary to discount the rents for months 2 through 12; then add in the nominal amount for the first month's rent.

For simplification, the following lease payments represent annual rent of $1000/year on a land lease discounted at 8 percent. The net present value is shown as calculated by spreadsheet, discount table factors, and the HP-12C business calculator, which is widely used in the real estate industry.

To calculate NPV, discount 11 rent payments and add back the nominal amount of the initial payment. For example (keeping in mind that formulas differ somewhat with different spreadsheets), enter the lease payments in the appropriate cells, as defined by rows and columns, and apply the NPV function built into the spreadsheet.

Spreadsheet

Row	Column: A	Spreadsheet formula
1	1000	NPV(A1:A11,8%)
2	1000	Therefore: NPV of A1:A11 = 7138.96
3	1000	Plus PV of first payment = 1000.00
4	1000	NPV of cash flows = 8138.96
5	1000	
6	1000	
7	1000	
8	1000	
9	1000	
10	1000	
11	1000	

In this example, the spreadsheet computes the NPV of Column A, Rows 1 through 11, which is written as cells A1:A11. The NPV formula discounts the amount in each cell and then sums the result to determine net present value. It is up to you to arrange the amounts in a meaningful time frame. That requires that the NPV function in the spreadsheet not be applied to the initial lease payment that is made before any time passes. To get the NPV of the entire cash flow series, the first lease payment must be added back to the NPV solution provided by the spreadsheet, as indicated in the above example. The same solution is found using the discount factors for 8 percent.

Discount Factors at 8%

1	1000	0.925926	925.926
2	1000	0.857339	857.339
3	1000	0.793832	793.832
4	1000	0.735030	735.03
5	1000	0.680583	680.583
6	1000	0.630170	630.17
7	1000	0.583490	583.49
8	1000	0.540269	540.269
9	1000	0.500249	500.249
10	1000	0.463193	463.193
11	1000	0.428883	428.883
		PV sum =	7138.96

The next step is to add the initial lease payment of $1,000 to the sum of the present values as calculated using the 8 percent discount factors in the above example.

PV sum per discount factors	$7,138.96
Initial lease payment	$1,000
Net present value	$8,138.96

The same computation can be made using the Hewlett-Packard 12C Programmable Financial Calculator, using the following key sequence for NPV.

Calculating NPV Using the HP-12C

1. Clear the calculator: f reg (clx)

2. Enter the initial lease payment: 1000

3. Press: g CFo

4. Enter the second lease payment: 1000

5. Press: g CFj

7. Enter the number of consecutive equal payments: 11

8. Press: g Nj

9. Enter the discount rate: 8

10. Press: i

11. Press: f NPV

12. Read the NPV: 8,138.96

This is an example of NPV calculation to a cash flow series using different computation tools. The purpose is to illustrate that the initial payment in a lease is not included in the spreadsheet cell when it occurs prior to the passage of time. In this case the cash flows are all negative for the tenant and positive for the landlord. Consequently, no change in sign to negative is used, since the net of the present values is not affected.

Calculating the NPV of First and Last Month's Rent and Deposits

One of the few positive cash flows received by a tenant occurs when a deposit is refunded at the end of a lease. Many buildings negotiate, when possible, for first and last month's rent and a deposit at the time of signing. These initial payments affect the financial value of the lease for the landlord and the financial cost to the tenant.

Variation in lease terms between buildings has a direct impact on the cost of a lease for a tenant. Sometimes the terms are more of an inconvenience than a significant dollar amount. Nevertheless, each cash flow component adds to or subtracts from the net present value amount over the life of the lease. When comparing lease offers from different buildings, the NPV of each cash flow, both negative and positive, can be accounted for in the spreadsheet.

In the following example, two leases are compared with slightly different terms regarding first and last month's rent and the refund of damage deposits.

Lease One terms: First and last month's rent on signing plus $2,000 deposit of which $1,000 is refundable.

Lease Two terms: First month's rent plus $2,000 refundable deposit.

Month	Lease one Year 1	Lease one Year 2	Lease two Year 1	Lease two Year 2
0	$12,000		$7,000	
1	$ 0	$5,000	$ 0	$5,000
2	$ 5,000	$5,000	$5,000	$5,000
3	$ 5,000	$5,000	$5,000	$5,000
4	$ 5,000	$5,000	$5,000	$5,000
5	$ 5,000	$5,000	$5,000	$5,000
6	$ 5,000	$5,000	$5,000	$5,000
7	$ 5,000	$5,000	$5,000	$5,000
8	$ 5,000	$5,000	$5,000	$5,000
9	$ 5,000	$5,000	$5,000	$5,000
10	$ 5,000	$5,000	$5,000	$5,000
11	$ 5,000	$5,000	$5,000	$5,000
12	$ 5,000	$ 0	$5,000	$5,000
13		−$1,000		−$2,000

This is how the cash flows for each lease appear in relation to the time they are paid. Applying the NPV function in a spreadsheet requires that the cash flow be treated somewhat differently so the initial payments are not included in the NPV calculation.

Also note that this lease is from the perspective of the tenant paying out the cash flows. Therefore, the deposit refund is entered as a negative amount so it will reduce the cost at the end of the lease.

Discounting amounts with negative signs occurring periodically in a lease or at the end of a lease is no different than the treatment of positive amounts. The only effect occurs when the positive and negative amounts are netted. In this example, the negative amount reduces the cost of the lease when it is returned to the tenant at the end of the term. Since time has passed, the deposit must be discounted.

The following grouping illustrates how to construct a spreadsheet to discount the cash flows in this example. The thing to keep in mind is the number of cash flows being discounted.

In the first year of both leases there are 11 rent payments made after the beginning of the lease. The first month's payment is made on signing before time has passed and is not included in the spreadsheet listing for application of the NPV formula. Therefore, in Leases One and Two there are 11 payments that are discounted the first year, since the first month is not.

Lease One also has 11 rent payments that are discounted in the second year because the last month is paid in advance. Lease Two has 12 rental payments in the second year. Both have a refund in month 13. Therefore, Lease One has 23 cash flows (22 rent, 1 deposit refund) that are discounted plus the initial rent and deposit that are not. Lease Two has 24 cash flows (23 rent, 1 deposit refund) that are discounted plus the initial deposit that is not.

These are monthly rent payments, and therefore, the monthly discount rate must be used in the spreadsheet formula. This requires simply dividing the annual discount rate of 8 percent by 12; for example: NPV(A1:B13,8%/12).

	Lease one		Lease two	
Month	Year 1	Year 2	Year 1	Year 2
1	$5,000	$5,000	$5,000	$5,000
2	$5,000	$5,000	$5,000	$5,000
3	$5,000	$5,000	$5,000	$5,000
4	$5,000	$5,000	$5,000	$5,000
5	$5,000	$5,000	$5,000	$5,000
6	$5,000	$5,000	$5,000	$5,000
7	$5,000	$5,000	$5,000	$5,000
8	$5,000	$5,000	$5,000	$5,000
9	$5,000	$5,000	$5,000	$5,000
10	$5,000	$5,000	$5,000	$5,000
11	$5,000	$5,000	$5,000	$5,000
12		$ 0		$5,000
13		−$1,000		−$2,000
PV of payments		$101,145.74		$104,584.54
Initial payment		12,000.00		7,000.00
NPV		$113,145.74		$111,584.54

The NPV function built into the spreadsheet discounts the cash flows for the cells as instructed. After that discounted amount is obtained, the initial payments, which represent present value amounts, are included to determine the NPV of the two leases.

The net present value amounts of these two leases represent the financial cost when discounted at 8 percent. By discounting the cash flows you can determine which lease represents the best financial value—the one that is less expensive.

Calculating the Financial Value of Rent Abatements

Variations in lease terms during competitive markets often include free rent during the first part of the lease. One or two month's free rent can reduce the cost of a lease over the term. Since most office buildings compete on the basis of rent/ft^2, it can be useful to run the rental payments for the term of the lease, determine the net present value, and reduce it to a cost ft^2/year.

The following example illustrates two lease alternatives with the following terms: Both are three-year terms for 10,000 ft^2; Lease one is $21/ft^2; Lease Two is $21.75/ft^2. Lease One requires the first month's rent on signing. Lease Two has three month's free rent with the fourth month's rent paid at signing; therefore, there is no rent due in the fourth month of Lease Two.

Lease One			Lease Two		
$17,000	$17,500	$ 17,500	0	$18,125	$ 18,125
$17,500	$17,500	$ 17,500	0	$18,125	$ 18,125
$17,500	$17,500	$ 17,500	0	$18,125	$ 18,125
$17,500	$17,500	$ 17,500	0	$18,125	$ 18,125
$17,500	$17,500	$ 17,500	$18,125	$18,125	$ 18,125
$17,500	$17,500	$ 17,500	$18,125	$18,125	$ 18,125
$17,500	$17,500	$ 17,500	$18,125	$18,125	$ 18,125
$17,500	$17,500	$ 17,500	$18,125	$18,125	$ 18,125
$17,500	$17,500	$ 17,500	$18,125	$18,125	$ 18,125
$17,500	$17,500	$ 17,500	$18,125	$18,125	$ 18,125
$17,500	$17,500	$ 17,500	$18,125	$18,125	$ 18,125
$17,500	$17,500	$ 17,500	$18,125	$18,125	$ 18,125
Total		$612,500			$580,000
First payment		17,500			18,125
Total value		$630,000			$598,125
Ave./ft^2/yr		21			19.94
Difference		1.06			
PV		$544,679.65			$508,485.84
Initial month		17,500.00			18,125.00
NPV		$562,179.65			$526,610.84
Ave. NPV/ft^2		18.74			17.55
Difference		1.19			

Calculating the financial value of free rent in monthly leases requires running the cash flows for the months in question so that the NPV can be applied to the appropriate cash flow in the appropriate time sequence.

Simplifying Calculation of Lease Escalations

Net present value can be used to evaluate the terms of a lease based solely on the rate/ft^2 per year. During negotiations after a particular building has been selected, NPV can be useful in working out the details of alternative methods of structuring the lease rate.

For example, the building owner may be open to several methods of structuring escalation of the lease rate, including a percentage increase, a lower percentage with a bump in rate into the lease term, and a fixed dollar escalation in the rate. These alternative calculations can be simplified for purposes of comparison by viewing them on the basis of net present value per year per ft^2.

In the following example, three alternative methods of escalating the yearly rate/ft^2 are presented. The first alternative is a 2 percent/year increase with a $2 bump in rental rate in the sixth year of the seven year term. The second alternative is a 3 percent fixed annual increase. The third is a fixed dollar increase each year.

The spreadsheet computes the net present value of each alternative on a square footage basis. In addition, the average nominal rental rate is also computed.

Comparing Lease Escalation Provisions

Year	2%/bump	3%	Fixed
1	28.70	28.70	28.70
2	29.27	29.56	29.70
3	29.86	30.45	30.70
4	30.46	31.36	31.70
5	31.07	32.30	32.70
6	33.69	33.27	33.70
7	34.36	34.27	34.70
NPV/ft^2	22.88	23.15	23.35
Ave. rate	31.06	31.42	31.70

Signing a lease without knowing the financial consequences of the terms puts the tenant and the landlord at a disadvantage. It is like negotiating in the dark. You can compare the financial effect of different lease terms more efficiently by discounting the annual square footage rates.

Most leases can be analyzed sufficiently using the annual rental rate on a square footage basis. In fact, building a spreadsheet using the cost and income components on a square footage basis can take much of the complexity out of the calculation.

Determining the Financial Value of Tenant Improvements

One of the important considerations for tenants is the amount of tenant improvement (TI) allowance provided by a building. Frequently, the building standard is insufficient for the needs of the tenant. Consequently, lease negotiations can rapidly lead to questions about who will pay for the tenant improvements above the standard allowance. Typically, the landlord finances the amount in excess of the allowance and amortizes it over the term of the lease. Usually, the amount amortized bears interest, and the monthly payment is treated as a component of base rent.

For example, if the building standard allowance is $15/ft² and the improvements the tenant wants are $20/ft², the amount above standard is $5/ft². On a 13,000 ft², lease that amount would be $65,000. If it is amortized over the five-year term of the lease with interest of 10 percent, the payment would be $1,381.06/ month. This amount would be added to the monthly lease payments, representing an increase of $1.28/ft² in rent.

Per ft² Cost of Above-Standard Improvements

$$\$1{,}381.06 \times 12 = \frac{\$16{,}573}{13{,}000} = \$1.28 \text{ per ft}^2/\text{yr.}$$

In the following example the lease rate is $19/ft² the first year with 3 percent/year increases for years four and five. The above-standard tenant improvements are amortized monthly including 10 percent interest over the term of the lease, which is five years. Therefore, there are three rent components:

1. Base rent
2. Escalation of 3%/year
3. Amortization payments on above standard TIs

These rent components can be summarized in the spreadsheet as follows, and the monthly rent payments can be determined and discounted to determine the financial effect for the tenant.

Summarizing Rent Components

	Year 1	Year 2	Year 3	Year 4	Year 5
Base rent (adjusted)	19.00	19.00	19.57	20.16	20.76
Escalation, 3%	0	0.57	0.59	0.61	0.62
Improvements	1.28	1.28	1.28	1.28	1.28
Total	20.28	20.85	21.44	22.05	22.66

At this point there is a choice of discounting the cash flows per ft² on an annual basis or running the cash flows as monthly amounts and discounting them as actually received. Both approaches are used in practice. The monthly series provides a more accurate figure. The annual per foot rents are easier to deal with and require less time to compute and are useful for comparison of variation of financial terms within a single lease.

As the cash flow analysis below indicates, there is a variation in the per ft² present value amounts when discounted based on monthly rents or annual square footage rates.

	Year 1	Year 2	Year 3	Year 4	Year 5
	$ 21,970	$ 22,588	$ 23,227	$ 23,888	$ 24,548
	$ 21,970	$ 22,588	$ 23,227	$ 23,888	$ 24,548
	$ 21,970	$ 22,588	$ 23,227	$ 23,888	$ 24,548
	$ 21,970	$ 22,588	$ 23,227	$ 23,888	$ 24,548
	$ 21,970	$ 22,588	$ 23,227	$ 23,888	$ 24,548
	$ 21,970	$ 22,588	$ 23,227	$ 23,888	$ 24,548
	$ 21,970	$ 22,588	$ 23,227	$ 23,888	$ 24,548
	$ 21,970	$ 22,588	$ 23,227	$ 23,888	$ 24,548
	$ 21,970	$ 22,588	$ 23,227	$ 23,888	$ 24,548
	$ 21,970	$ 22,588	$ 23,227	$ 23,888	$ 24,548
	$ 21,970	$ 22,588	$ 23,227	$ 23,888	$ 24,548
	$ 21,970	$F22,588	$ 23,227	$ 23,888	$ 24,548
	$ 21,970	$ 22,588	$ 23,227	$ 23,888	$ 24,548
PV 8%	$252,562	$492,578	$720,958	$938,558	$1,145,944
PV/RSF	19.43	18.95	18.49	18.05	17.63

The monthly rent is discounted based on the monthly rate for 8 percent, which is calculated by dividing 8 percent by 12 to get

0.6667 percent (0.00667). This percentage represents the periodic rate for the cash flows received for each period or month. If the rent had been paid quarterly, the periodic rate for an 8 percent discount factor would be 8 percent (0.08) divided by 4, or 2 percent (0.02).

Furthermore, the present value of the monthly cash flows is slightly higher because of the timing of the cash flows. The annual rental rate discounted at 8 percent indicates a present value of 17.06, while the monthly cash flows for the same office space indicate a present value of $17.63/ft^2$. This difference may not be significant for decision purposes when both lease terms are compared on an equal basis (monthly to monthly; yearly to yearly). But if the lease terms are close, it may be necessary to compare them based on actual cash flow amounts and timing.

Year	
1	20.28
2	20.85
3	21.44
4	22.05
5	22.66
8 percent rate	
PV/RSF	17.06

In both the monthly example and the yearly rate example, all cash flows are discounted including the initial month and the initial year. This was done for explanation purposes and is commonly used by some analysts because of the way the NPV function works on spreadsheets. The built-in function will discount each cash flow as if it occurred at the end of the period in question. That is why the initial payments are best not included in the discounted cash flows and added back to the discounted value (NPV) after the computation. The initial cash flow usually occurs before any time passes, and therefore its nominal and present values are the same.

The method of calculating NPV used by spreadsheets can be duplicated on the HP-12C by entering a zero for the initial cash flow (CFo). This adjustment to simulate the calculation of the spreadsheet produces a net present value of 85.302479 at the 8 percent discount rate in the above example as did the spreadsheet.

Converting NPV Lease Amounts to Square Footage Amounts

Net present value is calculated as a single dollar amount for the cash flow series. Each cash flow is discounted based on the time it occurs. Then the discounted amounts are summed, which nets the positive and negative cash flows and generates a net dollar value.

The net present value dollar amount must then be converted to $/ft^2/year. In the example above the actual present value of the yearly rates discounted at 8 percent was $85.30, which is then divided by five years to get the average present value of the rental rate of the lease ($17.06/ft^2).

The $85.30 amount can also be used to determine the present value of the lease over the five-year term by multiplying it by the square footage of the lease.

Computing the Total Present Value of a Lease

$$\$85.30 \times 13{,}000 \text{ ft}^2 = \$1{,}108{,}900$$

Note that this is a lower amount when compared to the total present value calculated based on the monthly rental payments. That amount is $1,145,944 as indicated on the spreadsheet example appearing above.

The conversion of gross present value amounts appearing in the spreadsheet requires additional work. The running total or cumulative amounts that appear at the bottom of each column in the example represent the present value for the accumulated time period and must be divided by the product of the years and size of the lease to get the present value to date per ft^2.

For example, in the third year the present value of the cash flows discounted at 8 percent monthly is $720,958. In order to convert this amount to the present value per ft^2 at the end of the third year, it must be divided by the total square footage of the lease multiplied by the number of years over which the cash flows were discounted.

Converting Cumulative Present Value to ft^2/yr

$$\frac{\$720{,}958}{13{,}000 \text{ ft}^2 \times 3 \text{ years}} = \$18.49 \text{ PV/ft}^2/\text{yr}$$

The calculation of a running total or cumulative amount using a spreadsheet should be done with caution so that the totals for each year are not entered at the base of the initial years prior to calculation of the NPV for subsequent years. Since NPV is part amount and part time, the ultimate value can only be calculated by including the values in all the previous cells. Therefore, if you calculate the NPV for the first year and put it at the bottom of the column, the spreadsheet will pick up and include that amount when computing the NPV for the first and second years. This danger occurs only when you put the NPV solution at the base of the column when moving left to right in time.

One way to avoid this is to calculate the cumulative NPV at the end of the lease first. Then calculate the NPV for the next to last year moving right to left in time. Therefore, in a five-year lease the cumulative amount for the entire lease at the end of five years would be calculated first. Then the NPV for four years would be calculated. This allows you to put the totals at the bottom of the columns as calculated without interfering with the sequence of time-amount computation of the built-in NPV function. Another way is to do the calculations to the side of the cash flow series and transfer the amount to base of each yearly column.

Calculating Load Factors in the Private and Government Sectors

In these examples net rentable square footage is used because that is the basis for calculation and payment. In office leasing, tenants actually base space requirements on the usable space they need. The difference between usable and rentable space is the load factor of the building. The load factor amount is stated as a percentage and varies from building to building, depending on the efficiency with which it was designed.

Load factors can range from the low range of 8 percent to 15 percent and higher. This percentage is the amount added to the usable space rented by the tenant, which increases the monthly rent. It is a charge for the lobby, hallways, and other common areas in the building.

With leases involving privately owned buildings, these charges are routinely accepted and in some cases become a factor for tenants in selecting space. A building with a lower load factor means the tenant can rent the same space for a lower rental rate.

For example, a tenant who needs 15,000 ft² of usable area will actually pay for 15,000 ft² plus the additional charge computed for the building's load factor. A building renting for $16/ft^2 that has a load factor of 8 percent has a lower net rentable cost than a building renting for the same amount with a 15 percent load factor.

Comparison of Net Usable and Net Rentable Square Footage

	Building A	Building B
Usable space	15,000 ft^2	15,000 ft^2
Load factor	8%	15%
Load	1,200 ft^2	2,250 ft^2
Rentable space	16,200 ft^2	17,250 ft^2
Rate	$ 16	$ 16
Annual rent	$259,200	$276,000

Difference $16,800/year

Customary practices in office leasing regarding load factors are not followed by government agencies. The General Services Administration (GSA) looks at each building and makes a determination as to the load factor acceptable to the agency. Consequently, the net to the building owner from a government lease may be reduced when compared to a private sector lease. There are really no guidelines for what the government is likely to do with a specific building. Challenges to the rental structure depend on the building and the way it is designed.

If a review of the building indicates that government employees will not enter through the lobby, the charge allocated to the lobby is likely to be refused by the government.

The net effect of this is that it costs the owner to rent space to the government, and an adjustment in cash flow will be necessary. Essentially, the refusal to accept the standard building load factor lowers the rental income of the landlord.

Using Spreadsheets to Determine the Value of Land Leases

One of main benefits of using a spreadsheet to calculate net present value is the ability to discount cash flows over very long time periods without special programming.

This capability allows you to generate the cash flows for long-term land leases and determine the present value with ease. For example, say you are presented with an opportunity to lease a corner location to a bank. There are two ways the bank is willing to structure the deal. The first way is a 30-year lease payable monthly at $2500/month. The total nominal value of this lease is $900,000.

Thirty-Year Lease

$2,500
× 360
$900,000

The other alternative is a 20-year lease for $3000/month which has a nominal value of $720,000.

Twenty-Year Lease

$3,000
× 240
$720,000

Which of these two offers is most financially valuable? On the face of it, the 30-year lease appears to offer more value because it has a higher nominal value, but the higher payments of the 20-year lease make a difference in the financial value.

By entering the lease payments in your spreadsheet straight down for 360 cells for the 30-year lease at $2,500, and 240 cells at $3,000 for the 20-year lease, and applying the NPV function you can determine the relative financial value of these monthly cash flows. The formula make look something like this:

NPV(A1:A360,10%/12), which generates an NPV of $284,877 (30 yr)

NPV(B1:B240,10%/12), which generates an NPV of $310,874 (20 yr)

Consequently, the financial value of the 20-year lease exceeds the value of the 30-year lease by $25,997 when discounted at a 10 percent monthly rate.

Formulas and Discount Factor Tables

Discounting is the reciprocal of compounding. Compounding produces future value by multiplication.

$$FV = PV \times (1 + i)^n$$

Discounting produces present value by division.

$$PV = \frac{FV}{(1 + i)^n}$$

Both use the same basic formula, but apply it differently to cash flows occurring at different times.

Both calculations measure change in the amount of funds with the passage of time, but under different circumstances. Compounding calculates future value by applying a chosen interest rate to an amount during a time period extending from the beginning of the investment into the future.

Discounting calculates present value by applying a chosen interest rate (called a *discount rate*), to future amounts during a time period extending from the future back to the present, or beginning of the investment period. As a result, discounting solves for the present value that would grow to the future value at the compounded interest rate. Discounting is literally compounding in reverse and nothing more.

The tables in this appendix are discount rate factors for calculation of present values.* Each factor is based on the receipt of one

---

*The discount rate factors in the following tables were generated by computer and published in Ward S. Curran, *Principles of Financial Management* (New York: McGraw-Hill Book Company, 1970).

dollar at the end of the year and is calculated using the present value formula to create a factor, simplified as:

$$P = \frac{1}{(1 + i)^n}$$

Present value factors are actually the discounted value of one dollar at the discount rate and time indicated. Consequently, you can use a factor by multiplying it times an actual cash flow to produce the present value dollar amount.

Net present value is the sum of the present values of all cash flows associated with an investment, both negative (money invested) and positive (money received). Net present value (NPV) is calculated by applying the discounting formula (present value formula) to all cash flows paid into and received from an investment project, then summing or "netting" the present value amounts. Negative cash flows are treated the same as positive cash flows in this calculation. NPV can be calculated with a financial calculator, computer, or by summing the present value amounts produced by the discount rate factors in this appendix.

The formula for net present value is the formula for present value with the added function of summation, signified by the Greek letter sigma.

$$NPV = \Sigma \frac{FV}{(1 + i)^n}$$

Net present value is simply the sum of present values of a series of cash flows. Consequently, the formula can be expanded as follows [11]:

$$NPV = C_0 + \frac{C_1}{1 + i} + \frac{C_2}{(1 + i)^2} + \cdots \frac{C_n}{(1 + i)^n}$$

$C_0 =$ the initial cash flow in year zero, before time has passed, usually a negative amount signifying money paid into the investment.

$C_1 =$ the cash flow occurring at the end of the first period.

$C_2 =$ the cash flow occurring at the end of the second period.

$C_n =$ the cash flows occurring in subsequent periods.

$i \;\; =$ the interest rate (discount rate).

Therefore, a $1000 investment that generates annual cash flows of $200 for three years and returns the original $1000 would produce a net present value as follows when discounted at 8 percent:

$$NPV = -1000 + \frac{200}{1.08} + \frac{200}{1.08 \times 1.08} + \frac{1200}{1.08 \times 1.08 \times 1.08}$$

$$NPV = -1000 + 185.19 + 171.47 + 952.60$$

$$NPV = 309.26$$

Present Value of 1

Year	1%	2%	3%	4%	5%
1	0.990099	0.980392	0.970874	0.961538	0.952381
2	0.980297	0.961169	0.942596	0.924556	0.907030
3	0.970591	0.942322	0.915143	0.888997	0.863838
4	0.960981	0.923846	0.888488	0.854804	0.822703
5	0.951467	0.905731	0.862610	0.821927	0.783527
6	0.942047	0.887972	0.837486	0.790314	0.746216
7	0.932720	0.870560	0.813093	0.759917	0.710682
8	0.923485	0.853491	0.789411	0.730690	0.676841
9	0.914342	0.836755	0.766418	0.702587	0.644610
10	0.905289	0.820348	0.744096	0.675564	0.613914
11	0.896326	0.804263	0.722423	0.649581	0.584680
12	0.887452	0.788493	0.701382	0.624597	0.556838
13	0.878666	0.773033	0.680953	0.600574	0.530322
14	0.869966	0.757875	0.661120	0.577474	0.505069
15	0.861353	0.743015	0.641864	0.555264	0.481019
16	0.852825	0.728446	0.623169	0.533908	0.458113
17	0.844381	0.714163	0.605019	0.513373	0.436299
18	0.836021	0.700160	0.587397	0.493629	0.415523
19	0.827744	0.686431	0.570289	0.474643	0.395736
20	0.819549	0.672971	0.553678	0.456387	0.376891
21	0.811434	0.659776	0.537552	0.438834	0.358944
22	0.803401	0.646839	0.521895	0.421956	0.341851
23	0.795446	0.634156	0.506694	0.405727	0.325573
24	0.787571	0.621722	0.491937	0.390122	0.310070
25	0.779773	0.609531	0.477609	0.375117	0.295304

Present Value of 1

Year	6%	7%	8%	9%	10%
1	0.943396	0.934580	0.925926	0.917431	0.909090
2	0.889996	0.873439	0.857339	0.841680	0.826446
3	0.839619	0.816298	0.793832	0.772184	0.751314
4	0.792093	0.762896	0.735029	0.708425	0.683013
5	0.747258	0.712987	0.680583	0.649931	0.620921
6	0.704960	0.666343	0.630169	0.596268	0.564473
7	0.665057	0.622750	0.583490	0.547034	0.513158
8	0.627412	0.582010	0.540268	0.501866	0.466507
9	0.591898	0.543934	0.500249	0.460429	0.424098
10	0.558394	0.508350	0.463194	0.422412	0.385543
11	0.526787	0.475094	0.428883	0.387534	0.350494
12	0.496969	0.444013	0.397114	0.355535	0.318631
13	0.468839	0.414965	0.367698	0.326179	0.289664
14	0.442301	0.387818	0.340461	0.299247	0.263331
15	0.417265	0.362447	0.315241	0.274539	0.239392
16	0.393646	0.338735	0.291890	0.251870	0.217629
17	0.371364	0.316576	0.270269	0.231074	0.197845
18	0.350344	0.295865	0.250249	0.211995	0.179859
19	0.330513	0.276509	0.231712	0.194490	0.163508
20	0.311805	0.258420	0.214548	0.178432	0.148643
21	0.294155	0.241514	0.198656	0.163699	0.135130
22	0.277505	0.225714	0.183940	0.150182	0.122846
23	0.261797	0.210948	0.170315	0.137782	0.111678
24	0.246979	0.197148	0.157699	0.126405	0.101525
25	0.232999	0.184250	0.146018	0.115968	0.092296

Present Value of 1

Year	11%	12%	13%	14%	15%
1	0.900901	0.892857	0.884956	0.877193	0.869565
2	0.811623	0.797194	0.783147	0.769468	0.756144
3	0.731191	0.711780	0.693050	0.674971	0.657516
4	0.658731	0.635518	0.613319	0.592080	0.571753
5	0.593451	0.567426	0.542760	0.519368	0.497178
6	0.534641	0.506631	0.480319	0.455587	0.432328
7	0.481659	0.452349	0.425061	0.399638	0.375938
8	0.433927	0.403883	0.376160	0.350559	0.326902
9	0.390926	0.360610	0.332885	0.307508	0.284263
10	0.352185	0.321973	0.294589	0.269744	0.247185
11	0.317284	0.287476	0.260698	0.236618	0.214944
12	0.285841	0.256675	0.230707	0.207559	0.186908
13	0.257515	0.229174	0.204165	0.182070	0.162528
14	0.231996	0.204620	0.180677	0.159710	0.141329
15	0.209005	0.182696	0.159891	0.140096	0.122895
16	0.188293	0.163121	0.141496	0.122892	0.106865
17	0.169633	0.145644	0.125218	0.107800	0.092926
18	0.152823	0.130039	0.110813	0.094561	0.080805
19	0.137678	0.116107	0.098064	0.082948	0.070265
20	0.124034	0.103667	0.086782	0.072762	0.061100
21	0.111743	0.092560	0.076799	0.063826	0.053131
22	0.100669	0.082643	0.067963	0.055988	0.046201
23	0.090693	0.073788	0.060145	0.049112	0.040174
24	0.081705	0.065882	0.053225	0.043081	0.034934
25	0.073608	0.058823	0.047102	0.037790	0.030377

Present Value of 1

Year	16%	17%	18%	19%	20%
1	0.862069	0.854701	0.847458	0.840336	0.833333
2	0.743163	0.730514	0.718184	0.706165	0.694444
3	0.640658	0.624371	0.608631	0.593416	0.578704
4	0.552291	0.533650	0.515788	0.498669	0.482254
5	0.476113	0.456112	0.437109	0.419050	0.401878
6	0.410442	0.389839	0.370431	0.352143	0.334898
7	0.353830	0.333196	0.313925	0.295918	0.279082
8	0.305026	0.284783	0.266038	0.248671	0.232568
9	0.262953	0.243404	0.225456	0.208967	0.193807
10	0.226684	0.208038	0.191065	0.175603	0.161506
11	0.195417	0.177810	0.161919	0.147565	0.134588
12	0.168463	0.151974	0.137219	0.124005	0.112157
13	0.145227	0.129893	0.116288	0.104205	0.093464
14	0.125195	0.111019	0.098549	0.087567	0.077886
15	0.107927	0.094888	0.083516	0.073586	0.064905
16	0.093040	0.081101	0.070776	0.061837	0.054088
17	0.080207	0.069317	0.059980	0.051964	0.045073
18	0.069144	0.059245	0.050830	0.043667	0.037561
19	0.059607	0.050637	0.043076	0.03669S	0.031301
20	0.051385	0.043279	0.036505	0.030836	0.026084
21	0.044298	0.036991	0.030937	0.025913	0.021736
22	0.038188	0.031616	0.026217	0.021775	0.018114
23	0.032920	0.027022	0.022218	0.018298	0.015095
24	0.028379	0.023096	0.018829	0.015377	0.012579
25	0.024465	0.019740	0.015957	0.012922	0.010482

Present Value of 1

Year	21%	22%	23%	24%	25%
1	0.826447	0.819672	0.813008	0.806451	0.800000
2	0.683013	0.671862	0.660982	0.650364	0.639999
3	0.564474	0.550706	0.537384	0.524487	0.511999
4	0.466508	0.451399	0.436898	0.422974	0.409600
5	0.385544	0.369999	0.355201	0.341108	0.327680
6	0.318631	0.303278	0.288782	0.275087	0.262143
7	0.263331	0.248589	0.234782	0.221844	0.209715
8	0.217629	0.203761	0.190880	0.178907	0.167772
9	0.179859	0.167017	0.155187	0.144280	0.134217
10	0.148644	0.136899	0.126168	0.116354	0.107374
11	0.122846	0.112213	0.102576	0.093834	0.085899
12	0.101526	0.091977	0.083395	0.075673	0.068719
13	0.083905	0.075391	0.067800	0.061026	0.054975
14	0.069343	0.061796	0.055122	0.049215	0.043980
15	0.057308	0.050652	0.044815	0.039689	0.035184
16	0.047362	0.041518	0.036435	0.032007	0.028147
17	0.039142	0.034031	0.029622	0.025812	0.022518
18	0.032349	0.027894	0.024083	0.020816	0.018014
19	0.026735	0.022864	0.019579	0.016787	0.014411
20	0.022095	0.018741	0.015918	0.013538	0.011529
21	0.018260	0.015361	0.012941	0.010918	0.009223
22	0.015091	0.012591	0.010521	0.008804	0.007378
23	0.012472	0.010321	0.008554	0.007100	0.005902
24	0.010307	0.008459	0.006954	0.005726	0.004722
25	0.008518	0.006934	0.005654	0.004618	0.003777

Present Value of 1

Year	26%	27%	28%	29%	30%
1	0.793651	0.787401	0.781250	0.775193	0.769321
2	0.629881	0.620001	0.610351	0.600925	0.591716
3	0.499907	0.488190	0.476837	0.465834	0.455166
4	0.396751	0.384402	0.372529	0.361111	0.350128
5	0.314882	0.302678	0.291038	0.279931	0.269329
6	0.249906	0.238330	0.227374	0.217001	0.207176
7	0.198338	0.187661	0.177636	0.168218	0.159366
8	0.157411	0.147764	0.138778	0.130401	0.122589
9	0.124930	0.116350	0.108420	0.101086	0.094299
10	0.099150	0.091614	0.084703	0.078361	0.072538
11	0.078691	0.072137	0.066174	0.060745	0.055798
12	0.062453	0.056801	0.051699	0.047089	0.042922
13	0.049566	0.044725	0.040389	0.036503	0.033017
14	0.039338	0.035216	0.031554	0.028297	0.025397
15	0.031220	0.027729	0.024652	0.021935	0.019536
16	0.024778	0.021834	0.019259	0.017004	0.015028
17	0.019665	0.017192	0.015046	0.013181	0.011560
18	0.015607	0.013537	0.011755	0.010218	0.008892
19	0.012386	0.010659	0.009183	0.007921	0.006840
20	0.009830	0.008393	0.007174	0.006140	0.005261
21	0.007802	0.006608	0.005605	0.004760	0.004047
22	0.006192	0.005203	0.004379	0.003690	0.003113
23	0.004914	0.004097	0.003421	0.002860	0.002395
24	0.003900	0.003226	0.002672	0.002217	0.001842
25	0.003095	0.002540	0.002088	0.001718	0.001417

Present Value of 1

Year	31%	32%	33%	34%	35%
1	0.763358	0.757575	0.751879	0.746268	0.740740
2	0.582716	0.573920	0.565322	0.556916	0.548696
3	0.444822	0.434789	0.425055	0.415610	0.406442
4	0.339558	0.329385	0.319590	0.310156	0.301068
5	0.259205	0.249535	0.240293	0.231460	0.223013
6	0.197866	0.189041	0.180672	0.172731	0.165195
7	0.151043	0.143213	0.135843	0.128904	0.122367
8	0.115300	0.108495	0.102138	0.096197	0.090642
9	0.088015	0.082193	0.076795	0.071788	0.067142
10	0.067187	0.062267	0.057741	0.053573	0.049735
11	0.051288	0.047172	0.043414	0.039980	0.036840
12	0.039151	0.035736	0.032642	0.029836	0.027289
13	0.029886	0.027073	0.024543	0.022265	0.020214
14	0.022814	0.020510	0.018453	0.016616	0.014973
15	0.017415	0.015537	0.013874	0.012400	0.011091
16	0.013294	0.011771	0.010432	0.009253	0.008216
17	0.010148	0.008917	0.007843	0.006905	0.006085
18	0.007746	0.006755	0.005897	0.005153	0.004508
19	0.005913	0.005117	0.004434	0.003846	0.003339
20	0.004514	0.003877	0.003334	0.002870	0.002473
21	0.003445	0.002937	0.002506	0.002141	0.001832
22	0.002630	0.002225	0.001884	0.001598	0.001357
23	0.002007	0.001685	0.001417	0.001192	0.001005
24	0.001532	0.001277	0.001065	0.000890	0.000744
25	0.001170	0.000967	0.000801	0.000664	0.000551

Present Value of 1

Year	36%	37%	38%	39%	40%
1	0.735294	0.729927	0.724638	0.719424	0.714285
2	0.540657	0.532792	0.525099	0.517571	0.510203
3	0.397542	0.388900	0.380507	0.372353	0.364431
4	0.292310	0.283869	0.275730	0.267880	0.260308
5	0.214934	0.207204	0.199804	0.192719	0.185935
6	0.158040	0.151243	0.144786	0.138647	0.132810
7	0.116206	0.110396	0.104917	0.099746	0.094864
8	0.085445	0.080581	0.076027	0.071759	0.067760
9	0.062827	0.058818	0.055092	0.051625	0.048400
10	0.046196	0.042933	0.039921	0.037140	0.034571
11	0.033968	0.031338	0.028928	0.026720	0.024694
12	0.024976	0.022874	0.020963	0.019223	0.017638
13	0.018365	0.016696	0.015190	0.013829	0.012599
14	0.013503	0.012187	0.011007	0.009949	0.008999
15	0.009929	0.008895	0.007976	0.007157	0.006428
16	0.007300	0.006493	0.005780	0.005149	0.004591
17	0.005368	0.004739	0.004188	0.003704	0.003279
18	0.003947	0.003459	0.003035	0.002665	0.002342
19	0.002902	0.002525	0.002199	0.001917	0.001673
20	0.002134	0.001843	0.001593	0.001379	0.001195
21	0.001569	0.001345	0.001154	0.000992	0.000853
22	0.001153	0.000982	0.000836	0.000713	0.000609
23	0.000848	0.000716	0.000606	0.000513	0.000435
24	0.000623	0.000523	0.000439	0.000369	0.000311
25	0.000458	0.000381	0.000318	0.000265	0.000222

References

1. Robert J. Barro, *Macroeconomics* (New York: John Wiley & Sons, Inc., 1984).
2. Peter F. Drucker, "Schumpeter and Keynes," *Forbes* 23 (May 1983): 124–132.
3. Jay W. Forrester, "Innovation and the Economic Long Wave" [Paper delivered at the Symposium on Technology, Innovation, and Corporate Strategy," London, England, November 16, 1978 (Revised December 12, 1978, Paper No. D-2990-1, System Dynamics Group, Alfred P. Sloan School of Management, Massachusetts Institute of Technology)].
4. Joseph A. Schumpeter, *Business Cycles* (New York: McGraw-Hill Book Co. 1939).
5. Paul Zane Pilzer, "The Real Estate Business and Technological Obsolescence," *Real Estate Review,* 19 (3) (Fall 1989): 30–33.
6. Paul Zane Pilzer, *Unlimited Wealth* (New York: Crown Publishers, Inc., 1990).
7. "The Early Warning Forecast Method," *Cahners Economics,* Cahners Publishing, Newton, MA.
8. Richard Mogey, "Cycles in Real Estate," *Cycles* (Foundation for the Study of Cycles, Irvine, California), 42 (3) (May/June 1991): 148–153.
9. George F. Warren and Frank A. Pearson, *World Prices and the Building Industry* (New York: John Wiley & Sons, Inc., 1937).
10. Arthur C. Holden, "The Menace of Mortgage Debts," *Harper's Magazine* (April 1933): 575–581.
11. Michael S. Young, "A Note on the Nonequivalence of NPV and IRR," *The Appraisal Journal* (July 1983): 459–461.
12. Tony Bizjak, "Capital Area's Housing Sales Have Gone From Boom To Bust," *The Sacramento Bee,* 29 September 1991, 1, A1.
13. Edward R. Dewey, "The 18-Year Rhythm," *Cycles: Selected Writings* (Foundation for the Study of Cycles, 1970).
14. Austin J. Jaffe and C. F. Sirmans, *Real Estate Investment Decision Making,* (Englewood Cliffs, NJ: Prentice-Hall, Inc., 1982).

15. George Leland Bach, *MicroEconomics,* 2nd ed. (Englewood Cliffs, NJ: Prentice-Hall, Inc., 1980).

16. Charles B. Akerson, "The Internal Rate of Return in Real Estate Investments" (Chicago: American Society of Real Estate Counselors,).

17. Foundation for the Study of Cycles, Inc., 2600 Michelson Drive, Suite 1570, Irvine, California 92715, (714) 261-7261, (for more on cycles).

Index

About the Author

William T. Tappan, Jr. is a specialist in commercial and industrial real estate investments, and a leading authority on real estate exchanges. He also teaches real estate investing courses, and is the author of the highly praised *Real Estate Exchange and Acquisition Techniques*, Second Edition.